King and People in
Provincial Massachusetts

R I C H A R D L. B U S H M A N

King and People in Provincial Massachusetts

Published for The Institute of

Early American History and Culture

Williamsburg, Virginia

By The University of North Carolina Press

Chapel Hill and London

The Institute of Early American History and Culture
is sponsored jointly by The College of William and Mary
and The Colonial Williamsburg Foundation.

Preface to the Paperback Edition
© 1992 by The University of North Carolina Press

© 1985 by The University of North Carolina Press

Manufactured in the United States of America

96   95   94   93   92   6   5   4   3   2

Library of Congress Cataloging in Publication Data

Bushman, Richard L.
King and people in provincial Massachusetts.

1. Massachusetts—Politics and government—Colonial
period, ca. 1600–1775.   I. Institute of Early American
History and Culture (Williamsburg, Va.)   II. Title.
F67.B97   1985   974.4′02   84-10383
ISBN 0-8078-1624-8
ISBN 0-8078-4398-9 (pbk.: alk. paper)

For Claudia Bushman

PREFACE TO THE
PAPERBACK EDITION

King and People in Provincial Massachusetts is an analysis of political culture in Massachusetts during the provincial period from 1691 to the Revolution. My aim in writing the book was to recreate the values and assumptions of the participants in politics insofar as those principles could be discovered in contemporaneous writings and actions. Above all, I wanted to recover the underlying structure of political culture as experienced at the time.

Concentrating on the writings of eighteenth-century politicians, I paid little heed to the debate over republicanism that was going on when the book appeared in 1985. In fact I implicitly exempted myself from the debate by using the words "republican government" rather than "republicanism" when outlining the book's themes in the Introduction. By focusing on republican government, I emphasized the constitutional changes made in 1776—the elimination of the monarch and the transfer of royal power to the people—rather than the implications of ideology for society and culture.

I focused on the change from monarchical to republican government in 1776 for two reasons: the revolutionaries themselves believed that the adoption of republican government was the most radical and important transformation in the Revolution; and it seemed to me that the end of monarchy was the culmination of colonial politics, the logical conclusion of its fundamental tendencies. I wanted to trace the developments in the provincial period that led to the people's taking government into their own hands. The writings on "republicanism" had gone off in a direction that would detract from this central purpose.

Yet *King and People* does bear on the question of republicanism, especially as the discussion has developed in recent years. Currently, republicanism as a political and social system has been defined in contrast to liberal individualism. Republicanism has been conceived as the political culture of a traditional society, made up of people generally equal and independent, who are devoted to the general good of family and neighborhood. Liberal individualism, on the other hand, is the culture of an unhindered market economy, in which individualism and profit seeking prevail, and little concern is shown for the general good. Republicanism and traditional society are counterposed to liberal individualism and budding capitalism.

King and People implicitly comments on this view of republicanism. The book reminds readers of another context of republicanism, one which during the Revolution was far more significant than liberal individualism. Republicanism arose in opposition to evils in royal government, not to the consequences of capitalism. Republican values aimed to halt the oppression of conspiring individuals who managed the patronage system for their own gain, not to protest exploitation by powerful figures in the market economy. *King and People* underscores the opposition of republicanism to the monarchical political order.

Two key republican ideas, "virtue" and "independence," derived their primary meanings from the critique of monarchical society. In monarchical culture, social relationships were grounded in protection and dependence. At the top of society, the king protected his people; in return the people were loyal and obedient; allegiance was given in exchange for protection. Social relationships throughout society paralleled this primary bond between king and people, creating elaborate chains of patrons and their dependents everywhere, but most notably in government. In the eighteenth century, the corruptions of this system were widely decried, and virtue and independence were considered the means of escaping its control.

Before the Revolution, virtue—devotion to the public good above private interest—primarily meant the willingness to resist the influence of the patronage networks. Resistance was virtuous because it entailed the sacrifice of personal interest. People could best serve their own interests by joining the network of dependents who benefited from the rewards of government. But dependents were obligated to yield to the wills of their masters, no matter how oppressive their actions; people who were entangled in the patronage system were incapable of resisting. The virtuous sacrificed the benefits of office and favor and withstood power rather than succumbing to it. It required high moral courage to turn away from the seductive temptations of patronage to oppose incursions on the rights of the people.

Independence, it can be seen, was a prerequisite of virtue. Independence meant living outside the bonds of dependence that ensnarled the "tools" and "creatures" of men in power. Only people with property of their own could be truly independent. The independent person, because not beholden, could resist the temptations of the influence networks and oppose the incursions of power. When tyranny threatened, only independent people could be counted on to resist—that is, to act virtuously on behalf of the general good.

This entire scenario of compliance and resistance, the republican drama, was enacted within the context of monarchical culture, not in a developing market economy. When the Revolutionaries spoke of virtue and independence, they meant resistance to patronage networks and conspiracies in government, not opposition to merchants and manufacturers.

Later, republican principles were used for many other purposes, among them criticism of industrial enterprise with its many dependent workers. But in the eighteenth century, government power was the primary target. Republicanism was locked in combat with monarchy, an old political order, rather than with capitalism, a new economic system. If we forget this primary relationship, we will inevitably misunderstand republican ideas. By emphasizing the place of monarchy in provincial politics, *King and People* reminds readers of the original context of republican culture.

The attention given to republican government rather than to republicanism brings readers closer to what I believe was the mind-set of the revolutionary period. Politics loomed much larger in eighteenth-century minds than in our minds today. Now we see politics as an overlay on a social structure of class relationships and on an economic system of production and trade. Eighteenth-century people saw politics as much more fundamental. By focusing on republican government, *King and People* restores politics to the center of analysis.

In the eighteenth century, power and eminence were to be found first of all in the state, not in the economy. To begin with, government office was the surest mark of high standing in society. Moreover, the power to tax, to mobilize for war, to regulate property in the courts, to grant land, and to issue currency overshadowed all other powers in society. For officeholders, government itself was an instrument for gaining wealth. More power converged in government than in any other human institution. For all these reasons, the Revolutionaries believed that their greatest achievement was the change they made in the constitution of government.

King and People attempts to recover this eighteenth-century sense of politics and thus to explain why a change in government was revolutionary. Political writings and the actions of the legislature during the provincial period reveal a profound fear that the powers of government will fall into the hands of self-serving officials, who will use the authority of office for personal gain. Above all, people were concerned that self-interest would override the limitations on power. The desire to control self-interested government officials explains the course of politics in eighteenth-century America more fully than any other fact. To bring those officials under the control of the people was to regulate the single most powerful force in their lives. When people gained the right to choose their rulers, they took a long step toward taming the powers they had so long feared. The adoption of republican government in 1776 was the logical culmination of colonial politics and, from an eighteenth-century perspective, truly revolutionary.

When *King and People* was published in 1985, it was at odds with historiographical trends. The book disregarded the furious debate over republicanism and focused instead on other issues. But the enthusiasm for republicanism as presently understood may have gone too far. I hope that the book will lead readers to keep in mind the monarchical context of republican ideas and reconsider the preeminence of politics in eighteenth-century thinking. *King and People* will have fulfilled its highest purpose if it brings us closer to the Revolution as the Revolutionaries themselves experienced it.

Chapel Hill
April 1992

ACKNOWLEDGMENTS

Research on this book was aided by grants from Brigham Young University, Boston University, and the American Council of Learned Societies. Work commenced at the Charles Warren Center, where I was particularly stimulated by conversations with Charles Strickland on the meaning of Independence. I worked mainly at the Houghton Library of Harvard University, the Boston Public Library, the Massachusetts Historical Society, and the Massachusetts State Archives at the State House in Boston. The librarians in all of these institutions were helpful and courteous.

I submitted the manuscript to the Institute of Early American History and Culture because of its reputation for rigorous editing, and I was not disappointed. Three editors read the manuscript and commented in detail: Norman Fiering, Thomas Doerflinger, and David Ammerman. Their criticisms, along with an astute letter from Oscar Handlin, who also read the manuscript, enabled me to see the final form the book should take. Gilbert Kelly, an alert and erudite copyeditor, caught a host of small errors and made useful stylistic suggestions. David Ferguson checked the citations with the help of Margaret Bushman and Karl Bushman. Gail Brittingham and Marie Perrone transformed disheveled manuscript into beautiful typescript.

As editor and friend, Claudia Bushman was always the moving spirit behind the work.

CONTENTS

*King and People in
Provincial Massachusetts*

INTRODUCTION

Books have a history of their own, especially those as long in the making as this one. I began some years ago with a general question about eighteenth-century culture. I was impressed with the prevalence and strength of the word "interest." It was a word that was used frequently in religion and politics to describe motivation, and I thought there must be some general relationship associated with "interest" that would illuminate eighteenth-century culture as a whole.

In time the scope had to be narrowed. Dealing with both religion and politics, I found myself working at a level of generality far removed from actual events and people. The connections were so abstract that probably no one in the eighteenth century comprehended them, and I was in danger of creating a mythical colonial mind with no real existence. There was, on the other hand, no question that political ideas really existed in the minds of politicians, particularly the politicians in one colony such as Massachusetts. They knew one another personally, read the same newspapers and pamphlets, and engaged each other in conversation and debate. Their discourse attested to the actuality of a common political culture.

As I focused on this one group, it became evident that "interest" was indeed a potent word for them, as I had suspected. Moreover, values, conceptions, and attitudes emanating from such words could be seen to affect political action. Through the study of one colony's politicians, I concluded, I could get a purchase on eighteenth-century culture, assured of the reality and the significance of the ideas under examination. The aim of the study thus became the reconstruction of political culture among Massachusetts politicians during the provincial period, from 1691 to 1776.[1]

---

1. I am content with the definition of political culture offered by Gabriel A. Almond and Sidney Verba, as being "the political system as internalized in the cognition, feel-

In searching for that culture in the politicians' writings—their addresses, legislation, pamphlets, and newspaper essays—I came across ideas that I had not expected to find, at least not in such quantity. The most important were those connected with the king. The monarch, though not an active politician in the colonies, was indeed a powerful symbol. Many forms of political discourse could be related to the king: the obligatory respect paid in ceremonial openings and closings, his personal voice in royal instructions, and the frequent references to his goodness, to the people's loyalty, and to zeal for his service.

But there was much more to monarchical influence than etiquette and custom. I came to see that the king was an anchor for a social system based on the protection which the powerful offered to the weak—and that the effects of this principle were felt throughout politics and society.

Because the implications of monarchical culture have not been fully recognized, I have elaborated that part of colonial political culture somewhat more fully than others. I do not wish to exaggerate the importance of monarchical ideas; they did not much affect the small controversies which made up the bulk of political history. But monarchical culture did shape politics by prescribing the kind of arguments available to politicians, by setting limits on criticism of rulers, and, paradoxically, by justifying riot and revolt. More important still, the very foundation of the state was the covenant to obey the king in return for his protection. That principle gave a general form to virtually all political activity, as democracy does today, and made the colonists into monarchists by habit and custom. Monarchical political practices and even monarchical sentiments were second nature to virtually every provincial politician.

The other word that stood out besides "king" was "people." As a cultural symbol, the people were the moral equal of the king. The word "people" had power to invest politicians with moral authority just as did the word "king." In the name of the people the members of the assembly could resist government officials, disobey royal instructions, and claim power for themselves. In the state, the people were to be represented, at least symbolically, in all major decisions along with the monarch. The processes of legislature and courts were designed, to

---

ings, and evaluations of its population." *The Civic Culture: Political Attitudes and Democracy in Five Nations* (Princeton, N.J., 1963), 16.

a great degree, to reconcile the desires and needs of king and people. Thus the title of the book.[2]

The king and the people were not, however, separate or opposing moral centers. The rights and privileges of the people did not constitute a culture outside of monarchy; they were integral to it. Supposedly, royal power was devoted entirely to the well-being of the people. While they were defending popular rights, the popular party claimed perfect loyalty to the monarch, because the king himself was the foremost defender of those rights. The opposition party was not composed of incipient republicans, secretly hostile to monarchical government. The popular party formed within monarchical culture and embraced all of its values.

The scope of monarchical culture, as I eventually realized, presented a problem for the understanding of colonial political history. How did republican government emerge from provincial political culture if popular rights, the foundation of republicanism, were fundamental to monarchy as well? The British crown had long before learned to accommodate popular elements in the mixed monarchy, including elections and electoral campaigns, riots, protests, and published criticisms of rulers. Equal or greater liberties were enjoyed in the colonies. In Massachusetts, the popular party which flourished at the beginning of the eighteenth century lapsed into inactivity by mid-century because the major constitutional issues having to do with popular rights had been successfully resolved. The colonists had no need of republican government in order to enjoy a generous measure of democracy.

Moreover, history worked against the adoption of republican government. The model for the American Revolution should have been the Glorious Revolution of 1688, the revolution honored by all Britons, including colonials, as the culmination of their constitutional development. In that revolution Britain had exchanged one king for another, rather than ending kingship altogether. Yet Americans rejected the Glorious Revolution as a model in 1776 and followed instead the bloody Puritan Revolution, when England had executed its king.

As these contradictions dawned on me, the old problem—Why a republic in 1776?—became newly perplexing. Eventually the governing theme of the book became the emergence of American republican

2. Reinhard Bendix treats the same theme much more broadly in a massive comparative study of Japan, Russia, Germany, England, and France, in *Kings or People: Power and the Mandate to Rule* (Berkeley, Calif., 1978).

government from the monarchical culture of the provincial period. The momentous change from monarchy to republic, the essence of the Revolution for the revolutionaries themselves, occurred so naturally, with so little debate, we are tempted to think it was inevitable. I wanted to know what logic made republican government a necessity both for whig leaders and for farmers in remote country towns.

We are mistaken to give the classical republican theorists too much credit for inspiring republican government in America. To be sure, John Adams referred to Sidney, Harrington, and Locke when formulating a model of republican government in his *Thoughts on Government* in 1776.[3] But more than the handful of provincials who had read these writers wanted a republic in 1776. The adoption of republican government won approbation from every level of society, including the unlearned. Even at the highest levels, there is no evidence of reasoned debate or lengthy contemplation. Republican government was scarcely mentioned in the colonies until the very eve of revolution.[4] The absence of discussion makes it difficult to believe that political speculation won the colonists over to republicanism.

It seems apparent that republican government could have been the obvious course in 1776 only if ingrained political habits and widely recognized problems pointed toward radical change. And here the notions associated with "interest," the word with which I began, become absolutely crucial. For concern about interest interlaced colonial political culture from the seventeenth century onward and shaped nearly every major political controversy. An elaborate structure of apprehensions, defenses, and stereotypes had grown up around the problem of interest, and it was the interplay of events with this entrenched system of thought that led to the renunciation of the king and the adoption of republican government.

King and people were the towering symbols around which formal political thought was organized, but ideas about interest dominated the underside of political culture. By interest, colonial politicians meant primarily self-interest, what we would call selfishness or, still more narrowly, greed. They worried about its terrible power over human conduct and particularly over the behavior of rulers. It was the combination of innate human selfishness with the power of government

3. Charles Francis Adams, ed., *The Works of John Adams*, IV (Boston, 1851), 194.
4. W. Paul Adams, "Republicanism in Political Rhetoric before 1776," *Political Science Quarterly*, LXXXV (1970), 397–421.

that most deeply troubled politicians. They thought of officials as a class, the way Marxists think of owners and employers. Colonial politicians believed that rulers by nature and by virtue of their positions were driven to exploit and oppress the people they ruled. Power and self-interest together constituted a nearly uncontrollable force. The management of overweening self-interest in all its complexity was, in fact, the central problem of provincial politics. The main point of the popular party was to dam those interests, or, better yet, to make them converge with the people's. The Revolutionary crisis was brought on by changes in the controls on official avarice, and republican government was primarily an effort to prevent self-interest from ravaging society.

The Revolution thus grew out of commonplace, deeply ingrained assumptions about politics, assumptions so old and so common that they were as much feelings as ideas. Apprehensions about how power combined with interest were not the particular possessions of any one school of thought or circle of politicians. The problem of interests troubled everyone, the imperial administrators in London along with the representatives from country towns. It was part of the great tradition descending from the parliamentary struggles of the seventeenth century, and nearly everything written about politics on either side of the Atlantic reinforced those ideas. The dangers of oppression alarmed some politicians more than others, notably England's country party, and country party rhetoric did come into vogue in Massachusetts after mid-century, as I explain in the Appendix, in time to play a large role in the Revolution. But the colony was not dependent on the spread of one variety of English political thought to mount a resistance movement. A much more general concern about self-interested rulers, broadly diffused through provincial society, alerted people to the danger signals.

I had not intended at the outset to write about the Revolution; it was the structure of the materials, as I gradually came to understand them, that forced me toward 1776. The emphasis on monarchy seemed to require an explanation of how it was sloughed off, and the provincial concern about interests flowed so directly into the Revolutionary struggles that a continuation beyond 1763 seemed to be necessary. The organization of the book reflects the development of my thinking. The first part explicates political culture from the establishment of royal government in 1691 through to mid-century, with some slight attention to specific political issues. The second part focuses on the influence of that culture on the movement toward Independence. I have not attempted a full-scale analysis of the Revolution in Massachusetts, but have offered a schematic description, emphasizing the interaction of traditional cultural ideas with the course of events.

Focusing on political culture appears to leave aside the stresses and strains in society which our histories usually emphasize. I have not actually disregarded such matters, but, rather, have approached them from another perspective. Beginning with culture enables us to see how the participants themselves understood experience. People's words indicate what social and economic conditions registered in their consciousness and how they thought social forces motivated their contemporaries. In the end I believe it will be clear that eighteenth-century political culture was not far removed from social reality. The preoccupation with interest and self-interest brought considerations of wealth and economic power to the center of politics. As the politicians themselves revealed in the moments of crisis, the force of political language came in large part from the connection of common political words like "oppression" and "slavery" with lands, houses, and goods. The provincials knew more was at stake in political controversies than the establishment of empty principle. In defending their political rights, they were guarding their society as well.

The question will naturally arise whether Massachusetts was exceptional among the colonies. In the matter of monarchical culture, it is likely that if monarchy influenced Massachusetts, reputedly the most independent colony, monarchy had influence in all. Beyond that, while certain issues such as the governor's salary received greater attention in Massachusetts than elsewhere, and the timing of controversies varied, the same general themes were expressed in the politics of all the English provinces of North America.

A rereading of documents one has labored to understand is always humbling. They contain so much more than can be accounted for by a single analytical scheme. The minds of the writers were far richer, far more diversely furnished, and much more disorganized than appears in subsequent explanations. It always seems possible that a different emphasis, a different selection of words, or a different manner of presentation might have resulted in another picture. But chastened as I am by the complexities of even one American colony, I believe that what follows will illuminate the most important ideas constituting provincial political culture in Massachusetts, and that these ideas lead us toward the eighteenth-century meaning of America's passage to republicanism.

PART I

Political Culture, 1691–1763

CHAPTER 1

The King in Massachusetts Bay

The provincial period of Massachusetts history began officially in October 1691, when King William III issued the colony its second charter of government. The first charter, granted by Charles I in 1629, had been dissolved in Court of Chancery in 1684, and the new charter was the replacement. The charter of 1691 once again gave powers of government to the colony, now styled the Province of Massachusetts Bay, but reserved to the king the right to appoint the governor, to veto laws, and to select the provincial Council from nominees of the House of Representatives. Originally the freemen had elected the governor and the assistants each year, and the king had no veto. By enlarging the king's powers, the second charter made Massachusetts a royal province. Taking its meaning from the political changes, the word "provincial" in Massachusetts history has come to signify the period from 1691 to 1776, when the colony became more fully integrated into the British Empire, economically and culturally as well as politically.[1]

The Governor and Company of Massachusetts Bay under the first charter had enjoyed extraordinary powers. Besides annually electing all of its officers—governor, deputy governor, and members of the General Court—the colony had the right to make all of its own laws.

1. The relevant portions of the two charters are reprinted in William Macdonald, ed., *Select Charters and Other Documents Illustrative of American History, 1606–1775* (New York and London, 1914), 37–42, 205–212.

The charter of 1629 gave authority to legislate to the freemen of "the Company." They chose deputies to represent them, and these along with the elected officials formed the General Court, or assembly. Massachusetts claimed that no other legislature, including the Parliament of Great Britain, had the right to interfere in the colony's affairs.[2] The General Court told Charles II in a letter of 1678 that "the lawes of England are bounded within the fower seas and doe not reach Amerrica."[3] Massachusetts even refused to acknowledge Parliament's authority to pass trade laws for the colony, and submitted to the Navigation Acts only after repassing each one in its own assembly. Imperial officials found this state of affairs intolerable. Eventually the Privy Council submitted the charter and complaints about the colony's insubordination to the Court of Chancery, which proceeded to vacate the charter and dissolve the government.[4]

During those fifty-five years while Massachusetts exercised virtually every privilege of republican government—electing all of its officers and making all of its laws—the colony continued to avow its loyalty to the king. Immediately after the Restoration of 1660, the General Court instructed its agents to present the colony "to his Majesty as his loyal and obedient subjects."[5] After 1662 all official writs and judicial processes ran in the king's name. In 1678 the Court ordered the king's arms "carved by an able artist, and erected in the court-house."[6] In

2. On the structure of government under the first charter, see George Lee Haskins, *Law and Authority in Early Massachusetts: A Study in Tradition and Design* (New York, 1960).

3. Nathaniel B. Shurtleff, ed., *Records of the Governor and Company of the Massachusetts Bay in New England* (Boston, 1853–1854), V, 200. Edward Randolph reported a conversation with Gov. John Leverett in which Leverett said with regard to the Navigation Acts "that the *laws made by your Majesty and your Parliament obligeth them in nothing* but what consists with the interest of that colony, that *the legislative power is and abides in them solely* to act and make lawes by virtue of a charter from your Majesties royall father." Quoted in Michael Garibaldi Hall, *Edward Randolph and the American Colonies, 1676–1703* (Chapel Hill, N.C., 1960), 24–25.

4. The story has been well told in David S. Lovejoy, *The Glorious Revolution in America* (New York, 1972); Richard R. Johnson, *Adjustment to Empire: The New England Colonies in the Era of the Glorious Revolution, 1675–1715* (New Brunswick, N.J., 1981); and J. M. Sosin, *English America and the Revolution of 1688: Royal Administration and the Structure of Provincial Government* (Lincoln, Nebr., 1982).

5. John Gorham Palfrey, *History of New England* (Boston, 1858–1890), II, 524n.

6. Palfrey, *History of New England*, III, 322. In 1643 someone suggested at the annual election of assistants in Massachusetts Bay that, by making war on the Parliament, the

April 1689 Massachusetts rose in revolt, spurred by the example of the Glorious Revolution in England; royal officials were rounded up and imprisoned, and a provisional government of colonials took over. And still the colony promptly pledged its allegiance and appealed to the king for another charter. Through its period of republican freedom in the seventeenth century, through the loss of its charter in 1684, through a revolution against the king's governor in 1689, Massachusetts refused to snap the last cord that bound it to Britain: loyalty to the king. Massachusetts as a whole submitted to the royal charter unhappily. The most influential popular leaders recommended in 1691 that the new charter be rejected. For eighty-five years every effort was made to limit royal power and enlarge the rights of the people. And yet monarchy itself was never challenged. The people celebrated the accession of each new king, pledged their loyalty in addresses and petitions, and seemed perfectly happy with monarchy as a form of government.

Then in 1776 the colonists declared their independence from monarchy as well as from Great Britain. At first the significance of rejecting the king as sovereign was little mentioned. In the obsession to rid themselves of British oppression, Americans paid little attention to the alteration in the form of government. Jefferson commented to Franklin in August 1777 that the people "seem to have deposited the monarchical and taken up the republican government with as much ease as would have attended their throwing off an old and putting on a new suit of clothes."[7] But it soon dawned on the nation that it had entered into a new order of the ages. Breaking the tie with the king, it came to believe, transformed their government and reoriented their culture. The essence of the American Revolution was understood as the momentous change from monarchy to republic.

It is difficult now to understand what the colonists abandoned when they repudiated the king. Monarchy rested so lightly on Massachusetts Bay in the seventeenth century as to seem weightless. In the provincial period the king's presence was little felt amidst the clamor of everyday politics. The king was a ceremonial personage, entering into rhetoric

---

king had forfeited his right to the people's allegiance. The General Court, the colony's legislative body, henceforth omitted reference to the king from the oath of office and dropped his name from the writs for election. *Ibid.*, I, 161, 614.

7. Jefferson to Franklin, Aug. 13, 1777, in Julian P. Boyd *et al.*, eds., *The Papers of Thomas Jefferson*, II (Princeton, N.J., 1950), 26.

and political ritual. The colony was already so democratic that Independence scarcely affected many of the forms of government. As we look back, the American passage from monarchy to republic appears to have been short and painless.

But a change in the fundamental nature of government cannot be dismissed as merely cosmetic. The conception of the state at the heart of government was basically altered in 1776. It would not be considered trivial today to revert from democracy to monarchy. Rather than discount the participants' own sense of undergoing a revolution, we should ask what difference monarchy made in provincial politics. And since there is little evidence of the king's influence on everyday affairs, we should look for monarchical influence at some other level of political culture.

We begin to grasp the meaning of monarchy when we view the incessant round of ceremonies exalting the king and listen to the ceaseless flow of monarchical rhetoric. The repetitiveness and simplicity of the language may be misleading. The words were formulaic and ritualistic, it is true, but that does not mean they were empty of meaning. To the contrary, both words and pageantry expressed in varying forms a single, powerful idea, from which flowed the basic rules of politics under a king.

The central monarchical principle was the belief that the king was the protector of his people. Protection and allegiance were reciprocal obligations. Although as much myth as reality, the idea of a protector king lay at the foundation of the state. The influence of that idea was felt throughout political life, shaping the underlying patterns of political behavior. At the Revolution this central principle was abandoned, and a new one took its place. Since relatively few adjustments in the form of colonial government were required at the time, the significance of the change can be overlooked. But a fundamental outlook was altered, with consequences for political and social conduct down to our own time.

i. Celebrations

On a Saturday in late December 1760, news of the death of George II reached Boston. The royal governor, Francis Bernard, at once issued

an order that the old king's grandson, Prince George, was to be proclaimed the new king, to reign as George III. The town readied itself
for two days and then on Tuesday morning, December 30, began the
solemn ritual which was occurring at many places in the empire at this
season. The governor, lieutenant governor, the Council, the House of
Representatives, and a number of principal gentlemen left the old
statehouse under military escort and proceeded to the Council chambers. There assembled were a regiment of militia and "a vast Con-
course of People of all Ranks." From the balcony of the courthouse the
proclamation was read in a loud voice.

> We . . . do now, with full Voice and Consent of Tongue and
> Heart, Publish and Proclaim, That the High and Mighty Prince
> GEORGE, Prince of Wales; is now . . . become our only Lawful
> and Rightful Liege Lord GEORGE the Third. . . . To Whom we
> acknowledge all Faith and constant Obedience, with all hearty
> and humble Affection: Beseeching GOD . . . to bless the Royal
> King GEORGE the Third, with long and happy Years to Reign
> over us.

After the concluding "God save the king!" three huzzahs rang out from
the throng, and the militia fired three volleys. At a signal, sixty-three
cannon were discharged at Castle William in the harbor, echoed immediately by batteries on the Boston and Charlestown shores. In the evening candles illuminated the town, and a handsome entertainment was
provided in Faneuil Hall, "where the Health of his Majesty King George
the Third, the Royal Family, and many other loyal Healths were drank."
Two days later the town mourned the passing of George II. Bells tolled
from early morning until late in the day, soldiers discharged seventy-
seven minute guns, one for each year of the dead king's life, and the
General Court with the governor listened to sermons morning and
afternoon.[8]

The display of affection for His Britannic Majesty was not new to
Boston, nor did it soon disappear from the town's public life. Boston
celebrated the king's birthday and the anniversary of his coronation an-

---

8. *Boston-Gazette, and Country Journal,* Jan. 5, 1761. On English coronation rituals, see
Percy Ernst Schramm, *A History of the English Coronation,* trans. Leopold G. Wick-
ham Legg (Oxford, 1937); Leopold G. Wickham Legg, ed., *English Coronation Records*
(Whitehall and New York, 1901).

nually until the eve of the tea party in 1773.[9] Cannons, toasts, and huzzahs echoed through the century before the Revolution, leaving a long record of monarchical celebrations. In the seventeenth century, the colony lavishly praised Charles II upon his restoration to the throne. In a petition of 1664 begging for a continuation of political privileges, the Massachusetts General Court acknowledged the king's sovereignty in language so obsequious as to be offensive to our ears.[10] His brother was similarly honored. Massachusetts had small cause to love James II, with his known sympathies for France and Roman Catholicism. Yet when ordered to proclaim him king, thousands swarmed into Boston's High Street. Drums beat, trumpets sounded, volleys were fired, and huzzahs were heard on all sides.[11] New England could much more happily honor William, and Mary his Protestant Stuart wife. Boston proclaimed him king on May 29, 1689, in the most joyous celebration the colony had ever seen. People flocked to the city from distant places for the procession. The provisional rulers attended by the principal gentlemen passed on horseback through the streets, followed by the town regiment and companies of horse and foot from the countryside. The better sort ate dinner at the town house, while wine was served to the people in the streets. Acclamations filled the air until the bell rang at nine o'clock and the people dispersed to their houses.[12]

From that point on, royal celebrations became fixed points in the Massachusetts calendar. Samuel Sewall reported that the birthday celebrations honoring William were well attended and that grief was widespread at his death in 1701.[13] Increasing prosperity and the urge to emulate England enlarged the celebrations as the years went by. At the

9. *Massachusetts Gazette; and the Boston Weekly News-Letter* (Boston), Sept. 23, 1773. On the continuation of loyalty to the king up through 1775, see William D. Liddle, "'A Patriot King, or None': Lord Bolingbroke and the American Renunciation of George III," *Journal of American History*, LXV (1978–1979), 951–970.

10. Shurtleff, ed., *Records of the Governor and Company of Massachusetts Bay*, IV, 129–133. The petition is conveniently reprinted in Jack P. Greene, ed., *Great Britain and the American Colonies, 1606–1763* (New York, 1970), 62–68.

11. Palfrey, *History of New England*, III, 322; Ola Elizabeth Winslow, *Samuel Sewall of Boston* (New York, 1964), 84.

12. Palfrey, *History of New England*, III, 590.

13. Samuel Sewall, *Diary of Samuel Sewall, 1674–1729* (Massachusetts Historical Society, *Collections*, 5th Ser., V–VII [Boston, 1878–1882]), I, 462; II, 58, 101, 123, cited hereafter as Sewall, *Diary*; Perry Miller, *The New England Mind: From Colony to Province* (Cambridge, Mass., 1953), 163.

accession of George II in 1727, the lieutenant governor, Council, and Representatives assembled in General Court (no governor was in the colony at the moment) and proclaimed George II king, "being here assisted with Number of Gentlemen Merchants and other Principal Inhabitants" to the number of 127. The *New-England Weekly Journal* reported that the "*King* was proclaim'd in Boston, with all possible demonstration of loyal zeal and affection, and with much more state solemnity and magnificence than was ever before seen among us." Three regiments of militia and five troops of horse under command of the lieutenant governor formed in the street before the statehouse, while people covered the roofs on every side.

> As soon as the *Herauld* had said his *Amen* to *God Save the King*, the loud and joyful *Huzza's* of so great a multitude rent the skies, the Regiments made a tripple discharge, the Castle Forts and Ships fir'd their cannon; and a splendid Entertainment follow'd for the Lieut. Governour and his Majesty's Council, Officers, Justices, and the Revd Ministers present; with suitable provisions for the Regiments and Troops.

Bells rang in the church through the day. In the evening the people lit bonfires and set off fireworks. In a grand illumination, three or four rows of candles burned in the windows of the houses in the principal streets. The *Journal* said, "The streets were fill'd all the Evening with the *Gentry* of both *Sexes*, who appear'd with much decency and gravity, and with gayety and chearfulness." On Sunday the clergy honored the old king, welcomed the new, and admonished their hearers to rejoice in the glorious British constitution.[14]

ii. Protection and Allegiance

The meaning of the coronations, royal birthdays, anniversaries of coronations, and all the other declarations of loyalty and allegiance can be glimpsed through the eyes of Thomas Prince, the young Harvard graduate who stood among the throngs watching the coronation pro-

14. *New-England Weekly Journal* (Boston), Aug. 21, 1727.

cession of George I in 1714. Thirteen years later in a sermon in Boston at the accession of George II, Prince recalled his reactions:

> I shall never forget the Joy that swell'd my Heart; when in the Splendid Procession at his *Coronation*, preceeded by all the Nobles of the Kingdom, and then his Son and Heir apparent, our other Hope, with their Ermine Robes and Coronets—That *Royal Face* at length appear'd, which Heaven had in that Moment sent to Save these Great Nations from the Brink of Ruin. Nor do I speak it as my case alone, but as what appear'd to be the equal Transport of the Multitudes round about me. The Tears of Joy seem'd to rise and swim in every Eye: And we were hardly able to give a Shout, thro' the labouring Passions that were swelling in us.

It is noteworthy that Prince, the young provincial, did not look on as an outsider. Observant and self-conscious as he was, he entered into the feelings of the multitude. Passions swelled in his breast, and tears swam in his eyes. Moreover, he thought it appropriate to repeat it all to his congregation thirteen years later, including a report on his emotions.[15]

Much of the culture of monarchy was implicit in the scene Prince viewed in 1714.[16] Processions were designed for the very purpose of educating onlookers. Tradition had carefully crafted the coronation to display the social order in all its splendor and to evoke awe and respect in the multitude. Although each procession departed in detail from its predecessors, the general structure persisted from reign to reign. The order was published in advance and, later in the century, was reprinted in provincial newspapers. The coronation of George III appeared in the *Boston-Gazette, and Country Journal,* November 16, 1761. At the head, the king's herb woman with her six maids strewed sweet herbs in the path, followed by fife and four drums in livery coats of "scarlet richly laced," a drum major, "Eight Trumpeters, four a breast, in rich Liveries of Crimson Velvet," kettle drums with crimson banners, and

---

15. Thomas Prince, *A Sermon on the Sorrowful Occasion Of The Death Of His late Majesty King George of Blessed Memory, An The Happy Accession Of His present Majesty King George II. to the Throne* (Boston,1727), 20. Another local man attempted a description of his reaction in *New-Eng. Weekly Jour.*, Aug. 21, 1727.

16. For a sociologist's perspective on the coronation, see Edward Shils and Michael Young, "The Meaning of the Coronation," in Edward Shils, *Center and Periphery: Essays in Macrosociology* (Chicago, 1975), 135–152.

eight more trumpeters. Thence the procession rose gradually—there were eighty-seven entries in all—from six clerks in Chancery, chaplains, sheriffs of the City of London, aldermen, the king's solicitor, gentlemen of the Privy Chamber, through baronesses and barons in their "Robes of Estate," bishops, viscountesses and viscounts, countesses, earls, duchesses, and dukes, to the lord chancellor and the archbishop of Canterbury. The penultimate climax was the queen in her royal robes attended by the lords bishops of London and Westminster, covered by a canopy and preceded by her ivory rod with dove, her scepter with cross, and her crown, and followed by the trainbearer with sixty-seven ladies of the bedchamber. At the peak of the procession came the king, also preceded by the regalia from which he was never to be separated—Saint Edward's staff, the golden spurs, the scepter with cross, the sword of state, Saint Edward's crown, the orb with cross, the chalice and paten—and followed by supporters of the train, master of the robes, gentlemen of the king's bedchamber, standard-bearers, captains, yeomen of the guard, and others. The king in his royal robes proceeded under a canopy supported by the barons of the Cinque Ports and accompanied by the bishops of Durham and of Bath and Wells.[17]

The shape of the procession was obviously an inclined plane reaching up to the king. Besides the ascent of titles, which all could recognize just as people today know the relative standing of captain and colonel, there was in the procession a steady crescendo of magnificence in costumes and trappings. The impact of the king's appearance lay not in his splendor alone but in the fact that he stood at the peak of a pyramid. "In the Splendid Procession at his Coronation," Prince observed, the king was "preceeded by all the Nobles of the Kingdom, and then his Son and Heir apparent, our other Hope, with their Ermine Robes and Coronets." All were wreathed in splendor with their ermine and coronets, but the king was the greatest of the great, the noblest of the noble.

The monarch stood at the top of virtually every pyramid of power. He was head of state, commander in chief, head of the church, wealthiest of the wealthy, largest landowner, the leader of society, and the

17. For a modern description of coronations with historical reflections, see Randolph S. Churchill, *The Story of the Coronation* (London, 1953). For other forms of pageantry, see David M. Bergeron, *English Civic Pageantry, 1558–1642* (London, 1971).

fountain of honor. Might that is divided in pluralistic societies came to a single focus in the monarch.[18] Above all, the myths of monarchy attributed moral goodness to the king. An aura of sacred power hovered over the throne. The Stuarts, including Queen Anne, practiced the royal touch to cure scrofula, the King's Evil. Conventional eighteenth-century usage permitted references to the king's "sacred person." Of kings above all other rulers, a Massachusetts preacher said, "with respect to that Power, Rule and Authority, which they have over others, they resemble *the Almighty* who is *the Original* of All Dominion, Might and Majesty."[19]

Awesome as royal magnificence was, the king's power and glory of themselves did not arouse the strong feelings. Prince's description dwelt on the watching multitude as much as on the procession. Their laboring passions, their cheers, and their very presence were part of the scene. The power and splendor were not as affecting as the juxtaposition of the concentrated glory of the realm moving between the masses of grateful and joyful people. The relationship of king and people generated the electricity.

Prince remembered that the succession of nobles in ermine and coronets at last gave way to "That *Royal Face* . . . which Heaven had in that Moment sent to Save these Great Nations from the Brink of Ruin." Prince was thinking of the disarray among the European powers in 1714, but the sentiment could be generalized. The king was, above all, the protector of his people. It was that knowledge which moved the multitude. All that concentrated power and glory, it was made to seem, were amassed to protect and defend the people of Great Britain and the empire. The sublimity of the scene lay in the great king's implied promise of protection and the people's reciprocal gratitude and allegiance.

No word was more potent or fundamental in the culture of mon-

18. Curtis Brown Watson, *Shakespeare and the Renaissance Concept of Honor* (Princeton, N.J., 1960), 372.
19. Samuel Mather, *The Fall of the Mighty lamented. A Funeral Discourse upon the Death of Her most Excellent Majesty Wilhelmina Dorothea Carolina* . . . (Boston, 1737–1738), 11. See also Jonathan Mayhew, *A Discourse Occasioned by the Death of King George II. And The Happy Accession of His Majesty King George III.* (Boston, 1761), 30–34; Samuel Checkley, *The Duty of a People, to Lay to Heart and Lament the Death of a Good King.* (Boston, [1727]), 19; Sir William Blackstone, *Commentaries on the Laws of England*, 12th ed. (London, 1793–1795), I, 241, 246–247; Sir William S. Holdsworth, *A History of English Law*, III, 3d ed. (Boston, 1923), 463–468; VI (1927), 309; IX (1926), 4–7; David L. Keir, *Constitutional History of Modern Britain, 1485–1951*, 5th ed. (London, 1953), 280.

archy than the word "protection." In the ancient tradition the king was anointed to be "defender of al the people." "By his great travails, study, and labors, they injoy not only their lives, lands, and goodes, but al that ever they have besids, in rest, peace and quietnes."[20] Out of regard for the archetypical role as commander of armies, the king at his accession announced his intention in case of war to command the army personally. Governor Bellomont noted in his praise of William III before the General Court that the king had "hazarded his Royal Person in the Front of Our Battles," thus restoring "the Almost lost Character of Bravery, and Valour."[21] At the beginning of the mid-century wars with the French, the House of Lords assured the king, "Nothing can more clearly demonstrate your Majesty's paternal Concern for the Welfare and Prosperity of your People" than his resolution "to maintain the just Rights and Possessions of Your Crown against all Encroachments."[22]

Just as the army and navy shielded the nation from foreign threats, royal courts offered protection against domestic disorders. Sir William Blackstone observed, "His majesty, in the eye of the law, is always present in all his courts, though he cannot personally distribute justice."[23] All offenses were against the king's peace or against his crown and justice. He enforced the laws. But that was not all. Beyond punishing specific breaches, the king was the guarantor of the constitution. His "chief" care was the preservation of all the liberties bound up in the constitution. In his first speech to Parliament in 1727, George II repeated the important assurance that "as the Religion, Liberty, Property, and a due Execution of the Laws, are the most valuable Blessings of a free People," it was the king's "constant Care" to "preserve the Constitution of this Kingdom," and thus "to secure to All My subjects, the full Enjoyment of their religious and civil Rights."[24]

In the sustaining myth of monarchy to which politicians of every

---

20. Quoted in Charles H. McIlwain, *The High Court of Parliament* (New Haven, Conn., 1910), 337–338.
21. Lord Bellomont to the General Court, June 2, 1699, Court Records, VII, 6, Archives Dept., State House, Boston. See also *Bost.-Gaz.*, May 15, 1727.
22. *Bost.-Gaz.*, June 2, 1755.
23. Blackstone, *Commentaries*, I, 269.
24. *New-Eng. Weekly Jour.*, Sept. 18, 1727. See also Holdsworth, *A History of English Law*, X (1938), 414–415; *New-Eng. Weekly Jour.*, Aug. 12, 1727; *Bost.-Gaz.*, Jan. 12, 1761.

variety necessarily subscribed, liberty and royal power were comple-mentary, not opposed.[25] It was a necessary convention, suspended only in revolution, that the king's authority was always exercised for the good of his subjects. It was in that faith that the Puritans jailed Governor Edmund Andros in 1689 and expected a royal blessing. By the same token George III received credit when Parliament repealed the Stamp Act in 1766. As one jubilant clergyman reconstructed the scene, the bill for repeal, having passed Parliament, arrived before the king. "And does *he* hesitate?—has he any struggle in *his* mind whether his American subjects shall be free? No.—he stops not a moment. The cries of the oppressed had before reached his royal ears, always open to their distresses. When he signed, 'tis reported, that he said, 'If he had known it would have given his good Subjects in America so much uneasiness, he never would have signed the former act.'"[26] A corollary of the monarchical axiom that the king could do no wrong was the belief that he would protect the people's rights whenever endangered, from whatever quarter, even by his own officers or the Parliament.

In this spirit, it was perfectly consistent for conservative monarchists to concur in the formula, "Salus Populi suprema lex esto" ("The good of the people shall be the supreme law").[27] It was believed true of all monarchs as it was said of Anne, "Your Majesty measures Your Hon-our and Glory by Your Benifience to Your People." Royal protection went beyond armies and courts to encompass the total well-being of the people. The Lords honored Queen Anne for "Your care of the general welfare and happiness of Your People, extended even to the poorest and meanest of Your Subjects."[28] George II told the Parlia-ment, "It is the fix'd Purpose of my Heart, to promote the true Hap-piness of My Kingdoms."[29] Traditional, feudal protection included food and presents for vassals. One way to signify loyalty in the Civil War was to say, "I have eaten the king's bread."[30] In a latter-day ex-

25. J. R. Western, *Monarchy and Revolution: The English State in the 1680s* (Totowa, N.J., 1972), 30.

26. Joseph Emerson, *A Thanksgiving-Sermon Preach'd at Pepperrell, July 24th, 1766* (Boston, 1766), 15.

27. For a discussion of the principle, see Francis D. Wormuth, *The Royal Prerogative, 1603–1649: A Study in English Political and Constitutional Ideas* (Ithaca, N.Y., 1939), 111–114.

28. *Boston News-Letter*, Sept. 15, 1707; May 22, 1704.

29. *Ibid.*, June 23, 1743.

30. Marc Bloch, *Feudal Society*, trans. L. A. Manyon (London, 1961), I, 163.

pression of that down-to-earth interest in his subject's welfare, George III, in 1772, noted his "real concern" that the "produce of the late harvest has not given us the relief we had hoped for in respect to the dearness of corn."[31] More often in the eighteenth century, the royal goodness was credited with the general prosperity of the realm. Anne's purpose, along with protection of "Her Subjects in the Enjoyment of all their Rights and Privileges," was "to Promote their Good, and to Establish their Peace and Prosperity, upon sure and lasting Foundations." She was conceived as surveying all the interests of the realm and exercising her power in behalf of "the true Interest" of the kingdom.[32] The happiness of the people was ultimately attributed to the king's intelligence, power, and good will.

No encomiums were too grandiose for the protector monarch. The clergy found scriptural reason for styling kings as gods. Anne was told that "by doing all the Good possible" to her people, she resembled "God, whose Viceregent Your Majesty is."[33] Governor Bellomont in his enthusiasm for William III declared in his maiden speech in Massachusetts, "There is Something that is Godlike in what the King has done for us."[34] More commonly, the appellations were familial. Thomas Prince observed upon the death of George I that in relation to his subjects, "he appeared constantly to be their affectionate and common Father."[35] On the same principle, the clergy extended the commandment to honor parents to rulers. Obedience was not all they intended by the characterization. The fatherhood of the king and the reciprocal childhood of the subjects were modes of relating. The king was "tender" in his care, and the subjects were affectionate. In its idealized, mythic form, obedience was not forced, and the exercise of power was not raw. The warmth and mutual affection of family were the sinews of national unity as well. "We can assure your Majesty of Hearts full of Loyalty and Affection to your Person and Government," dissenting ministers told the new king in 1727.[36] The royal protector was the model of fatherhood at its best.

31. Rind's *Virginia Gazette* (Williamsburg), Mar. 4, 1773.
32. *Bost. News-Letter*, Apr. 28, 1707; Apr. 6, 1713.
33. *Ibid.*, Sept. 15, 1707.
34. Bellomont to General Court, June 2, 1699, Court Recs., VII, 6.
35. Prince, *Sermon*, 20.
36. *New-Eng. Weekly Jour.*, Sept. 18, 1727. See also Blackstone, *Commentaries*, I, 371.

The people then obeyed the king not from fear, but from self-interest, because the monarch protected their rights and advanced the prosperity of the kingdom. More important, they yielded out of gratitude. Gratitude was the cement of monarchical culture. Gratitude turned submission into a moral duty, performed not grudgingly, but willingly, cheerfully, and affectionately. This was the bond in the ancient formula that tied allegiance to protection. Blackstone called allegiance "the tie, or *ligamen*, which binds the subject to the king, in return for that protection which the king affords the subject." It went into effect at birth, for a child was immediately "under the king's protection; at a time too, when (during their infancy) they were incapable of protecting themselves. Natural allegiance is therefore a debt of gratitude."[37]

The protection-allegiance formula did not remain the unspoken assumption of political activity; it was repeated over and over again. Parliamentary rhetoricians volubly construed every major action of the monarch as confirmation of his benevolence and took every possible occasion to pledge their allegiance. "These many and great Instances of your Majesty's Goodness, and Concern for the Happiness and Welfare of your People," the Commons told the king in 1727, "call upon us for the highest Returns of Duty, Zeal and Affection to your Majesty's Person and Government."[38] The simple protection-allegiance formula, often couched in complex syntax and august diction, entered into virtually every address to the crown. Thus the City of London to the queen in 1713 declared, "*Your Majesty hath so wholly devoted Your Self to procure the Ease and Welfare of Your Subjects, that the strictest Loyalty and most unalterable affection, would be unequal Return, did not Your Majesty assure Us, You want no other Guaranty but That.*"[39] It was mirrored back and forth in the speeches and replies passing between the crown and Parliament. The king promised protection of rights and asked for allegiance; the Lords or Commons promised obedience and expressed gratitude and affection.

Such language justified the inequalities in society, the exercise of power, the necessity for submission, and even civil cruelty in terms that made those conditions morally and psychologically acceptable. Taxes, to take one example, were seen as the gift of the people. "Sup-

37. Blackstone, *Commentaries*, I, 366, 369.
38. *New-Eng. Weekly Jour.*, Sept. 18, 1727.
39. *Bost. News-Letter*, Dec. 4, 1713. See also *Bost.-Gaz.*, June 15, 1761.

plies granted in parliament," Thomas Pownall wrote, "are of good will, not of duty: the free and voluntary act of the giver; not obligations and services which the giver cannot, by right, refuse."[40] Whatever the actual jealousies of power, reference to the myth of the state revived confidence in the ultimate benevolence of the government. "We humbly assured Your Majesty," the Commons declared in 1732,

> that having the truest Sense of the many Blessings we have enjoyed during the Course of Your Majesty's Reign, and how much our present Happiness is owing to Your Paternal Love and Care of Your People, we will with the greatest Chearfulness grant the necessary Supplies for the current Service of the Year; and Your Majesty will always find such Returns of Duty and Gratitude from us, as the best of Kings may expect from the most loyal Subjects, fully convinced that the only End of Your Majesty's auspicious Government, is the Protection and Prosperity of Your People.[41]

Those formulaic words, however much they disguised actual resentments and struggles, reassured all parties of fundamental trust and thus enabled the struggle to continue without endangering the state.

The word that summarized the entire relationship was "dependence." "Dependence" implied a hierarchy of power, with great ones above exercising their power on behalf of lesser ones below, and the lesser ones returning obedience out of gratitude, affection, duty, and interest. "Dependence" described the archetypical relationships of king and people, of father and family, and could be extended to include virtually every other relationship of superior and inferior. Exemplified and justified by the king's tender care of his people, "dependence" was the fundamental module of monarchical culture and the wellspring of the emotion that flowed through the multitude in 1714 when Thomas Prince watched the coronation procession move toward Westminster.

40. Thomas Pownall, *The Administration of the British Colonies*, 5th ed. (London, 1774), I, 176.
41. *Weekly Rehearsal* (Boston), Apr. 17, 1732. For similar affirmations in the various addresses which passed between the Parliament and the crown, see *Bost. News-Letter*, June 29, 1731; *New-Eng. Weekly Jour.*, Sept. 18, 1727; Oct. 2, 1727; *Bost.-Gaz.*, Feb. 13, 1750.

iii. Securing Moral Advantage

The powerful and far-reaching ideas of protection, allegiance, and dependence appear far less important when we look at everyday politics. Monarchical principles had no more (and no less) effect on the measures which the assembly enacted than the idea that the people are sovereign affects legislation in a democratic congress. Monarchical culture shaped the forms of politics more than it did the contents, shaped the modes of argumentation and acceptable political styles rather than the measures passed. We would not discover the importance of monarchical ideas in the colony by reviewing the bills passed in the Massachusetts assembly. That the king was a force in political culture, a presence in the mind of every politician, has to be deduced from the formalities of government rather than its business.

The king himself scarcely ever interfered personally in provincial politics. He did not select governors as he chose his chief ministers in England.[42] His wishes for the colony, if he had any, filtered through layers and layers of officialdom before reaching America. Until the late years of the Revolutionary movement, eighteenth-century colonial policy showed little evidence of the king's hand. The Board of Trade, the Privy Council, the secretary of state for the southern department, the chancellor of the Exchequer, the Admiralty, and so on and on, formed colonial policy, not the king.

The combined force of royal bureaucracy, the crown as contrasted to the king, had limited influence as well. The charter of 1691 reserved to the crown the appointment of the governor and lieutenant governor, and the approval of Council members from nominations submitted by the House of Representatives. The governor had to assent to all legislation, and the crown could in addition disallow laws in conflict with the laws of England. But those powers did not guarantee colonial compliance with royal policies. The crown stated its desires in royal instructions, a long list of dos and don'ts which the governors brought over with them. But instructions were addressed to the governor, not the people of the colony, and had no force of law. Before instructions were binding, the assembly had to support them with legislation. The

42. Sir Lewis Namier, *England in the Age of the American Revolution* (New York, 1930), 58–60.

taxes, the salaries, the troops to support royal policies had to come from the colonial assembly, and the assemblies consistently disregarded the instructions when they interfered with colonial interests. Threats and pleas of the governors accomplished nothing in the face of the assembly's obstinacy. At times the royal governors wrote home in frustration that the crown had no authority and the people claimed all. Royal rule in Massachusetts did not imply royal dominance.[43]

Because the crown lacked controlling power, the significance of monarchical government in the colonies had less to do with royal policies than with moral forces and rhetorical strategies. Judging from the words of the politicians themselves, political activity took place in a highly charged moral realm. Blame and obligation were mentioned in virtually every exchange in the assembly. The colonists rehearsed their rights, protested their innocence and loyalty, and laid claim to the king's favor. The governors reminded the assemblies of their obligations to the monarch and accused them of disloyalty. Although the language may sound like empty rhetoric to us, the representatives and the royal governors attended to the moral issues with meticulous care, as if the struggle for moral advantage made a difference. The symbolic figure of the king loomed large in these disputes, and it is here, in the moral realm, that monarchical principles manifested themselves most strongly.

For royal governors, the culture of monarchy was an instrument of politics. Whatever moral authority governors exercised in the provinces derived from the king, and in a remote province with no troops or police, moral authority was all-important. Governors presented themselves as surrogates of the king and equated loyalty to the servant with loyalty to the master. They were aided by the fact that monarchical government was conceived, as Blackstone observed, as resting in the king's will alone.[44] Instructions to the governors were couched in the first person, the royal "We." Each command was an expression of

43. Leonard Woods Labaree, *Royal Government in America: A Study of the British Colonial System before 1783* (New Haven, Conn., 1930); and Labaree, ed., *Royal Instructions to British Colonial Governors, 1660–1776* (New York, 1967 [orig. publ. n.p., 1935]).

44. Blackstone, *Commentaries*, I, 249–250. Colonial governors were not exceptional in their dependence on opinion. Speaking generally, David Hume wrote, "The governors have nothing to support them but opinion." *Essays: Moral, Political, and Literary*, ed. T. H. Green and T. H. Grose (London, 1882), I, 110. See also Gordon S. Wood, *The Creation of the American Republic, 1776–1787* (Chapel Hill, N.C., 1969), vii–viii.

"our will and pleasure." The governor presented himself as the agent of that will.

Moreover, like every official entrusted with the king's authority, the governor claimed, with fitting humility, to embody the king's own prime virtue, a tender regard for the well-being of the people. "And that I may acquit my selfe towards you as I ought," Bellomont said, "I shall as well as my Weekness will Permit me, Copy after the example of our Great Master the King, who thrô the whole Course of his Administration, has shewed a Tenderness of his People not to be equalled."[45] The governor cast himself as a subsidiary protector, executing the wishes of the royal master, and therefore entitled to the people's allegiance and obedience.[46]

Governors had access to other moral resources. They were commonly the beneficiaries of the preachments at the annual elections. The oft-quoted text from Romans 13 on subjection to the higher powers— "For there is no power but of God; the powers that be are ordained of God"—was almost without exception applied on behalf of the governors. But significantly, they never chose to use that language themselves and never spoke to the assembly of respect due rulers as beneficiaries of divine authority. Though many were Massachusetts-bred, the governors limited themselves to the connection with monarchy to justify the exercise of power. By so doing they established the terms of rhetorical controversy in the legislature. The governors' reliance on royal authority compelled the assembly to answer in language derived from the culture of monarchy.

The assembly did not waver before that challenge. The House and Council lavishly expressed admiration and affection for the king. "We reflect, with Reverence to his late Majesty's most Sacred Memory, upon the various Instances of his Favour and Benignity to this Province," the Court said in an address to the throne in June 1761. "His paternal Care in delivering us from the Dangers to which we were exposed by the unjust Views and Measures of the French Enemy . . . hath made such Impressions upon us, as can never be effaced, and the Remembrance thereof will descent to our latest Posterity. We were

45. Bellomont to General Court, June 2, 1699, Court Recs., VII, 5.
46. After an exhausting battle with the assembly in 1739, Gov. Belcher bluntly told the Representatives, "You seem to be desirous to enter into a Controversy with His Majesty, upon His repeated Royal orders to me." *Bost. News-Letter*, Oct. 4–11, 1739; *Journals of the House of Representatives of Massachusetts* (Boston, 1919–), VIII, 308.

preparing an humble Address, to acknowledge our Obligations to Duty, Loyalty and Affection to His late Majesty," the address said, when death intervened, and the assembly "freely and chearfully" transferred their allegiance "to our rightful Lord and Sovereign his Royal Successor."[47]

The assembly did not intone these phrases merely out of habit or courtesy. Failure to appear zealously loyal had consequences. The instructions to Governor William Burnet in 1728 bluntly said that if the Representatives "hope to recommend themselves to the Continuance of Our Royal Grace and Favour," they must show it by providing "a fixed and honourable Sallary for . . . Our Governor."[48] The same threat and promise applied to an act for preserving mast trees or raising money for a military company. "After all the Royal Favours and Protections We have had from her Majesty," Joseph Dudley observed to the House in 1705, "our Neglect and Disobedience will be very much aggravated And attended with very evil Consequences."[49] In the instruction on the salary, the king said the whole matter "may require the Consideration of the Legislature," presumably a parliamentary statute to settle the affair. The assembly's insistence on its dutiful allegiance to the crown was an attempt to ward off the consequences of royal wrath.[50]

In the midst of a dispute over the governor's salary in 1729, a moderate correspondent of the *New-England Weekly Journal* submitted a parable meant to warn Massachusetts of the inevitable outcome of resistance to royal instructions. The parable told of a robin favored by its old master for its beautiful voice. When the old man died, the son con-

47. *Bost.-Gaz.*, June 15, 1761. See also *Journals of the House*, II, 219; VIII, 250–251. The addresses to the throne from various New England groups in 1705 echoed the sentiments of English addresses currently appearing in the *Bost. News-Letter. A Modest Enquiry into the Grounds and Occasions of a Late Pamphlet, intituled, A Memorial of the Present Deplorable State of New-England* (Mass. Hist. Soc., *Colls.*, 5th Ser., VI [Boston, 1879]), 88–94. See also the loyalist protestations of the leader of the opposition in 1720: Elisha Cooke, Jr., *Mr. Cooke's Just and Seasonable Vindication: Respecting some Affairs transacted in the late General Assembly at Boston, 1720* ([Boston, 1720]).

48. *Journals of the House*, VIII, 247.

49. Joseph Dudley to the House of Representatives, Sept. 5, 1705, Court Recs., VIII, 147. See also *Journals of the House*, IV, 4.

50. *Journals of the House*, VIII, 247; see also 370. See also Noel Sainsbury *et al.*, eds., *Calendar of State Papers, Colonial Series, America and West Indies* (London, 1860–), XXXVI, 340, cited hereafter as *Cal. St. Papers.*

tinued to honor the bird. But the robin perversely took to biting the golden wires of which its cage was made. The kindly son provided a larger golden cage for fear of losing the pretty bird. The bird not only kept up its habit of biting the golden wire but sang so loudly as to drown out the other birds. At last the robin grew so "Proud and Haughty" that the master resolved to wring the bird's neck. A council was called, however, and the master determined only to place the bird in an iron cage. The author drew no moral. The point was clear. A proud and haughty Massachusetts put its own political privileges in jeopardy.[51] The colony was in danger of an iron cage.

Through these exchanges, we get an idea of what monarchical culture meant in provincial politics. The protection-allegiance bond became in the give-and-take of political exchange a formula for bargaining, just as it was in other contexts a formula for submission. Protection and allegiance were conceived as two sides of a balance scale. Weighting or lightening one side required a change in the other. The moral of the bird cage story was that a troublesome and disobedient province, one manifesting less allegiance, merited less protection or fewer rights. By the same token, when the monarch increased his protection, through aid in war or the bestowal of a privilege, greater compliance was expected from the people. After the king reimbursed Massachusetts for subduing Louisburg, Governor William Shirley told the assembly that failure to pay him an honorable and fixed salary would be looked on by the king as an instance of ingratitude. When the crown removed an offensive surveyor of the king's woods, Jonathan Belcher said the least the colony could do in return was to dispatch soldiers to defend Maine.[52] The reason for the assembly's respectful language was that "dutiful expressions and assurances" to the king "would undoubtedly engage His Majesty to do everything on His Part" for the "ease and benefit" of the colony.[53] It was a form of quid pro quo politics. Without ever precisely weighing obligations, there were a strong sense of moral expectation on both sides and strenuous efforts by both the crown and the assembly to generate moral advantage for themselves.

51. *New-Eng. Weekly Jour.*, May 19, 1729. For a more blunt warning from a governor, Dudley to the House, March 11, 1703, Mass. Arch., VII, 363.
52. *Journals of the House*, XXV, 53; XI, 174.
53. *Ibid.*, VII, 107. See also *ibid.*, XVII, 158; Dudley to the House, June 16, 1702, Mass. Arch., VII, 292.

The bargaining went on in deadly earnest, for the stakes were high. Ultimately the colony was defending its measure of freedom. The governors persistently told the assembly that they enjoyed unusual privileges. In the eyes of many royal officials the privileges were excessive—the very cause of the turmoil in provincial administration. Many believed the empire would benefit from a restriction of the rights granted by charter. The standard tactic for these reforming officials was to exhibit the disloyalty of the colonists. It was often said that Massachusetts aimed at outright independence.[54] The consequences were obvious to everyone familiar with the standard equation. A diminishment of allegiance meant less obligation to protect and thus the need for fewer favors in the form of aid or privileges. Independence in the colonies justified a curtailment of liberties.

Events gave the province reason to believe that the threats were not mere words. Massachusetts had lost its first charter in 1684 and been reduced to virtual slavery when Edward Randolph persuaded the crown of the colony's dubious loyalty. Proprietary charters were falling on every side in the decades after the Glorious Revolution. Connecticut's charter was in continual jeopardy. By an explanatory addition to its charter in 1726, the lower house in Massachusetts lost the right to elect its speaker. The change was forced on them after Governor Samuel Shute sailed home bearing tales of the colony's recalcitrance in obeying royal instructions. Whatever the economic or political interests behind the attacks on colonial rights, in the British courts and council chambers where each case was ultimately decided, disloyalty, manifest in failure to comply with the royal will and pleasure, was the pretext for suspending liberties. Conversely, the province's defense had to be made on grounds of loyalty and dutiful subjection.[55]

Looking back, it is impossible to assess the sincerity of the assembly's devotion to the king, and in the last analysis it is unnecessary. The point is that provincials conducted themselves according to the political imperatives of the culture of monarchy. The permutations of protection-allegiance were ingrained in their thinking because that basic relationship fixed the broad rules of political conduct. Whether

54. *Cal. St. Papers*, XXXII, 371–374, 412–413; XXXVI, 341; J. M. Bumsted, "'Things in the Womb of Time': Ideas of American Independence, 1633 to 1763," *William and Mary Quarterly*, 3d Ser., XXXI (1974), 537; George Louis Beer, *British Colonial Policy, 1754–1765* (New York, 1907), 166–169; Palfrey, *History of New England*, IV, 290–291.
55. *Journals of the House*, III, 97–98.

they were deeply moved by love of the king did not matter. Political necessity required the assemblies to declare their allegiance repeatedly and passionately and thus to immerse themselves in royal political culture.

Massachusetts' most bitter rage was reserved for those who detracted from the image of loyalty and hence threw the colony's liberties into jeopardy. Edward Randolph, whose distorted reports were held responsible for the loss of the first charter, was vilified ever after.[56] In the eighteenth century Chief Justice Thomas Hutchinson's frank letters to Thomas Whateley on conditions in Massachusetts were believed by Benjamin Franklin to have been the cause of "exciting jealousies in the crown and provoking it to wrath against so great a part of its most faithful subjects." In its official condemnation, the Massachusetts House said that Hutchinson's letters "had a natural and *efficacious* tendency to interrupt and alienate the affections of our most gracious sovereign King George the Third from this his loyal and affectionate province, to destroy that harmony and good will between Great Britain and this colony which every friend to either would wish to establish, to excite the resentment of the British administration against this province," and eventually "*to produce the severe and destructive measures* which have been taken."[57] The refusal of the king to come to the defense of the colony was accounted for by the fact that "every avenue to the Royal Ear Seems to be blocked up by the gross Falsities and Designd Misrepresentations . . . from sum of whom at Least we might have expected better Things."[58]

In the maneuvering for moral advantage, the colonists were not always on the defensive. They knew how to turn the axioms of monarchical culture against the crown and build up credit that laid the king under obligation. Within the protection-allegiance bond was the potential for pressuring the king, and Massachusetts knew how to manip-

56. Thomas Danforth, leader of the extremist faction, warned Randolph as he boarded ship for England in 1783 that he was commending himself to God on the high seas, and not to be an enemy to "this poor people," whom Randolph had seen to have a sincere desire "to serve God and honor the King." Palfrey, *History of New England*, III, 375.

57. Quoted in Bernard Bailyn, *The Ordeal of Thomas Hutchinson* (Cambridge, Mass., 1974), 238, 241.

58. Amherst, Jan. 26, 1774, Letters and Proceedings received by the Boston Committee of Correspondence (photostat), Massachusetts Historical Society, Boston.

ulate the formula to its advantage. Jeremiah Dummer used such arguments in *A Defence of the New-England Charters*. Dummer, a Harvard
graduate who took up permanent residence in England in 1704, was
Massachusetts' agent from 1711 to 1728. More conscious than the assembly of the absolute necessity of orderly and submissive conduct,
Dummer cautioned the colony against the very appearance of independence. But to the British ministry he argued eloquently for colonial
rights. When he wrote the *Defence* in 1715, a bill to alter the Rhode
Island and Connecticut charters was before Parliament. He delayed
publication when the bill failed and then issued it six years later when a
violent clash between Governor Shute and the Massachusetts assembly
revived the movement to vacate New England charters.[59]

Of the various arguments Dummer made, one of the most intrigu-
ing included an elaborate calculation of the cost of settlement:

Freight of passengers	£95,000
Transport of stock	12,000
Provisions	45,000
Building materials	18,000
Miscellaneous	30,000
Total	200,000

Dummer took pains to sum up expenditures ninety years after the fact
to show at what cost the colonists had expanded the British dominions
without risk to the crown. That imposed an obligation. Charles I
granted the New England charters "on this express Condition of set-
ling Colonies for the Benefit of the Crown." The planters had performed their side of the agreement. New Englanders had "at a vast Expence, and through incredible Difficulties accomplish'd the Work even
beyond what was ever hop'd or expected." To withdraw the colony's
rights would be a terrible miscarriage. "To strip the Country of their
Charters after the Service has been so successfully perform'd, is abhor-
rent from all Reason, Equity and Justice." The colonists' act of unpaid

59. Palfrey, *History of New England*, IV, 407–422, 486–487; Perry Miller, *New England
Mind: Colony to Province*, 386–390; Clifford K. Shipton, *Sibley's Harvard Graduates: Biographical Sketches of Those Who Attended Harvard College*, IV (Cambridge, Mass., 1933),
454–468. For information on Dummer, besides Shipton's sketch, see Sheldon S. Cohen, "The Diary of Jeremiah Dummer," *WMQ*, 3d Ser., XXIV (1967), 397–422.

service to the crown entitled them at the very least to a continuation of their original privileges.[60]

Dummer was of course more familiar with monarchical political morality than were ordinary provincial politicians and could ring the changes on the protection-allegiance formula more expertly, but he was not the inventor of this line of reasoning. The General Court in 1664, when appealing to the crown for exemption from the authority of the royal commission, observed that the first planters "did at their oune charges transport themselves, their wives, and families over the ocean, purchase the lands of the natives, and plant this colony with great labour, hazards, costs, and difficulties; for a long time wrestling with the wants of a wildernes, and the burdens of a new plantation." The Court did not explicitly say that the king was obligated to them for their services, but it did say that it was hard to be asked "to yeild up our liberties, which are farr dearer to us than our lives, and which had wee had any feare of being deprived of, wee had never wandered from our fathers houses into these ends of the earth, nor layd out our labors and estates therein, besides engaging in a most hazardous and difficult warre with the most warlike of the natives, to our great charge and the losse of some of the lives of our deare friends." The petition's framer knew that this picture of the founders permitted the colony to ask that, "if wee have found favour in the sight of the king . . . let our government live, our patent live, our magistrates live, our lawes and liberties live, our religious enjoyments live."[61]

A variation on the theme was heard following the Seven Years' War. At first the province gratefully acknowledged the protection of the crown and cheerfully pledged a return of willing submission. As the Revolutionary agitation gained momentum in the 1760s, the colonists recognized that Britain's war effort in North America could be used against them. The refusal to pay parliamentary taxes appeared as gross ingratitude in view of the vast exertion of the crown on their behalf. "I am equally grieved and surprised at the waywardness and ingratitude of the Americans," wrote an essayist in the *London Chronicle* in January

60. Jeremiah Dummer, *A Defence of the New-England Charters* (London, 1721), 13.
61. In Greene, ed., *Great Britain and the American Colonies*, 63, 37. For similar incantations, Palfrey, *History of New England*, II, 449; III, 380, 389; *Bost.-Gaz.*, June 19, 1750. See also Miller, *New England Mind: Colony to Province*, 168–169; Paul R. Lucas, "Colony or Commonwealth: Massachusetts Bay, 1661–1666," *WMQ*, 3d Ser., XXIV (1967), 91.

1766, "to make such an undutiful return to the mother-country, for that parental care and tenderness with which she has fostered and protected them. . . . Has not it cost us upwards of fifty millions to defend America from the assaults of foreign enemies, under whom she would have groaned with every kind of oppression and tyranny? . . . though they have been supported with so much blood and treasure; and are at present protected, at the expence of between three and four hundred thousand pounds a year, notwithstanding all this, refuse to bear a light and modest part of the grievances of government, and shew a disposition to shake off all dependance and subjection."[62]

The colonists evaded this charge by changing their attitude toward the war. It was not fought for the colonies' advantage, they began to say. Britain had her own interests in view. America had paid heavily and gained little. "In that large expence of the money and blood of these colonies [in] the last war, the crown alone had the profit; we supplied men and money much beyond our proportion . . . not a foot of the lands conquered have fell to our share; not a ship stationed upon our coast, for our defence in a time of war to protect our trade, the whole of the operations in America, were with a view to their own advantage, without any regard to our interest." The colonists gave their best to the struggle. "None but a colonist can conceive of the ardour and zeal with which these colonies put to their shoulders, what treasures expended, and what number of lives lost, in the several enterprizes in which they were engaged; and yet not they, but others have the profit." The crown took possession of the acquisitions, and "the wealth of the British nation is amazingly encreased." How bitterly ironical it seemed by 1775! "Good heaven's!—must all this be forgot by those who have had the profit of our toils and BLOOD;—and now in a time of peace must we have ships and troops in plenty, not to protect, but to ENSLAVE US." Even at that date, in an angry mood, the writer drew the familiar moral about the obligations of the crown to protect subjects of proven loyalty. "Every attempt to *wrest* Liberty and Property from us must be exceeding unrighteous, and fraught with pe-

---

62. *London Chronicle*, Jan. 28, 1766, reprinted in Edmund S. Morgan, ed., *Prologue to Revolution: Sources and Documents on the Stamp Act Crisis, 1764–1766* (Chapel Hill, N.C., 1959), 132. On the initial gratitude to Britain, see Jack P. Greene, "The Seven Years' War and the American Revolution: The Causal Relationship Reconsidered," in Peter Marshall and Glynn Williams, eds., *The British Atlantic Empire before the American Revolution* (London, 1980), 99.

culiar turpitude, for we have never forfeited one iota of our Charter Rights, we have been as fast friends to our Mother-country, as loyal to our king, and as peaceable and governable a people as any under heaven, and have afforded to *Great Britain* immense wealth."[63]

The effects of the colony's argumentation cannot be accurately measured. The crown and Parliament obviously did not yield before the colonists' claims. But one fact is clear: the participants on both sides struggled continually for moral advantage. They wrote extensively, vigorously, and frequently to put themselves in the right and their opponents in the wrong, as measured by the moral standards of monarchical culture. The distance of Massachusetts Bay from the throne of England did not dissolve the protocols of royal government. New England of necessity carried on political discourse according to principles which prevailed at court and which applied to subjects of the crown throughout the empire. The king as protector was a powerful presence in every politician's mind.

iv. The Defiance of Authority

The painful efforts to demonstrate loyalty and the fear of retribution against dissent gave monarchical government a repressive cast. It is possible to conceive of the crown as gagging the opposition and tolerating no form of resistance to the royal will. The king's great authority sometimes seems to have hung like a weight on the human spirit. And yet the record of English politics under its king is not one of repressive domination. To the contrary, English history is filled with riots, insur-

63. Oliver Noble, *Some Strictures Upon The Sacred Story Recorded In The Book of Esther, Shewing The Power and Oppression of State Ministers tending to the Ruin and Destruction of God's People* . . . (Newburyport, Mass., 1775), 27, 22–23. See also [John Allen], *An Oration, Upon the Beauties of Liberty, or the Essential Rights of the Americans*, 3d ed. (Boston, 1773), xi; Samuel Mather, *An Attempt to Shew, That America Must Be Known To The Ancients* (Boston, 1773), 28–35; Mendon, Mar. 1, 1776, to Boston Committee of Correspondence, Letters and Proceedings; Joseph Warren, *An Oration Delivered March 5th, 1772 At The Request Of The Inhabitants Of The Town of Boston* . . . (Boston, 1772), 9; Oct. 18, 1702, Mass. Arch., LI, 134–135. The Tory picture of Britain's protection and of America's obligation was the reverse of the radical's view. Janice Christine Potter, "The Lost Alternative: The Loyalists in the American Revolution" (M.A. thesis, Queen's University, 1970), 54–63.

rections, and threats to government, quite the opposite of what we would expect, given the assumptions of monarchical culture.

It would be an error to interpret the instances of resistance as a contradiction of monarchical principle. Kings did seek to repress the opposition, of course, but resistance was as integral to monarchical political culture as obedience. Although monarchy has been more enduring than any other form of government, it was vulnerable because of the ambiguity in its central justification. Protection obligated people to submit; failure to protect dissolved the obligation. The extravagant proposition that the king could do no wrong had to be believed, whether true or not, because failure to uphold that idea jeopardized the state itself. A king who did wrong deserved to be overthrown.[64] Protection and allegiance, the bond of unity and submission, was a formula for revolt as well as a formula for bargaining.

On its reverse side, the protection covenant opened vast possibilities for defiance. Many of the rules of political conduct arose from the need to protect the crown against its own weakness. To shield the king, monarchical political culture forbade open criticism of rulers and required that complaints take the form of petitions which pledged allegiance while seeking redress. These rules and forms infused all of government and gave colonial politics their monarchical cast. But repression was only half of it. The ambiguity in the protection covenant justified both the stifling of dissent and shameless resistance.

Precautions were necessary because people well understood the revolutionary side of the protection formula. In the 1630s, the Commissioners for Plantations requested that Massachusetts Bay return its charter. In 1638 John Winthrop wrote home to explain why the colony refused to comply. The concluding reason was, "If our patent be taken from us, (whereby we suppose we may claim interest in his Majesty's favor and protection,) the common people here will conceive that his

---

64. Fritz Kern pointed out that medieval notions of kingship implied that "the instant a ruler interferes with the rights of others without their consent, he ceases to be king, becomes a tyrant, and simultaneously loses his claim to obedience, without any necessity for formal legal proceedings on the part of the community." He argued that constitutional government under monarchy evolved from the possibility of conflict between "the right of resistance or absolutism." *Kingship and Law in the Middle Ages*, trans. S. B. Chrimes (Oxford, 1939), 196, 132. For Harvard students toying with the revolutionary potential of the protection covenant, see John C. Miller, *Sam Adams: Pioneer in Propaganda* (Boston, 1936), 16.

Majesty hath cast them off, and that hereby they are freed from their allegiance and subjection."[65] Likely Winthrop spoke for himself as much as for the common people, but even the pretense is evidence that ordinary men were believed capable of throwing off allegiance when protection failed.

In the course of the seventeenth century, fifteen attempts were made to overthrow colonial governments. Virginia had two such revolts (the most famous being Bacon's Rebellion), Maryland had five, the Carolinas three, New York one, New Jersey two, New Hampshire one, and Massachusetts one. In each case disaffected elements forcibly attempted to remove the governor and confine him to prison. The insurgents accused him of failure to offer protection, often against attacks by Indians or French, but equally often against the corrupt impositions of friends and appointees. Justified morally by the terms of their covenant with rulers, the colonists withdrew allegiance until the king appointed more trustworthy officials, and assumed in the meantime the responsibility of defending themselves. No new revolutionary doctrines had to be imported to justify their uprisings. The right to revolt was inherent in the first principle of royal government. Under its mandate, the insurrectionists could feel the righteous outrage so necessary for revolutionary action.[66]

By the same token, the revolutionary corollary permitted men of all ranks to join the insurrections. The Mathers, Simon Bradstreet, and Wait Winthrop took the lead in the overthrow of Governor Andros in 1689. They were not desperate, marginal men. They had vested interests in both the economic and social order and did not conceive of themselves as rebels. And yet the part they took in overthrowing Andros did not embarrass them. The protection-allegiance formula had

---

65. Quoted in Palfrey, *History of New England*, I, 558. See also S[amuel] N[owell], *Abraham in Arms* . . . (Boston, 1678), 10. Traditionally people had distinguished resistance to lesser officials from resistance to the monarch. Just three kings were executed in the Middle Ages, while innumerable vassal lords were deposed and killed. Bloch, *Feudal Society*, II, 381.

66. Richard Maxwell Brown, "Violence and the American Revolution," in Stephen G. Kurtz and James H. Hutson, eds., *Essays on the American Revolution* (Chapel Hill, N.C., 1973), 85. Brown passes over the jailing of Governor Harvey in Virginia in 1635. Richard L. Morton, *Colonial Virginia* (Chapel Hill, N.C., 1960), I, 137. For contemporaneous explanations of many revolts and for a modern attempt to suggest social causes, see Michael G. Hall *et al.*, eds., *The Glorious Revolution in America: Documents on the Colonial Crisis of 1689* (Chapel Hill, N.C., 1964).

the merit of justifying resistance without totally discrediting the insurgents. After overthrowing a royal governor, they needed only to reassert allegiance to the crown to regain a place in respectable society.[67]

The key issue was not the ruler's competence, but his intent. Election sermons pleaded for tolerance of human failings. John Winthrop instructed the Massachusetts General Court, in his famous "little speech" following the Hingham militia case, that rulers were not to be removed merely because they exhibited the infirmities common to all men. People must run the hazard of inadequate skill and ability. Only if the wrong was ill will was the ruler to be brought to judgment, that is, if "the error is not in the skill, but in the evil of the will."[68] The critical question in times of suffering was whether the failings of the government were by accident and circumstance or by design. Should the ruler actually turn on the people, in contravention of his oath of office, and oppress and abuse them, allegiance was at an end.

To guard the reputation of rulers and particularly of their motives, they had to be depicted as moved entirely by good will. The ultimate guarantee of order was the maxim that the king could do no wrong. The principle of royal innocence forever preserved him from the imputation of malice toward his people. Whatever went awry in the state, the blame lay elsewhere—with evil counselors or conniving foreign potentates. To believe otherwise was treason.[69] But the immunities of lesser officials were less certain. On the one hand, it was believed that since popular discontents would erupt whenever doubts were cast on a ruler's intentions, the governor's reputation had to be carefully safeguarded. On the other hand, there was the widespread belief that the people rightfully resisted when a malevolent official endangered their liberty or well-being. Not only words but clubs and cutlasses could be raised against bad rulers.

In the seventeenth century, the proper recourse against an evil minister was impeachment for treason. Evil ministers were construed as

67. The routine nature of these lesser revolts made it possible for deposed officials to return to office as Joseph Dudley did. Jailed with Andros in 1689, Dudley came back as governor of Massachusetts Bay in 1702.
68. John Winthrop, *The History of New England from 1630 to 1649*, ed. James Savage (Boston, 1853), II, 280. John Dickinson repeated the point with perfect clarity in *Letters from a Farmer in Pennsylvania, to the Inhabitants of the British Colonies* (Philadelphia, 1768), 15–16.
69. Wormuth, *Royal Prerogative*, 109–111.

enemies of the nation who merited death on the gallows. In the eighteenth century, impeachment fell into disuse, and the press and a loyal parliamentary opposition became the instruments of the opposition.[70] Both forms of criticism developed under a cloud of guilt and recrimination, because both lacked unambiguous moral justification. Chief Justice John Holt's famous opinion in 1704 held through the century: "If people should not be called to account for possessing the people with an ill opinion of the government, no government can subsist. For it is very necessary for all governments that the people should have a good opinion of it."[71] The House of Commons resolved in 1721 that a comparison of conditions in 1721 and 1641, the year of revolution, was "false, malicious, scandalous, infamous and traitorous libel; tending to alienate the affections of his Majesty's subjects, and to excite the people to sedition and rebellion."[72] Direct criticism could bring down the government.

The defenders of John Peter Zenger in the famous trial in New York in 1733 admitted that "abuses that dissolve society, and sap the foundations of government, are not to be sheltered under the umbrage of the liberty of the press."[73] They went on, of course, to say that Zenger's newspaper did not dissolve and sap the foundations of government, but they began with the assumption that opposition had to be carried on within limits. A London reprint in the *Boston Evening-Post* in 1737 summarized the common sense of the period when it said, "No Man, I presume, will contend, that by the *Liberty of the Press* any Man should have the Privilege of reviling the Person of the King, or of traducing his Government; or of treating the two Houses of Parliament contumeliously; or of persuading the People that they are *oppressed* and *enslaved*, and *ought to revolt*; or of spreading Calumnies at random upon Men and Women of all Ranks, or of any Rank." The Pretender's at-

---

70. On the general theme of a formed opposition, see Archibald S. Foord, *His Majesty's Opposition, 1714–1830* (Oxford, 1964). After 1696 no political offenders were impeached for treason with the exception of Jacobites in 1715 and 1745 and Lord Macclesfield in 1725. Keir, *Constitutional History*, 290, 39, 192–194. Until 1641 the publication of domestic news of any sort was a legal offense. There were no printed newspapers, only privately circulated newsletters. Christopher Hill, *The Century of Revolution, 1603–1714* (London, 1961), 98–99.

71. Quoted in J. R. Western, *Monarchy and Revolution*, 66.

72. Quoted in Laurence Hanson, *Government and the Press, 1695–1763* (Oxford, 1936), 44.

73. Stanley Nider Katz, ed., *A Brief Narrative of the Case and Trial of John Peter Zenger, Printer of the New York Weekly Journal* (Cambridge, Mass., 1963), 14.

tempt on the throne in 1714 was the horrible example. "Such was the Force of monstrous Misrepresentations, false Tales and poisonous Libels, that the Sense of Protection was lost in the Spirit of Disaffection, and Liberty ungratefully perverted into Revolt."[74] Such ambiguities enveloped the opposition press throughout the eighteenth century.[75]

In view of these principles arising from the monarchical idea of protection, all branches of the Massachusetts government—governor, Council, and lower house—cooperated to contain criticism. Never did Massachusetts libertarian thinking lead England on questions of freedom of the press. An early act of the Representatives under the interim government after the Glorious Revolution ordered that any persons printing papers "tending to the disturbance of the peace and subversion of the government of this theire Majesties Collonie" were to be "accounted enemies to theire Majesties present Govemt" and "proceeded against as such with uttermost Severity."[76] The Massachusetts House took the lead in quashing James Franklin's *New-England Courant* in 1721 and in punishing the publisher and editor Daniel Fowle in 1754.[77] In Massachusetts the phrase "liberty of the press" was used mainly in the seventeenth-century sense of freedom to publish without license from an official censor, not the right to criticize rulers freely.

Not until 1768, when the prosecution of John Wilkes in London for his attack on the ministry in the *North Briton* sent shock waves through

74. *Boston Evening-Post*, July 4, 1737, reprinted from the *Daily Gazette* (London), May 2, 1737. English Tories and libertarians rejoiced at the outcome of Zenger's trial. James Alexander, the attorney who contributed largely to Andrew Hamilton's brief on behalf of the printer, was highly conscious of English interest. As with so many provincial controversies, the Zenger case was self-consciously played out before a transatlantic audience. Patricia U. Bonomi, *A Factious People: Politics and Society in Colonial New York* (New York, 1971), 74, 112–120; Katz, ed., *A Brief Narrative of the Case and Trial of John Peter Zenger*, 26–28; *Bost. Eve.-Post*, June 5, 1738; Livingston Rutherford, *The Trial of John Peter Zenger (1734) and the Freedom of the Press* (San Francisco, 1940), 249–255.

75. Holdsworth argued in a Whiggish vein that the established doctrine of popular rights required means to check government, and that restraints on the press in the eighteenth century were contradictory. True as that may be, the countervailing force of regard for rulers under the principles of monarchical government prevented the elimination of the contradiction for a century. Holdsworth, *History of the English Law*, X, 672–696. See also Hanson, *Government and the Press*, 32–35, 57; Leonard William Levy, *Legacy of Suppression: Freedom of Speech and Press in Early American History* (Cambridge, Mass., 1960), 172–175.

76. Clyde Augustus Duniway, *The Development of Freedom of the Press in Massachusetts* (Cambridge, Mass., 1906), 67–68.

77. *Ibid.*, 101–102, 117–118.

the empire, did liberty of the press in its modern sense win a following among the representatives. For the first time, the House declared that "the Liberty of the Press is a great Bulwark of the Liberty of the People: It is therefore the incumbent Duty of those who are constituted the Guardians of the People's Rights to defend and maintain it."[78] Up to that time, the lower house as the vehicle of the popular party insisted on respect for rulers. Popular leaders seemed to have recognized that public accusations against rulers undermined the moral foundations of government and released popular resentments.

The public as a whole was less circumspect. The lower house acknowledged the necessity of safeguarding the governor's reputation as a protector of the people, but for grand juries, stifling criticism was less important than indicting those who failed to protect. The bulk of the ordinary people appear to have tolerated and perhaps favored forthright criticism. Four printers were brought before grand juries between 1695 and 1772 charged with seditious libel. The juries acquitted in every case, even though two of the charges originated from the joint action of Council and House. From 1690 to 1772, not a single printer or author was indicted by a Massachusetts jury for breach of the laws against seditious libel or for any offense which involved liberty of the press. Perhaps because of this consistent record, the General Court's requests for prosecutions became mere gestures. In five of the cases having to do with liberty of the press, one-quarter of the whole for the provincial period, prosecution was abandoned despite orders from the assembly to proceed. Even in the absence of a spokesman like Andrew Hamilton to advance the rights of a free press as he did in the Zenger trial, Massachusetts juries refused to bring printers and authors to judgment for seditious libel and related charges. The fact that the elected representatives of the people in the assembly backed the prosecution in two of the instances did not move the juries. They acted as if they understood the obligation of rulers and were not loath to criticize those who were found wanting.[79]

78. Quoted in *ibid.*, 127. James Allen, a radical in the House who himself suffered from a censure, took a strong stand for freedom of the press in 1749. John Schutz, *William Shirley: King's Governor of Massachusetts* (Chapel Hill, N.C., 1961), 142. For the printers' economic position in relation to free press ideology, Stephen Botein, "'Meer Mechanics' and an Open Press: The Business and Political Strategies of Colonial American Printers," *Perspectives in American History*, IX (1975), 127–225.
79. Tabulated from Duniway, *Freedom of the Press*.

The consistent popular support of critics raises questions about the state of public feeling regarding royal government. There is no reason to doubt popular affection for the king himself. The people of Boston entered into the public celebrations of royalty as heartily as the gentlemen. But the lower ranks of society appear to have harbored suspicions of royal officials that inclined people to believe the attacks in the press. The four grand jury actions, though few, confirm the conservatives' assumption in England and America that "the People are very apt in all Countries, to take groundless Disgusts at their Governors." "Public Incendiaries," if left at liberty to "infuse and improve those Disgusts, to spread and invent whatever inflammatory Tidings and alarming Grievances," could easily have rulers by the ears. "It is hardly possible that any Government could subsist a Month; but the Governours must be continually changed or butcherd." So restive were popular feelings, according to this common conservative view, that unless people were controlled, "there could be no Government at all, but a perpetual Struggle on one Side to govern, and on the other not to be governed."[80]

Even more than the grand juries' defense of government critics, rioters in Boston and across the Massachusetts countryside took advantage of the invitation to defiance in the protection-and-allegiance formula. Nearly two dozen riots occurred in Massachusetts between 1689 and 1760. If stones thrown through Council chamber windows are counted, the number would exceed fifty.[81] Governor Shirley said a "Mobbish Spirit" possessed Boston. If that claim was not always true, enough incidents occurred to demonstrate the capacity of ordinary people to take the law into their own hands.[82] They resisted government or assumed its powers themselves as if by right. They readily suspended allegiance when they believed the rulers were failing in their obligations.

Riots usually struck at something or someone other than govern-

80. *Bost. Eve.-Post*, July 4, 1737, borrowing from the *Daily Gaz.* (London), May 2, 1737. See also *New-Eng. Weekly Jour.*, July 21, 1729, and Aug. 25, 1729.

81. Dirk Hoerder, *Crowd Action in Revolutionary Massachusetts, 1765–1780* (New York, 1977), 40–84. See also Brown, "Violence and the American Revolution," in Kurtz and Hutson, eds., *Essays on the American Revolution*, 117–118.

82. G. B. Warden, *Boston, 1689–1776* (Boston, 1970), 137. For riots in France and England, see Natalie Zemon Davis, "The Rites of Violence: Religious Riot in Sixteenth-Century France," *Past and Present*, No. 59 (1973), 53–91; Max Beloff, *Public Order and Popular Disturbances, 1660–1714* (London, 1938).

ment, but as in England, the crowd's anger usually in time enveloped rulers. Natural conditions or external circumstances may have caused food shortages, a cause of ninety-six riots in England between 1740 and 1765, and four in Massachusetts before 1763, but rulers were held responsible.[83] In 1737, rioters pulled down one of the town's market houses and sawed through the foundation of another. Originally designed as a marketplace where sales could be restricted as in Europe, the houses were symbols of controls which the townsmen believed would raise prices. Following the attack, Benjamin Colman, a Boston clergyman, expressed his dismay at the "shameful and vile disorders at Boston, murmuring against the Government and the rich people among us as if they could (by any means within their Power, besides Prayer) have prevented the rise of provisions."[84] A letter circulating through Boston after the riot announced that five hundred men had signed a "Solemn League and Covenent" to resist any attempt to apprehend the rioters. The allusion to the Scottish covenant which marked the beginning of the English Civil War was a blunt if exaggerated threat.[85]

The people attacked the government more directly during the impressment riots in 1747.[86] Commodore Charles Knowles's naval squadron had suffered from desertions while laying off Nantasket in the fall of 1747. When he received orders to put to sea, the commodore, in defiance of British law, sent a press gang to the Boston waterfront. During the early morning hours of November 17, the gangs picked sailors off outbound vessels and swept up a few dockworkers and apprentices for good measure. A crowd of several hundred townsmen quickly armed themselves with clubs, cutlasses, and pitchmops and

83. Brown, "Violence and the American Revolution," in Kurtz and Hutson, eds., *Essays on the American Revolution*, 91.
84. Benjamin Colman to Samuel Holden, May 8, 1737, Benjamin Colman Collection, II, Massachusetts Historical Society, Boston. Carl Bridenbaugh, *Cities in the Wilderness: The First Century of Urban Life in America, 1625–1742* (New York, 1938), 66, 196, 383, 389; Warden, *Boston*, 121–123; Sewall, *Diary*, II, 280–281.
85. Warden, *Boston*, 122.
86. For accounts of the Knowles riot, see Schutz, *William Shirley*, 127–130; John Noble, "Notes on the Libel Suit of Knowles *v.* Douglass in the Superior Court of Judicature. 1748 and 1749," Publications of the Colonial Society of Massachusetts, *Transactions*, III (Boston, 1895–1897), 213–218; Carl Bridenbaugh, *Cities in Revolt: Urban Life in America, 1743–1776* (New York, 1955), 115–117. For an analysis of the context of the riot, John Lax and William Pencak, "The Knowles Riot and the Crisis of the 1740's in Massachusetts," *Perspectives in American History*, X (1976), 163–214.

drove off the commodore's boats. The outraged crowd then searched for naval officers to hold as hostages against the return of the kidnapped men. For three days the government was powerless. The militia refused to turn out, drummers were quashed, and only officers appeared at muster. The governor, though not involved at all, was immediately suspected of complicity and became the chief target of the crowd. He had to retreat to Castle William in the harbor, where he pleaded with Knowles to return the impressed Bostonians, and at the same time ordered militia regiments in Milton, Roxbury, and Cambridge to stand by to occupy the town.

After three days of conflict and negotiation, Shirley reentered the city. Shirley had persuaded Commodore Knowles to release the townspeople and had demanded and received an apology from the Boston town meeting for the violence. When he came ashore from Castle William on Friday, November 19, a large assembly of the same militia which had refused to turn out during the crisis escorted him up King Street to the courthouse. The crowd of spectators lining the street applauded as he came along. Thomas Hutchinson, then speaker of the House and a witness to most of the events, said that "the governor was conducted to his house with as great parade as when he first assumed the government."[87] He was embraced as warmly as he had been maligned two days earlier.

In quick succession, the feelings of the people passed through two long pendulum sweeps, from conventional gratitude and allegiance to anger and resistance when protection failed, and then back. The people showed their loyalty and submissiveness at the end, but during the riot they demonstrated their capacity for swift, violent action when they believed the governor had failed them. The outbursts suggest how loyalty and compliance were joined in provincial Massachusetts with rebelliousness and independence. They existed together not because people were fickle, but because the fundamental monarchical principle was itself ambivalent. It both required submission and justified revolt. Massachusetts provincials celebrated the king and honored the royal governor, but when events provoked resentment and suspicion, monarchical culture enabled them to take power into their own hands.

The forces of resistance, though widespread, operated differently

87. Thomas Hutchinson, *The History of the Colony and Province of Massachusetts-Bay*, ed. Lawrence Shaw Mayo (Cambridge, Mass., 1936), II, 333.

going from the top to the bottom of provincial society. The leading statesmen and clergy joined in to overthrow Governor Andros in 1689. The terms of the protection formula enabled them to pull down a royal official without guilt or disgrace when extreme circumstances warranted. But in the run of everyday politics, the political leaders of provincial society were more circumspect. They did not countenance riots or candid press criticism. Regard for political stability and the dangers of provoking the king required the lower house to discipline the press as well as their own tongues and pens.

Among the common people, anger and suspicion more frequently burst through the surface. The returns of the grand juries and the occasional riots are evidence of a restive spirit in the populace. Many who were normally loyal and submissive showed themselves capable of direct action when provoked. Their resistance was facilitated by the fact that they did not step out of the dominant political culture to oppose rulers. The people simply took advantage of one implication of monarchical principles, the right to defend oneself when government failed to protect. The ambiguity in the protection covenant introduced a continuing strain of instability and violence into monarchical political culture, otherwise so strong and resilient.

v. Petitions

Although in theory and practice monarchical culture was inhospitable to candid criticism of rulers, some means had to be provided to vent legitimate complaints. The government could not regulate the disparate interests of a large empire without a safety valve for releasing resentments and identifying abuses and injustices. The acceptable vent was the petition. The right of petition, guaranteed traditionally to every Englishman, permitted him freely to complain of wrongs, but the form and language registered the complaint without impugning the motives of rulers.

From the fourteenth century on, there were two sorts of petitions, petitions of grace and petitions of right. A petition of grace was an appeal to the generosity of the crown for an exercise of power on the petitioner's behalf. It prevailed on the king's benevolence by presenting the sufferings or grievances of the subject as graphically as possible. The king granted or denied the request as an act of grace. A petition of right was based on law. The appeal was not for grace, but to the remedy of wrongs done contrary to law, and was to be granted not out of royal generosity, but out of respect for the subject's rights. Since petitions of rights were most commonly entered against rulers who could not be taken to court, they implicitly protested governmental abuses.[88]

Virtually any grievance or wrong could be the subject of a petition, including all of the specific complaints that underlay the riots and partisan politics of the eighteenth century: food shortages, impressment, boundary conflicts, currency issues, and so forth. When the imposition of the stamp tax outraged colonists in 1765, that anger properly flowed into petitions of right to king and Commons and a memorial to the House of Lords. Monarchical culture did not bottle up society or gag every complaining voice. There were methods and places for hearing every person and every grievance.

The genius of the petition lay in its language. A petition reaffirmed loyalty to the government in the very act of complaining. Petitionary language by its very nature reduced the petitioner to subservience. Although extreme among petitions from Massachusetts to the throne, the opening lines of the "humble supplication" of 1664, objecting to the presumptions of the royal commissioners, exemplified the expected attitude of parties to a petition.

> Dread Soveraigne:—If your poore subjects, who have remooved themselves into a remote corner of the earth to enjoy peace with God and man, doe in this day of theire trouble prostrate themselves at your royal feete, and begg yor favor, wee hope it will be graciously accepted by your majestie, and that as the high place you susteine on earth doeth number you here among the gods, so you will imitate the God of heaven, in being ready to mainteyne the cause of the aflicted and the right of the poore, and to receive their cries and addresses to that end.[89]

The opening lines of petitions always established the petitioners' inferiority and absolute loyalty. The 1664 petition, because of Massachu-

---

88. Holdsworth, *History of English Law*, IX, 9–15. Until the fifteenth century, legislation was conceived as a parliamentary petition to which the crown gave the force of law. *Ibid.*, X, 696.

89. Shurtleff, ed., *Records of the Governor and Company of Massachusetts Bay*, IV, 129–130.

setts' awareness of its vulnerability and because it was the seventeenth century, dramatized the lowliness with a picture of "poore subjects" prostrate at the royal feet. A 1729 petition in the eighteenth-century style more simply said, "We your Majesty's loyal and dutifull subjects, the Representatives of yor. Province of the Massachusetts Bay in the General Court assembled humbly beg leave to approach yor. Royall Presence and offer the reasons and grounds of our proceedings and conclusions." The word "humble" was ubiquitous in both centuries.[90]

Besides lowering themselves before the king, petitioners took great pains to assure him of their loyalty. The 1664 petition again overdid the point with the reference to "the high place you susteine on earth doeth number you here among the gods." The more moderate 1729 petition closed with a hearty appeal in an otherwise cooly reasoned piece: "We hope we shall always enjoy your Majesty's Royal Grace and Favour which this universally loyall people, above all things desire; that the Crown may long flourish on your Royal Head, and continue so in your most illustrious family to the latest posterity."[91] The opening words of the Stamp Act Congress petition to the king declared that the colonists were "Unanimously devoted with the warmest Sentiments of Duty and Affection to your Majesty's Sacred Person and Government, Inviolably attached to the present Happy Establishment of the Protestant Succession in your Illustrious House, and deeply sensible of your Royal Attention to their Prosperity and Happiness."[92]

More critical still to the stabilization of governance was the acknowledgment of the king as protector, the basis of gratitude and obligation. In one way or another petitionary rhetoric depicted the king acting out the role which more than any other bound his people to him. The 1664 supplication, after numbering the king "among the gods," went on to appeal to Charles to "imitate the God of heaven, in being ready to mainteyne the cause of the aflicted and the right of the poore." The Stamp Act petition virtually restated the protection covenant in its closing appeal: "With Hearts therefore impressed with the most indelible Characters of Gratitude to your Majesty, and to the Memory of the Kings of your Illustrious House, whose Reigns have been Signally distinguished by their Auspicious Influence on the Prosperity of the

90. *Cal. St. Papers*, XXVI, 311.

91. *Ibid.*, 314.

92. *Proceedings of the Congress at New York* (Annapolis, Md., 1766), 17, conveniently reprinted in Morgan, ed., *Prologue to Revolution*, 64.

British Dominions, and convinced by the most affecting Proofs of your Majesty's Paternal Love to all your People, however distant, and your unceasing and benevolent Desires to promote their Happiness . . ."[93]

Apart from the verbal recognitions of the king's protective role, the very act of petitioning confirmed him as protector. A petition was the act of the helpless begging aid from the powerful. The appeal put the petitioner immediately under obligation. The request itself, apart from the wording, contained an implicit promise of allegiance. That was a key moral distinction. Rioters implicitly declared government protection had failed and took upon themselves the defense of their rights and interests. Apart from the violence and disorder, rioters withdrew by so much from the covenant with rulers and became independent, or in a state of nature, as they came to call it. The petition, though equally a sign of discontent, drew petitioners more deeply into the protection covenant and heightened their dependence.

Since the merit of a petition was that it implicitly pledged allegiance, tone was as important as content. The attitude of the petitioners, their loyalty, pliability, affection, and gratitude, were under scrutiny. The exact wording made a difference. It defeated the purpose to allow telltale signs of independence or insolence to seep in. Conflicts arose more than once within the assembly over how high the wording should be. House and Council debated at length the wording of a 1728 reply to Governor Burnet, when tone was all that divided them. Both opposed the grant of a permanent salary, Burnet's request, but the more truculent House wished "to make answer," while the Council preferred "we humbly offer." The House claimed "Rights and Priviledges inherent in Us in common with other His Majesties Freeborn Natural Subjects," while the Council contented itself with "our undoubted Right as Englishmen," and "a Priviledge vested in the General Court by the Royal Charter." The eventual compromise changed the Council's pious hope, "We desire that the Rights and Priviledges of His Majesties good Subjects of this Province may be preserved," to the more militant "It is our Duty to preserve and maintain the Rights and priviledges of his Majesties good Subjects of this Province." The sensitivity to the slight nuances suggests the delicacy and importance of the correct posture.[94]

The contest between pliability and militancy recurred over and over in the pre-Revolutionary crisis. In 1764, when the House, led by James

93. Morgan, ed., *Prologue to Revolution*, 65.
94. *Journals of the House*, VIII, 269–272.

Otis, and the Council, led by Lieutenant Governor Thomas Hutchinson, debated the wording of a petition in opposition to the impending Stamp Act, the substance of the protest was never in question. Parliamentary taxation was unacceptable in both houses. The language was all that was at issue. The Representatives' version again went for natural rights and strict constitutional guarantees. Hutchinson turned aside this "incautiously expressed" draft and pressed on the House the "imprudence" of offending the crown. After ten days of exhausting debate, his own draft received approval, wherein colonial taxation was made a privilege, "a matter of favor," and "not a claim of right."[95] The technicalities of the imperial constitution were not the issue. Hutchinson was searching for language to depict an attitude of compliance rather than of stubbornness and independence. On both sides of the Atlantic, politicians, accustomed to the rules of monarchical government, listened for small differences in tone of voice, knowing the crown would scrutinize the document for the colonist's underlying attitude.[96]

As the disagreements over wording reveal, petitions were not a completely satisfactory form of complaint. They were unequal to the task of containing the undercurrents of hostility and suspicion running through colonial politics. The ambiguities in the protection formula enabled petitioners all too easily to turn their words against rulers. An intended confirmation of government became a rebuke. The acceptable talk of royal protection trembled on the edge of resentment and threat. A plea for help, with the change of a word or two, became an indictment.

The crown had long recognized the dangerous potential. In the uneasy days following the Restoration, Parliament forbade the submission of petitions to king or Parliament signed by more than ten persons. James II construed some petitions as seditious libel, often with good cause. The Kentish petition of 1701 was called "scandalous, inso-

---

95. Quoted in Bailyn, *Ordeal of Thomas Hutchinson*, 64–65. See also Edmund S. Morgan and Helen M. Morgan, *The Stamp Act Crisis: Prologue to Revolution* (Chapel Hill, N.C., 1953), 54.

96. Patrick Henry's Stamp Act resolves disturbed the legislative leaders in Virginia, Jefferson said, "not from any question of our rights, but on the ground that the same sentiments had been at their preceeding session expressed in a more conciliatory form to which the answers were not yet received." Quoted in J. A. Leo Lemay, "John Mercer and the Stamp Act in Virginia, 1764–1765," *Virginia Magazine of History and Biography*, XCI (1983), 20–21.

lent, seditious."[97] The Stamp Act Congress, though it observed the correct form, obviously used petitions to the king and commons as instruments of protest.

The trouble lay not in the form, but in the contradictions in the protection covenant itself. Honoring the king for protection of the people's rights so easily verged toward a warning of the consequences of failure to respect those rights. "His Royal Highness, the Prince" understood, Samuel Mather explained in a sermon ostensibly intended to honor Prince Frederick on the occasion of his death in 1751, "that nothing was *lawful* in the Administration but what was *allowed by the Laws* of the Realm; and that He, who wears the Crown by the National Consent and Choice, is not above the Laws, nor at Liberty to dispense with them."[98] If the press and the riot spoke for the discontent of ordinary people, the critical petition was the instrument of respectable politicians for admonishing rulers.

The mood of the petitions changed through the eighteenth century. The extravagant diction of the seventeenth century gave way to a more moderate tone of voice. It became poor form to address the king as "Dread Soveraigne" and to indulge in excesses of self-abasement and extravagant praise. Enlightenment aversion to enthusiastic display affected the style of petitionary language just as it modified religious discourse.[99] And besides the changes in style, there were changes in argument. Petitions came to incorporate what can be called a Lockean spirit. They emphasized the contractual nature of the protection-and-allegiance covenant. The king was obligated to protect the people's rights just as much as they were obligated to obey and serve.

The change in argumentation cannot be attributed primarily to John

97. E. Neville Williams, *The Eighteenth-Century Constitution, 1688–1815* (Cambridge, 1960), 410–411; J. P. Kenyon, ed., *The Stuart Constitution, 1603–1688: Documents and Commentary* (Cambridge, 1966), 361; Holdsworth, *History of English Law*, X, 698.

98. Samuel Mather, *A Funeral Discourse Preached On the Occasion of the Death of the High, Puissant and most Illustrious Prince Frederick Lewis* . . . (Boston, 1751), 27. See also Jonathan Mayhew, *A Discourse, Occasioned by the Death of King George II* . . . (Boston, 1761), 38–39; *Journals of the House*, XVII, 181; *New-Eng. Weekly Jour.*, Nov. 27, 1727.

99. Thomas Hollis told Benjamin Colman in 1727, commenting on a recent address to the crown from Massachusetts, that "your compliments to our court now are fifty if not one hundred years too ancient for our present polite style and court," and recommended that he read over some recent addresses from English dissenters for models of a proper tone. Josiah Quincy, *The History of Harvard University* (Cambridge, Mass., 1840), I, 385. Norman Fiering provided this reference.

Locke's direct influence. His political ideas were little known in the colonies until the second quarter of the century. When they quietly came into currency around mid-century, it was not for revolutionary purposes.[100] Locke's basic formulation was in essence a restatement of the ancient covenant: rulers were obligated to defend the rights of their people, and when they failed, the gratitude and allegiance on which obedience was grounded fell away. Like the protection covenant on which it was based, the idea of contract was as much a statement of obligation as a justification of revolt.[101] Locke was as versatile as monarchical culture itself in serving the submissive as well as the rebellious. One of the first presentations of Lockean political ideas in New England, John Barnard's 1734 election sermon, merely repeated conventional clerical conceptions of balance: rulers were to serve the people, and the people were to obey the rulers. Governor Jonathan Belcher liked the sermon so much he asked his son in England to slip a copy into the queen's bedchamber.[102]

But Locke's contract theory could also be used in the eighteenth-century spirit of bargaining, to insist on the king's respect for popular rights in return for the people's allegiance. As the Revolution drew near, Locke became a convenient resource for voicing the altered moral posture of Americans. He did not represent a new ideology, but helped to refocus an old one. Because Lockean ideas could be worded to emphasize the resistance side of traditional principles, Locke helped the colonies pass smoothly from submission to resistance without a

100. John Dunn could find no record of Locke's *Two Treatises of Government* in America before 1724. Locke was better known for his educational theories. A copy of *The Collected Works* was entered in the Harvard College Library in 1724, and reference was made to Locke in a pamphlet by the Anglican John Checkley published in 1730. The *Weekly Rehearsal* advertised Locke's *Works* on Apr. 30, 1733. The previous year the *Weekly Rehearsal* referred to Locke as the best guide to logic. John Dunn, "The Politics of Locke in England and America in the Eighteenth Century," in John W. Yolton, ed., *John Locke: Problems and Perspectives: A Collection of New Essays* (Cambridge, 1969), 45–80.

101. Kern has pointed out that "it was easy to consider the limitation imposed upon the king by the oath and homage of the people as the elements of a contract, in which it was tacitly or expressly stipulated that one party was bound to the other so long as each upheld the contract; and this view was argued from a very early date." *Kingship and Law in the Middle Ages*, 77, 196. For the doctrine of contract in the English Civil War, see Wormuth, *Royal Prerogative*, 118–119.

102. John Barnard, *The Throne Established by Righteousness . . .* (Boston, 1734); Shipton, *Sibley's Harvard Graduates*, IV, 509.

break in fundamental ideology.[103] The Congress did not need to search out a wholly new political philosophy. Monarchical political culture was as equal to the task of revolution as it was to enjoining submission. The Declaration of Independence itself conformed to the principles of the protection covenant. It was a bill of treason, indicting the king for assaulting his people rather than protecting them. The Lockean language in the Declaration simply stated explicitly the right to revolt which was always implicit in the monarchical covenant.

From the beginning to the last moment of membership in the empire, Massachusetts carried on its political life in the presence of the king. He was not a presence like John Winthrop or Elisha Cooke. Neither the Stuarts nor the Hanoverians interfered personally in colonial politics. The influence of the king was symbolic and moral, not practical. His moral power grew out of the conception of the state and, particularly, the covenant between king and people. But as a governing symbol, the king's moral influence was felt everywhere. According to the required fiction, the monarch played a role in every aspect of government. He commissioned every officer, symbolically fought every battle, conducted all diplomacy with other heads of state. The king sat in every court in the person of the judge. The laws were declarations of his will. All land titles derived from the king, who still had a claim, however slight and attenuated, to every piece of property in the realm or dominions.

In political discourse, politicians had always to speak with the king in mind. They jeopardized the province's privileges if they displayed any degree of disloyalty, and were thought to invite insurrection if they criticized the crown's appointees. Monarchical culture prescribed a language for petitions that turned complaints into loyal supplications for royal protection, increasing the petitioners' obligations to yield. The same language with a slight twist could be turned to remind the king of his obligation to protect the people, even to demand a defense of their rights. The simple principle of a protector king generated a pliable rhetoric, readily put to many purposes. But through it all, the king was never forgotten.

Though placing many restraints on politicians, monarchical political

103. Ronald Hamowy, "Jefferson and the Scottish Enlightenment: A Critique of Garry Wills's *Inventing America: Jefferson's Declaration of Independence*," *WMQ*, 3d Ser., XXXVI (1979), 503–523; Isaac Kramnick, "Republican Revisionism Revisited," *American Historical Review*, LXXXVII (1982), 629–664.

culture could not repress opposition. The protection covenant itself provided a direct justification for resistance. The government's failure to protect the people returned to them the right to protect themselves. In that special sense, rebellion could be conducted within the limits of monarchical culture. And in that sense, the king presided over the American Revolution.[104] For only by indicting the king for failing to protect his people could Americans, by the terms of the ancient covenant, free themselves from monarchical rule and declare their independence.

104. Ernst Kantorowicz has pointed out that because the king was both a natural person and the embodiment of a divine political ideal, his moral authority as an ideal could be used to justify opposition to him as a person. Hence the Puritan slogan in 1642, "fighting the king to defend the king." Ernst H. Kantorowicz, *The King's Two Bodies: A Study in Mediaeval Political Theology* (Princeton, N.J., 1957), 21–23.

CHAPTER 2

Dependence

i. Government and Society

The strength of monarchical government in Massachusetts came primarily from its command over the consciences of the people. That moral force enabled the crown to govern the colonies up through the middle of the eighteenth century largely without armies and with little control of the courts. There was always the threat of force, of course, but the provincials submitted to royal rule day by day less from fear than from belief in the legitimate right of the king and his officers to rule, as that right was grounded in the protection covenant of monarchical political culture.

Within England itself, and ideally elsewhere, an additional most powerful influence worked in behalf of royal government. Monarchical government rested on a social order that sustained and implemented its authority. It began with the king and his household and through a series of interlocking dependencies extended outward and downward through the nation. Through this network, influence from the throne supposedly extended to the lowest ranks of society and into the farthest reaches of the empire. Those myriad personal relationships gave vitality and force to the formal proceedings of government.

This social structure can be considered monarchical in the sense that the essence of the relationship between king and people, the principle of dependence, was replicated endlessly through society at every level. The whole people's dependence on the king came from the same pattern as the relationship of landlords and tenants, masters and apprentices, fathers and children—that is, of patrons and clients.[1] The relationships went beyond mere deference. Deference was born of the respect owed to all persons of a superior class. Out of deference people honored any who bore the outward marks of gentility: clothing, speech, bearing, equipage, housing, or the ability to lead. Strangers benefited as well as familiars. Dependence, by contrast, was a relationship between two specific individuals, not between classes of people. It was based on concrete and particular acts of favor and protection, and the bond was deeper and more compelling by far.

The word for the various forms of protection that accompanied dependence in the social sphere was "patronage." Frequently, in use, "protection" and "patronage" were nearly equivalent words. The Fellows of Harvard College, upon the arrival of Governor Shirley in 1741, promised to teach youth the principles of loyalty in hopes of recommending "the Security of all our Rights and Privileges to your kind Patronage."[2] Securing popular rights made a ruler a patron. On the other hand, office-seekers asked for the "protection" of the duke of Newcastle when all they wanted was a position.[3]

The forms of patronage were as varied as the needs of the people. An entire borough became dependent on a local aristocrat who used his influence in Parliament to obtain a favorable alteration in the town charter. Their patron expected in return the selection of his candidates for the House of Commons. Children and women were dependent on their fathers and husbands. The whole household of a gentleman, all the cooks, maids, gardeners, coachmen, and retainers forming his establishment, were dependents. Artists dedicated their work to great men and women in hopes of obtaining their patronage. Writers hoped

1. Technically, allegiance was sworn only to a lord with no superior, and in England only the king qualified. Sir William Blackstone, *Commentaries on the Laws of England*, 12th ed. (London, 1793–1795), I, 366–367.
2. *Boston Gazette, or, Weekly Journal*, Aug. 24–31, 1741.
3. William Shirley to the duke of Newcastle, May 12, 1740, in Charles Henry Lincoln, ed., *Correspondence of William Shirley, Governor of Massachusetts and Military Commander in America, 1731–1760* (New York, 1912), I, 21.

for a pension or a place in government in return for putting their pens to the service of the ministry. Dean Swift pleaded with Robert Walpole to get him out of Ireland, and only when refused did Swift commit himself to the opposition.

In England the most significant forms of patronage were land and office. The landlord's traditional functions went beyond those of an owner's renting land. In the eighteenth century, rural landlords still felt a responsibility for the general well-being of tenants, their health, morals, religion, and education. Landlords endowed churches, saw to the care of the sick, distributed gifts on holidays, mediated disputes, encouraged promising children, disciplined the reprobate, all in the expectation of reciprocal respect and compliance. "None but those who have been familiarized with English farmers and cottagers," an observer remarked early in the nineteenth century, "can conceive the degree of awe which actuated them in regard to their landlords. . . . The English landlord's influence does not slumber. We have ourselves seen farmers deprived of their farms for frequent drunkenness—for leading immoral lives—for being bad cultivators;—and we have seen a farmer compelled to marry a girl whom he had seduced."[4]

In the eighteenth century virtually every ambitious young Englishman's first need was to attract the attention of a potential patron. There was virtually no way to obtain office other than through the influence of a person in power. Every place was in the gift of someone who must be approached, cajoled, and promised return of some sort. And not only political office, but all the favors government had to bestow—on printers, merchants, surveyors, builders, clerics—were accessible only through a patron. The ambitious young Benjamin Franklin with an eye on advancement in England threw himself on the mercies of Governor William Keith in Pennsylvania. Only after Franklin learned by experience of aristocratic caprice did he attempt to rise in the world independently. Printers with strictly colonial aspiration hungered for government printing business, the staple of the trade; merchants yearned to be the commissary for a military expedition or to be granted a contract for provisions.

The workings of patronage politics do not have to be construed as corrupt. It was equally in the interest of society to identify talent and

4. Quoted in Harold Perkin, *The Origins of Modern English Society, 1780–1880* (London, 1969), 228.

elevate it to office. "Indeed, what later ages considered corruption," Harold Perkin has observed, "was, in the absence of impersonal examination and selection procedures, the inevitable method of recruitment."[5] The great politicians on whom the responsibility of governance rested could not afford to fill the imperial bureaucracy with undiluted incompetence. The positive side of what the opposition condemned as corrupt was the recognition of merit or service to worthy friends. The great lords of the realm went about the business of bestowing office and rewarding talent without embarrassment. Patronage was fully within the moral scope of their position in society and government. What was a patron to do if not patronize merit?

At the same time, the extent of a great lord's patronage measured his power. He was personally the beneficiary of the offices and pensions he dispersed. His own influence enlarged with the number of men in his interest. The essence of what made him great was not the high style in which he lived, the mere reflection of greatness, but his patronage. "The final assessment of any man's power," J. H. Plumb has written, "lay in his ability to influence voters."[6]

Patronage thus combined both good and evil. Self-interest, ambition, avarice, and the lust for power wound through the networks of dependents and patrons, joined with a justifying sense of duty and obligation. Beneath the surface of shifting alliances, betrayals, caprice, conniving, and vengeance lay a powerful and enduring structure of personal relationships. As Perkin put it:

> In the mesh of continuing loyalties of which appointments were the outward sign, patronage brings us very close to the inner structure of the old society. Hierarchy inhered not so much in the fortuitous juxtaposition of degree above degree, rank upon rank, status over status, as in the permanent vertical links which, rather than the horizontal solidarities of class, bound society together. "Vertical friendship," a durable two-way relationship between patrons and clients permeating the whole of society, was a social nexus peculiar to the old society, less formal and inescapable than feudal homage, more personal and comprehensive than the contractual, employment relationships of capitalist "Cash Payment." For those who lived within its embrace it was so much an integral

5. *Ibid.*, 48.
6. J. H. Plumb, *Sir Robert Walpole: The Making of a Statesman* (London, 1956), 54.

part of the texture of life that they had no name for it save "friendship."[7]

Politics in Great Britain was in large part the art of managing the more accessible networks of influence which composed the upper layer of the social structure. Along the broad margins of both Whig and Tory parties, where issues alone did not move the members of Parliament, the influence of patrons exercised discipline over that substantial body of men who desired office. The king's own patronage at the disposal of his ministry encompassed nearly a fifth of the Commons, and the recipients could be relied on for the most part to vote with the government.[8] Each of the great lords of the realm included in his sphere of influence a certain number of others, usually from a borough that had customarily deferred to his judgment because of proximity and familiarity or because of aid rendered and a debt incurred. The duke of Newcastle was said to control fourteen seats.[9] Other members would comply because of kinship, hope of office for themselves or friends, or for a hundred other reasons why the weak looked to the strong. From the group of powerful men who held the strings of power reaching into society and Parliament, the king selected his ministry. The choice was based on compatibility and competence first, but power and influence were important secondary qualifications. By careful management, the members in the ministry's aggregate interest, the group committed on principle and the recipients of the king's patronage, could be coalesced into a working majority.[10]

The governance of Britain (as contrasted to its politics) was almost entirely a function of the social structure. The formal institutions of law enforcement were primitive and frail. The constable, the practice of hue and cry, the justice of the peace, and insecure village jails could never have controlled the mass of criminal activity typical of later centuries. People kept within the law because most were under the sur-

7. Perkin, *Origins of Modern English Society*, 49.
8. Robert Walcott, Jr., *English Politics in the Early Eighteenth Century* (Cambridge, Mass., 1956).
9. James A. Henretta, *"Salutary Neglect": Colonial Administration under the Duke of Newcastle* (Princeton, N.J., 1972), 235; Plumb, *Walpole*, 26–27.
10. In addition to works by Plumb, Perkin, and Walcott cited above, see John B. Owen, *The Rise of the Pelhams* (London, 1957); Sir Lewis Namier, *The Structure of Politics at the Accession of George III*, rev. ed. (New York, 1957); J. H. Plumb, *The Growth of Political Stability in England, 1675–1725* (London, 1967).

veillance of a superior on whom they depended for favor and protection in innumerable ways. The effectiveness of the justice of the peace arose as much from his position as local magnate as from his official commission. His authority was multiplied through the gentlemen in his jurisdiction, all of whom were expected as a concomitant of their standing to arrest, rebuke, and discipline moral offenders. Their presence alone intimidated individuals with criminal ambitions. As the old society ran downhill in the early nineteenth century, observers commented admiringly on how a landlord's influence over farmers and cottagers operated in "the most powerful manner, in preventing vice and crime; and in giving the best tone to what may be called the rustic world."

> In the small communities, the villages and tiny towns, of the old society in which the average individual worked, lived and had his being, the source of income itself, with the rest of the "life-chances" of the individual, was controlled by a paternal landlord, employer or patron who regarded class attitudes as the insubordination of a dependent child. In a world of personal dependency any breach of "the great law of subordination," between master and servant, squire and villager, husband and wife, father and child, was a sort of petty treason, to be ruthlessly suppressed.[11]

The stupendous increase of crime in the nineteenth century occurred in English cities, where individuals floated free of the dependency networks and, under the pressure of desperate poverty, turned to theft and prostitution.[12] Large cities had to organize police forces in the modern sense of agencies for crime control to compensate for the failure of urban society to construct adequate dependency networks, which traditionally had disciplined the populace.

Even at its height, patronage never encompassed every individual. Economic adjustments, wars, epidemics, and unforeseen disturbances of every sort cast loose vagabonds, migratory laborers, soldiers of fortune, sharpsters, small traders, weavers, and professionals.[13] Moreover, certain segments of the population prided themselves on their inde-

---

11. Perkin, *Origins of Modern English Society*, 228, 37.
12. *Ibid.*, 162, 167.
13. For independent merchants, see Plumb, *Walpole*, 27–29. E. P. Thompson has argued against the independence of the middle class. "In general, the middle classes submitted to a client relationship. Here and there men of character might break free,

pendence and deprecated those enthralled by the obligations of office or tenantry. Backbench members of Parliament of both parties, many of them squires elected from their counties, distinguished themselves from the active politicians by a freedom of action impossible for the beneficiaries of patronage. Real Whig publicists, drawing on a prominent strain of Renaissance political thought, erected independence into an ideal of good citizenship, so much so that more traditional commentators complained with Oliver Goldsmith, "That independence Britons prize too high, / Keeps man from man, and breaks the social tie."[14]

But the ideal of independence was strictly limited. The country party advocates of independence did not intend to honor vagabonds, small shopkeepers, or even professionals like the city lawyers. The gentlemen who applauded Cato, the country party publicist, and were his ideal were men anchored in the traditional social structure. They were substantial patrons in their own small kingdoms with domains of dependents that included their families, a household establishment, local clerics, tenants and farm laborers, village tradesmen, and others who ate at their tables, received their charity, and depended on their protection in litigation. The country party proposed independence only for the small number of people who constituted the political community, not for the entire society. Even radical publicists, dedicated to discrediting patronage, yielded to its temptations when the opportunity presented itself. Thomas Gordon, the coauthor of *Cato's Letters*, a few years after their composition accepted a place from Walpole and dedicated his next work to Sir Robert and the Prince of Wales.[15] Dependence was not so disgusting that adequate compensation could not persuade an advocate to change his mind.

Far from proving the weakness of patronage, radical Whig writings attested to its strength. They prized independence because they knew the force of dependence. They feared that corruption was enveloping all of England. The patronage of the wealthy and powerful was luring

---

but even the arts remained coloured by dependency upon the liberality of patrons." "Eighteenth-Century English Society: Class Struggle without Class?" *Social History*, III (1978), 143.

14. Oliver Goldsmith, "The Traveller," lines 339–340, in Arthur Friedman, ed., *The Collected Works of Oliver Goldsmith* (Oxford, 1966), IV.

15. David L. Jacobson, ed., *The English Libertarian Heritage: From the Writings of John Trenchard and Thomas Gordon in "The Independent Whig" and "Cato's Letters"* (Indianapolis, Ind., 1965), xxviii.

more and more of the populace into debasing dependence. The world was filling up with flattery, servility, and blind obedience. However numerous in reality were the detached and masterless, in country party rhetoric, power lay with masters and their networks of dependents. Only by a mighty effort could the combined forces of a virtuous and independent citizenry hold that power in check.

Cato of the *Letters* believed that monarchy and dependency were inextricably intertwined. Dependence at lower levels was more than an imitation of the archetypal dependence of people on the king; the two were mutually reinforcing. The crown added to the strength of both magnates and the lesser gentry, just as it drew strength from them. The nature of the estates of nobility and gentry, "and particularly of their Mannors," Cato observed, led to the formation of dependencies.[16] It was in the interest of the aristocracy to intensify this dependence. Monarchy added to the advantages of the propertied classes, in Cato's analysis, by affording them further favors to bestow. The "Birth and Fortunes" of nobility and gentry "procure them easy Admittance into the Legislature," and thence "their near Approach to the Throne gives them Pretences to honourable and profitable Employments." Men of property were the ones most likely to receive government offices. The control of political patronage which the king placed in the hands of the privileged increased their power by creating "a Dependence from the inferior Part of Mankind."[17] The distribution of places added to the possession of estates gave nobility and gentry a steely grip on their advantageous position.

Naturally such men "must ever be in the Interest of Monarchy, whilst they are in their own Interest; since Monarchy supports and keeps up this Distinction, and subsists by it." Monarchy, a patronage society, and property distinctions were so intermingled that change was impossible. "It is senseless to imagine, that Men who have great Possessions, will ever put themselves upon the Level with those who have none, or with such as depend upon them for Subsistence or Protection." The gentry's superior position as protectors and providers lead them to believe "they have a Right to govern or influence" their dependents, and realistically the upper classes "will be ever able to

16. John Trenchard and William Gordon, *Cato's Letters: or, Essays, on Liberty, Civil and Religious, and other Important Subjects*, 3d ed. (New York, 1968 [orig. publ. London, 1724]), II, 160.
17. Trenchard and Gordon, *Cato's Letters*, III, 160–161.

govern, whilst they keep their Possessions, and a monarchical Form of Government, and therefore will always endeavour to keep it."[18] The combination of property and office was irresistible.

The larger liberty of a republic or commonwealth was out of the question, Cato said, "before Nature has prepared the way" by equalizing property. "An Equality of Estate will give an Equality of Power," and nothing short of that will work. No "Man or Number of Men" should be so foolish as to believe they "can ever get Power enough to turn all the Possessions of England topsy-turvy and throw them into Average." Nature alone can effect that, for no one desires it but such as have no estates.[19] Awaiting the disposition of nature to the contrary, monarchy, inequality, and dependence were fastened on England as securely as the love of property and distinction were ingrained in human nature.[20]

ii. Imperial Politicians

To exercise full effect in the colonies, monarchy required a social structure comparable to England's. It was not enough for Massachusetts to embrace the myth of the protector king and to promote a good opinion of the sovereign and his officers. The day-to-day power to govern was transmitted along the lines of influence reaching downward from the throne into individual villages and towns. Without the interlocking chains of dependency, the crown would have to rely solely on persuasion and claims to legitimate authority, weak reeds when unpopular measures had to be enforced.

In the colonies, the royal governors clearly were involved in this social structure both as dependents and as patrons. They were the beneficiaries of the largesse of English patrons, and at the same time, the bulk of colonial patronage lay in the governors' hands, making them the link between the imperial bureaucracy and colonial society. The varied agencies and ministries directed policies and instructions to the

18. *Ibid.*
19. *Ibid.*
20. For a discussion of how magnates and the crown mutually supported one another, see Reinhard Bendix, *Kings or People: Power and the Mandate to Rule* (Berkeley, Calif., 1978), 212–217.

governor from above, and the lines of colonial influence converged in him from below. He was expected to carry out imperial policies by managing the authority and influence inherent in his office.

Before inquiring into the extent and strength of the needed dependencies in Massachusetts, it is worthwhile to look more closely at the governors themselves. For besides practicing patronage politics, the governors, more than any other colonials, exemplified the ethics and etiquette of monarchical society. Dependency implied more than the manipulation of influence to serve political interests. A code of behavior accompanied the acceptance of a great man's favor, including the adoption of certain personal ideals. The requirements of getting and holding office in the imperial patronage system, by instilling values and habits useful in that world, made the governors exemplary of those values and thus cultural and social forces in the colonies. In them we see the full dimensions of monarchical society as it might have taken form in America.

The careers of two of Massachusetts' royal governors, Joseph Dudley and Jonathan Belcher, exhibit slightly different aspects of this patronage culture. Dudley, governor from 1702 to 1715, was a scion of one of Massachusetts' most distinguished families.[21] He was first recruited into royal government by Edward Randolph, the commissioner for the Lords of Trade in Massachusetts before the loss of the first charter. Randolph early recognized in Dudley a potential ally. Major Dudley "hath his fortune to make in the world," Randolph wrote the bishop of London, "and if his Majesty, upon alteration of the government, make him captain of the Castle of Boston and the forts in the colloney, his Majesty will gaine a popular man."[22] Randolph assumed that a man of large ambition could be won to the side of the crown, since crown patronage was the only avenue to advancement. On the other hand, Dudley's popularity, meaning his influence with the people, would extend the authority of the crown.

Dudley's career thereafter exemplified the typical course of a colonial placeman. He gained office, lost it, and regained it again. Through constant attention to potential supporters in England, he succeeded despite the hatred of the popular party in Massachusetts, which never

21. The narrative which follows is taken from Everett Kimball, *The Public Life of Joseph Dudley: A Study of the Colonial Policy of the Stuarts in New England, 1660–1715* (New York, 1911).

22. Quoted *ibid.*, 14.

forgave his collaboration with the Andros administration that took over after the loss of the first charter. When Bostonians jailed Governor Andros in 1689, Dudley was jailed too. Despite the repudiation, Dudley's darling ambition remained to return as royal governor, and after ten years of accumulating support, he received the appointment.

Dudley had two patrons in England: William Blathwayt, the clerk of the Privy Council, who became a member of the Board of Trade after its organization in 1696, and Lord Cutts, who was in favor with the king for bravery at the battle of Boyne. Cutts, who had been appointed governor of the Isle of Wight, made Dudley deputy governor in 1693. Besides the administrative experience, Dudley got a close-up of patronage politics. Even Cutts's rebukes taught Dudley the imperatives of patronage politics. Absent from the Isle of Wight most of the time to attend more important matters in London, Cutts managed Dudley and the governorship by letter. On April 1, 1698, in a peeved passage, Cutts told Dudley:

> I won't complain of your unkind behavior to me, that is not the matter now in dispute; tho' in a week (all things consider'd) some men would have shown some concern for One's health and affaires; but I don't insist upon it, your Personal Civilitys are most certainly your own, and dispose on 'em how you please; provided you trouble me no more if Fortune should chance to smile on me, then you doe now. . . . But this (as I sayd before) is not the matter now in dispute. That which I have just reason to complain of is your reall neglect of the King's service in your station. For if I neither see nor hear of a Lieut-Governour in a Week, I would fain know (when so many things are to be consider'd now the Spring comes on) what you are payd for. . . . when you come to the King's Levee (which you should doe if ever you expect any thing) you can make your reports, and take my Orders as you goe up. I have very good Neibours now and want no Company.[23]

In quick succession, Cutts admonished Dudley for failing in all the important points of patronage etiquette. Inquiries after the patron's "health and affaires" were not empty formalities. They were signals of continuing affection and loyalty (Cutts for the moment was out of

23. Robert C. Winthrop, Jr., ed., "Letters of Lord John Cutts," Massachusetts Historical Society, *Proceedings*, 2d Ser., II (Boston, 1886), 188–189.

favor at court) in a system where loyalties were constantly shifting and where patrons were as dependent on their clients as clients on patrons. Letters, despite the conventional apology for occupying the patron's time, were the veins and arteries of patronage. Silence and the withholding of information were the prelude to a break. Colonial governors pleaded with their protectors in England for a letter as a sign of favor. Cutts demanded a report from his client as a pledge of support and to help Cutts keep the reins of power firmly in hand.[24] Finally, Cutts reminded Dudley that friends were made and patronage distributed at levees as much as at court.

Lord Cutts gave Dudley his greatest boost when, in 1701, Cutts saw to his client's return as a member of Parliament for Newton, a rotten borough on the Isle of Wight. A seat in Parliament gave Dudley access to the centers of power and occasion to impress those in command of colonial patronage. He was invariably in attendance when needed, and always on the side of the ministry in critical votes. In London he widened his circle of friends and improved his reputation with a discourse on "the Several Juicies in Fruit Trees," and a paper contributed to the Society for the Propagation of the Gospel in Foreign Parts entitled "An Account of the State of Religion in the English Plantations in North America."[25] His views on colonial affairs were sought after all the more widely because they accorded with the policies of the current administration.

Through the assiduous pursuit of every advantage, Dudley accumulated an imposing array of supporters. The aggregate strength enabled him to return in 1702 to govern a colony that just thirteen years earlier had stripped him of authority, imprisoned him for ten months, charged him with 119 illegal acts, and sent him to England for trial. The hatred still burned brightly in the minds of the old charter party in 1702.[26] Throughout his administration they scrutinized every move and objected to every vaguely suspicious action. But Dudley stood firm against these varied onslaughts, thanks to the continuing confidence of

24. Dudley's friend, John Chamberlayne, later chastened Dudley for failing to write his English patrons. Mass. Hist. Soc., *Collections*, 6th Ser., III (Boston, 1889), 529, 531, 540, 546. Governor Belcher had an insatiable appetite for letters from the great. *Belcher Papers* (*ibid.*, 6th Ser., VI–VII [Boston, 1893–1894]), Part I, 2, 25, 32, 49, 204, 404; Part II, 247, 251, 418, cited hereafter as *Belcher Papers*.
25. Kimball, *Joseph Dudley*, 72.
26. *Ibid.*, 52.

his English patrons. They protected him in the places where power was actually exercised. The colonials' animosity was harmless so long as Dudley's name stood in good repute at home. He fell in Massachusetts only with the change of administration in Westminster in 1715, when a totally new political configuration left out his patrons. Lord Stanhope, a new secretary of state who knew not Joseph, dropped the governor in favor of one of his own clients, Colonel Elizeus Burgess, a former aide.

Up until the end, Dudley exemplified the assiduous placeman who studied the art of cultivating patrons. He learned from Cutts the significance of the letter, the royal levee, the inquiries after the patron's health, the apparent courtesies that were actually signals of allegiance. He displayed the proper tincture of learning with his treatise on fruit tree juices and showed a fitting interest in the colonial church. All that was necessary to do, Dudley performed, thereby earning the reward he had long sought. He was the quintessential colonial placeman and displayed in his person and career what would have happened to everyone in the upper levels of Massachusetts society had the patronage networks extended further.

Jonathan Belcher, also a native son of Massachusetts, did not lay the groundwork for his appointment in 1730 as carefully as did Dudley in the 1690s. Belcher did have the foresight to visit the court of Hanover on two of his three trips to Europe. In 1704, just twenty-two, and five years out of Harvard, he saw the Princess Sophia, heir to the crown of England. In 1708 he again called on the electress of Hanover "purposely to throw myself at your Royal Highness's feet," as he told her. This time he offered candles and an Indian slave as gifts from New England. Years later, in 1729, when his name was mentioned to George II as a candidate for the governorship, the king asked whether he was the same Mr. Belcher who twice was at Hanover.[27]

In the period between 1704 and 1729, Belcher spent six years in England, which gave him opportunity to widen his acquaintanceship. His "peculiar Beauty and Gracefulness of Person" and the marks of "the scholar, the accomplished Gentleman, and the true Christian," not to mention his large fortune, won him friends and admirers. Lord Town-

27. Clifford K. Shipton, *Sibley's Harvard Graduates: Biographical Sketches of Those Who Attended Harvard College*, IV (Cambridge, Mass., 1933), 435–436, 439. There is no full-length biography of Belcher. The best sketch is Shipton's cited here, but the governor reveals himself all too candidly in his letters. *Belcher Papers*, Parts I, II.

shend, secretary of state, was particularly instrumental in obtaining Belcher's commission in 1730. Belcher told Townshend in 1731, "I am fond of calling your Lordship my patron and the author of the favour and honour I enjoy under his Majesty."[28]

The governorship, however, was not the culmination of a campaign for Belcher as it was for Dudley or later for William Shirley. It was more the result of chance and circumstance. Governor Burnet died unexpectedly on September 7, 1729, when Belcher was in London on a mission for the Massachusetts House. The government had been paralyzed for two years while Burnet and the Representatives were locked in a death struggle over a permanent salary. Belcher was a native, educated, wealthy, and obviously in favor with the House. His mission in London was to present the case against a permanent salary to the Board of Trade. Belcher told the board that Burnet's problems were the result of personal dislike among House members. At the same time, Belcher promised faithfully to pursue the instruction to obtain a permanent salary. Since he had long been a prerogative man and only suddenly and mysteriously switched to the side of the Representatives, the board saw in him a likely candidate to break the stalemate. Just two and a half months after Burnet's death, Belcher received his commission.

Belcher's involvement in patronage politics is less evident in his own maneuverings for office than in his efforts on behalf of his favorite son, Jonathan Junior. It was not enough to obtain high office for oneself. The provincial gentleman of the eighteenth century was equally interested in establishing a family, a line of gentlemen who would be powers in their locales and of service to the king in their own generations. Joseph Dudley dreamed of a Dudley dynasty. His children married auspiciously into the Winthrop, Sewall, and Dummer families, and Dudley pressed Winthrop particularly to favor the Winthrop-Dudley marriage in the disposition of his estate. The reason Dudley gave was the great need of New England for aristocratic families.[29] Dudley himself practiced a limited form of primogeniture. He gave sizable farms and other valuables to each of his children, but to his eldest, Paul, he gave houses and lands in Roxbury, Oxford, Woodstock, Newton, Brookline, and Merrimack. He entailed his estate so that his land would

28. *Belcher Papers*, Part I, 91.
29. Joseph Dudley to John Winthrop, Feb. 5, 1714, Mass. Hist. Soc., *Colls.*, 6th Ser., V (Boston, 1892), 283–284.

descend to his heirs "after the manner of Englande forever, to the Male Heirs first, and after to the Females."[30] In such ambitions we glimpse the monarchical society that might have grown up in America under different circumstances.

Belcher's ambitions for his family took another direction, and through the career of his son we see the modes of personal conduct, the personal ideals, and the inner spirit of monarchical society. Rather than seek his fortune in New England, Jonathan Junior sailed for England. After assisting his father in the first year of his governorship, Jonathan left in the spring of 1731 to study law at the Middle Temple. Although Belcher sincerely desired a superior law training for his son, the governor lost no time in introducing young Jonathan to all of Belcher's own acquaintances in hopes of winning favor. A veritable blizzard of letters from the governor fell on England in the fall of 1731. Jonathan Senior wrote to the bishop of London, the bishop of Lincoln, the duke of Newcastle, Lord Chancellor King, Sir Robert Walpole, Horace Walpole, Sir Philip Yorke, Sir Charles Talbot, as well as a crowd of lesser lights: Sir Joseph Jekyll, Henry Bendish, Edward Carteret, Robert Dingley, Isaac Watts, and Edmund Calamy and other dissenters.[31] On his side it was Jonathan Junior's duty, as he was advised after a dinner with the speaker of the House, Arthur Onslow, "to take all possible occasions of paying your duty that you may keep your self in his knowledge and memory, which may prove to your great future advantage."[32] The governor obliged his English connections with favors as he could: a cage of flying squirrels for the Princess Royal, wild geese for the park of Horace Walpole, and a tea-table or dishes made of black ash knots for Newcastle or the queen.[33] In a more serious vein, he obtained the Naval Office in New Hampshire for the son of the bishop of Lincoln, who was Jonathan's most serious patron.[34]

Every detail of Jonathan's demeanor was the subject of Belcher's instruction. He was as concerned as Lord Chesterfield to make a gentleman of his son. Belcher charged Jonathan to intersperse his labors with the proper recreations: "walking, riding, bowling, and billiards." He

---

30. Dudley's will is reprinted in Kimball, *Joseph Dudley*, 202.
31. *Belcher Papers*, Part I, 26, 30, 53–61, 64–65, 71–72, 92, 455–456.
32. Jonathan Belcher to Jonathan Belcher, Jr., Nov. 11, 1731, *Belcher Papers*, Part I, 49.
33. Shipton, *Sibley's Harvard Graduates*, VIII (Boston, 1951), 345.
34. Jonathan Belcher to the bishop of Lincoln, Nov. 18, 1731, *Belcher Papers*, Part I, 53. See also *ibid.*, 61, 87.

advised Jonathan to "endeavour to be a fine dancer," and to learn fencing, "which will extend all the parts and members of your body, open your breast, and make you more erect."[35] Jonathan enlarged on his father's instructions and took up the bull viol, flute, and spinet and contributed an epithalamium to the Cambridge volume of poetry in honor of the Princess Royal on the occasion of her marriage to the prince of Orange.[36]

Father and son disagreed over hair versus wigs. The governor forbade Jonathan to cut his hair without his father's leave, even though dressing the hair cost as much as a good wig. "I think nothing a finer ornament to a young gentm than a good head of hair well order'd and set forth." He wanted Jonathan when he appeared "before persons of rank and distinction" to be "always handsomely drest (your hair especially)." When Jonathan persisted, the father finally relented and consented to cutting the hair on the anniversary of his second year in residence at the Middle Temple. There was a caution, however. "Always buy your wiggs at the Court End of the town. Altho' they'll cost more, they are so much more nice and genteel."[37]

There were nice manners to practice along with fencing and dancing. Belcher warned against "pride, supercilliousness, affectation, and stiffness" that would make Jonathan "the object of hatred and contempt." "I say let Mr. Belcher be admir'd for his real humility, condescention, courteousness, affability, and great good manners to all the world" that he might be "the object of love and esteem." Through "the study of humanity," these qualities would "become perfectly easy and natural to you."[38]

It was not all for show. Belcher wished his son to incorporate real virtues, particularly to ground himself in the law. For a time he would have to content himself "with living pretty much a recluse, for the advantage of study." But ultimately the payoff would come. Belcher put up as an example the eldest son of Governor Dudley, who came to the attention of the chief judge while young Dudley was assiduously taking notes during a court session at Westminster Hall. The judge called

35. Nov. 11, 1731, *ibid.*, 52.
36. Shipton, *Sibley's Harvard Graduates*, VIII, 345, 347.
37. Nov. 11, 1731, *Belcher Papers*, Part I, 52; Nov. 25, 1731, *ibid.*, 65; Apr. 23, 1733, *ibid.*, 265.
38. Nov. 25, 1731, *ibid.*, 65; Nov. 11, 1731, *ibid.*, 52.
39. Nov. 11, 1731, *ibid.*, 52, 51.

for the notes of several sergeants and barristers and after examining Dudley's pronounced them the best of the lot. "This I tell you," Belcher said, "to prick up your emulation."[39]

Belcher's vision of his son's future was of thorough, self-denying preparation followed by glorious recognition. Jonathan was to be beautiful, accomplished, learned, affable, and generous—a gentleman, and, with the help of a successful law practice, ultimately wealthy. The father related to his son a recurring experience that seemed to encapsulate the governor's expectation. "In my several voyages to London I have many times observ'd a gentm starting out of a court with a coach and six, fine liveries, etc, and upon enquiry, Who's that? Why 'tis such an one who has with great industry acquir'd a fine estate and hitherto liv'd obscurely, but now is able to make the figure you see." It all added up at last to that: the once obscure but well-grounded gentleman making a public figure which startled Londoners into asking, "Who's that?" Thus the provincial dream of glory.[40]

The seeds Belcher planted that first fall bore fruit almost too quickly. Within a year after his arrival in England, young Jonathan, just twenty-two, was thinking of standing for a seat in Parliament. Despite the encouragement of the bishop of Lincoln, the governor said no, until the *Rhode Island Gazette* forced his hand by publishing in December 1732 news of Jonathan's plans. Then the governor went to with a will. He persuaded Jonathan to stand for Tamworth in Staffordshire instead of Coventry, his initial choice. Belcher hoped for the support of Tamworth's large Quaker population because of aid rendered Massachusetts Quakers. Learning of the town's prevailing industry, the governor leaned on Boston merchants to place large orders with Tamworth's cloth manufacturers. The title of a twenty-thousand-pound estate in Connecticut was transferred to Jonathan to meet the qualifications for a seat, and two thousand pounds was sent for a campaign fund. All to no avail. Jonathan did not take the trouble to appear in person at the election and lost by a dozen votes in two or three hundred.[41]

That was a turning point. The bishop of Lincoln lost interest in Jonathan because of the governor's failure to find an adequate place for the bishop's son in Massachusetts. The law business never got off the ground, and Jonathan's yearly expenses of more than £2,000, more

40. *Ibid.*, 52.
41. Shipton, *Sibley's Harvard Graduates*, VIII, 348–349.

than the governor's total income from office, drained his father's resources and exhausted his patience. None of Jonathan's various love
interests matured. At thirty-one he was unmarried and a heavier and
heavier burden on his father. In 1741 the removal of Belcher from the
Massachusetts governorship drastically curtailed his influence in England. Young Jonathan was forced to pull back. He moved to Dublin
and resorted to the modest patronage of Belcher relations. William
Belcher, M.P., arranged the position of deputy secretary to the lord
chancellor of Ireland with a salary of £150 a year. There at last after
years of virtual invisibility, more mature fruit ripened. Immersing himself in legal studies as his father had long advised, Jonathan prepared
an abridgment of the Irish laws. The publication came to the attention
of Lord Halifax, who in 1754 nominated Jonathan to the office of chief
justice of Nova Scotia. Received there with great pomp, he went on to
serve honorably on the bench and then to become lieutenant governor.
Governor Belcher's dreams for his son were at least in part realized.[42]

The lengthy negotiations for position which Belcher conducted on
behalf of young Jonathan were all carried forward in strict conformity
to an etiquette which was as much a manifestation of patronage society as was the struggle for place itself. Belcher's language revealed
the underlying assumptions of the culture all the more sharply because
he yielded to the enthusiastic exaggeration of the provincial. After
Arthur Onslow, speaker of the House, agreed to see Jonathan, Belcher
could scarcely contain himself. "I find myself, Sir, under the strongest
tyes of respect and gratitude to Mr. Speaker for the mention you are
pleas'd to make of the youth, my son, and in so kind and condescending manner as that you wou'd endeavour to find him out and see him.
This is what neither I, nor he, dare expect, but it will be favour and
honour enough that you will allow him now and then to make his
obeisance to you, and that you wou'd drop your wise advice how he
may best proceed in the study of the law."[43] Informing those sentiments were the same conventions that structured petitionary rhetoric.
Speaker Onslow is cast as the powerful and condescending personage
to whom the lowly Jonathan turns for protection. Belcher repeatedly
portrayed his son and heir, to whom had been given every advantage
New England offered, as sadly disadvantaged, being "born and bred in

42. *Ibid.*, 350–355.
43. Oct. 30, 1731, *Belcher Papers*, Part I, 21.

the wilds of America." It was only with the aid of the "umbrage and protection" of such glorious personages as Onslow that Jonathan could "make some small figure in life." The honor of the speaker's "wise advice how he may best proceed in the study of the law" placed father and son "under the strongest tyes of respect and gratitude."[44] The bishop of Lincoln's patronage was so obligating, Belcher told his Lordship, as to bring the Belchers "within the Statute of Bankruptcy."[45]

Although, of course, the bond was not completed until favors were actually granted, the conventions of the protection covenant required such abasement to express gratitude and promise obedience. As he told his patron Lord Townshend, the governor would never forget "that great respect and duty I shall always owe to your Lordship for the favour and honour his Majesty has done me and my family, in appointing me to the government of my native country." For that reason, Belcher was eager to offer return of service. "I can't help repeating that the obligations your Lordship has laid me under can never be obliterated, and nothing wou'd be so pleasing to me as an opportunity of giving some convincing proofs of the great sense I retain of your Lordship's goodness to me."[46] Although there was no formal political authority binding the client to his patron, the pledge of obedience was nonetheless explicit. "I shall always with great pleasure pay a strict regard and obedience to the least of your Grace's commands," Belcher told the duke of Newcastle.[47]

The language, the personal cultivation, and the dreams of glory were all aspects of the patronage world into which Dudley and Belcher were drawn. Occasional lapses and awkward movements betrayed their provincial origins now and again. Belcher's language was overblown compared to the better-controlled letters of his successor in the governorship, William Shirley, who had been reared in England. But both Dudley and Belcher zealously cultivated their patrons, learned patronage etiquette, and enjoyed success. They alone are proof that the Atlantic had not isolated Massachusetts from monarchical society in England and that some provincials at least yearned for its rewards.

44. Jonathan Belcher to Arthur Onslow, Oct. 29, 1731, *ibid.* See also Belcher to Onslow, Dec. 30, 1731, *ibid.*, 92.
45. Nov. 18, 1731, *ibid.*, 55. See also Jonathan Belcher to Jonathan Belcher, Jr., Sept. 18, 1732, *ibid.*, 181.
46. Dec. 30, 1731, *ibid.*, 90.
47. Nov. 1, 1731, *ibid.*, 25.

Doubtless others shared such aspirations. How many is an important question. For after winning their appointments, Dudley's and Belcher's effectiveness as governors depended heavily on how far the structures and forms of monarchical society had penetrated Massachusetts as a whole.

iii. Massachusetts Society

Belcher's life would have been easier had the patron-client relationships in which he was enmeshed extended from the governor down through lesser offices and the assembly, through the minor aristocracies of the towns, and at last to the voters. A tug on the string at one end would have yielded compliance at the other. Under such perfect conditions, the governor would have enjoyed invariable cooperation in the legislature. Voters would have chosen friends of the government at the annual elections, and no representative would have resisted royal instructions. Though motivated by the desire for a patron's favor, each act of obedience would be represented as service to the crown for the well-being of the king's people. Idealized as the picture was, Sir Robert Walpole did govern England on these principles between 1721 and 1742. Although the chains of dependence were incomplete and frail, calling for consummate management, Walpole's power came from his control of the patronage networks.

A few critics charged Massachusetts' royal governors with the same practices. A British tract circulated in 1707 accused Joseph Dudley of manipulating military and court appointments. A Massachusetts address in favor of Dudley, the tract claimed, was the work of "particular Friends; such, who being either Related to him, or bore Commissions under him, dare not deny his Request."[48] Later in the century the assembly itself was said to be corrupted. "Popular as the Form of our Government appears to be, *they* have no lucrative Employments to bestow," a contributor to the *Boston Gazette* observed in 1750, "while on

---

48. *A Memorial of the Present Deplorable State of New-England with the many Disadvantages it lyes under in the Male-Administration of their Present Governour, Joseph Dudley* . . . (Boston, 1707) (Mass. Hist. Soc., *Colls.*, 5th Ser., VI [Boston, 1879]), 39. See also *ibid.*, 40, 46, 103, 104, 118, 119, 122, 124.

the other Side; [mili]tary Com[mis]sions, P[o]sts of Profit, and B[i]lls of Exch[an]ge have been the Reward of *signal Services*."[49] Publicists here and there through the century hinted that the governor had patronage networks at his command comparable to Walpole's.[50]

More practical men recognized the limits on the governor's patronage. "We have few places of any considerable profit," the Scotsman William Douglass wrote Cadwallader Colden in New York in 1727. The most profitable was the Naval Office, which worked with customs to enforce the Navigation Acts. "The captaincies of the forts to the eastward are at present of small value." There were others. "The governor has the nomination of the sheriffs of the several counties, (good small farms, that of Boston is the most profitable post in this Province, next to the treasurer and commissary in war time) of the register of probates in the several counties."[51] But all of these officers served without salary, dependent solely on modest fees for remuneration, and the appointee himself did the work. There were no pensions and sinecures in Massachusetts Bay.

The modesty of the returns did not discourage Douglass. In 1727, thinking of the profitability of office for a governor, Douglass observed that "a great many small farms well leased out may be equivalent to a few great farms." Twenty years later in his *Summary, Historical and Political*, speaking this time of politics, Douglass emphasized that the nomination of "all Judges, Justices and Sheriffs, which being, with the Militia Officers of the several Townships, a great Majority in the lower House, gives the Governor a very great Influence there."[52] There was truth in Douglass's judgment. The governor appointed the five members of the Superior Court of Judicature with the advice and consent of the Council, and the four members of each county court, the Inferior

49. Jan. 9, 1750. See also *A Letter from a Gentleman in Mount Hope, to His Friend in Treamount* ([Boston, 1721]), in Andrew McFarland Davis, ed., *Colonial Currency Reprints, 1682–1751* (Boston, 1910–1911), II, 263; and *A Letter to an Eminent Clergy-Man in the Massachusett's Bay* ([Boston, 1721]), in *ibid.*, 232–233, 238.

50. *Reflections upon Reflections: or, More News from Robinson Cruso's Island* . . . ([Boston], 1720), in Davis, ed., *Colonial Currency Reprints*, II, 116–117; Samuel Sewall, *Diary of Samuel Sewall, 1674–1729* (Mass. Hist. Soc., *Colls.*, 5th Ser., V–VII [Boston, 1878–1882]), II, 238, cited hereafter as Sewall, *Diary*.

51. Nov. 20, 1727, in Mass. Hist. Soc., *Colls.*, 4th Ser., II (Boston, 1854), 176.

52. *Ibid.*; William Douglass, *A Summary, Historical and Political, of the First Planting, Progressive Improvements, and Present State of the British Settlements in North-America* (Boston, 1747–1752), I, 472–473.

Court of Common Pleas. He similarly proposed justices of the peace, judges and registers of probate courts, and sheriffs. As captain general and commander in chief, the governor appointed military officers independently. The House nominated commissioners of impost and excise and notaries public to the governor for approval.[53] Alone among colonial legislatures, the Massachusetts House nominated members of the Governor's Council.

Jonathan Belcher sought conscientiously to live up to the potential of Massachusetts patronage which Douglass glimpsed. As the beneficiary of English patronage, Belcher envisioned himself wielding the same power in Massachusetts Bay. The criticism of his immediate predecessor William Burnet for giving offices to allies did not intimidate Belcher. When he promised in England to bring the opposition to rein, he had the judicious distribution of offices in mind. Thomas Hutchinson, writing the history of Massachusetts thirty years later, said Belcher made more frequent removes from office than any governor before or after.[54] He began in 1730 by claiming that all commissions required renewal at the entrance of a new governor into office. Over the next three years he confirmed all the current justices of the peace, with the implicit threat of dropping troublesome persons. During his eleven years in office he had a total of 71 provincial-level appointments to make, and 672 county-level appointments, including offices such as commissioners of impost and excise nominated from the House. The combined total of 743 places in which he had a voice exaggerates his patronage somewhat, because a number of individuals were appointed to more than one office. In Middlesex County, with 85 appointments in the eleven-year span, duplications reduced the number of individuals affected to 64. If the proportion applied to all appointments, the total for the province would be 557 appointments instead of 743. But to this number must be added military commissions and appointments to special courts.[55]

53. For gubernatorial patronage in the colonies generally, see Bernard Bailyn, *The Origins of American Politics* (New York, 1968), 72–76.

54. Thomas Hutchinson, *The History of the Colony and Province of Massachusetts-Bay*, ed. Lawrence Shaw Mayo (Cambridge, Mass., 1936), II, 276, 285 n.

55. John Gorham Palfrey, *History of New England* (Boston, 1858–1889), IV, 540. The number of appointees was tabulated from William H. Whitmore, *The Massachusetts Civil List for the Colonial and Provincial Periods, 1630–1774* . . . (Baltimore, Md., 1969 [orig. publ., Albany, N.Y., 1870]).

Belcher worked the patronage machinery for all it was worth. He appointed Elisha Cooke, leader of the popular party, to the Suffolk County Court of Common Pleas and for two years neutralized his influence.[56] During the conflict over the land bank in 1740, Belcher issued a proclamation threatening removal of all persons holding commissions under the governor. Four of the leading figures in the bank resigned as justices of the peace, and ten others were dismissed. Nine militia officers resigned, and eleven were dismissed.[57] A later tract said that when the land bank bills were before the legislature, Belcher had influence with "Friends and Dependants in the House."[58] And the number of "dependents" in the House was substantial. In 1731 at the beginning of his administration, just 25 percent of the House were military officers or held court appointments, usually as justices of the peace. By 1735 the number rose to a high of 60 percent and then tapered off slightly. The median for Belcher's entire administration from 1731 to 1740 was 51 percent of the House with appointments from the governor.[59]

Four years before Belcher's appointment, officeholding appears to have influenced House votes. In 1726 an Explanatory Charter issued by the crown came before the assembly. A few years before, the House had battled with Governor Shute over the right to dismiss itself and to appoint its own speaker without his approval, claiming the right on the basis of ambiguous wording in the charter. Shute had carried a complaint to England, and the Privy Council recommended the issuance of an Explanatory Charter to put the governor's powers beyond question. After a warm debate the House accepted the additional provisions by a vote of forty-eight to thirty-two. Among the thirty-two opponents of

56. Whitmore, *Massachusetts Civil List*, 78; Palfrey, *History of New England*, V, 540.

57. J. M. Bumsted, "Religion, Finance, and Democracy in Massachusetts: The Town of Norton as a Case Study," *Journal of American History*, LVII (1970–1971), 826; Andrew McFarland Davis, *Currency and Banking in the Province of the Massachusetts Bay* (American Economic Association, *Publications*, 3d Ser., II [1901]), 147–149; *Boston Weekly News-Letter*, Dec. 4, 1740; Palfrey, *History of New England*, IV, 551–552.

58. *An Account of the Rise, Progress and Consequences of the two late Schemes Commonly call'd the Land-Bank or Manufactory Scheme and the Silver Scheme . . .* (Boston, 1744), in Davis, ed., *Colonial Currency Reprints*, IV, 256.

59. The names and titles of the representatives are listed at the beginning of each session in *Journals of the House of Representatives in Massachusetts* (Boston, 1919–), X, 1–2, 135–136; XI, 3–4, 211–212; XII, 3–4; XIII, 3–4; XIV, 3–4; XV, 3–4; XVI, 3–4; XVII, 3–4; XVIII, 3–4; XIX, 3–4, 13–14.

the royal prerogative were five men with appointments; among the supporters were thirty holders of appointments, 63 percent of the total.[60]

Despite the success in this one instance, patronage politics failed Belcher. His was one of the most troubled administrations in provincial history. He battled the popular party in the House over three major issues, the issuance of money from the treasury, the permanent salary, and currency. In none of the three did he win through the manipulation of influence. The House finally backed down on treasury requisitions after the Privy Council ruled against them; the governor and Privy Council compromised on the salary; and only an act of Parliament stopped the land bank. Gubernatorial influence may have had its way on lesser issues, but on the big constitutional and fiscal questions, the governor's power crumpled. He was reduced to mere argumentation or to frantic appeals to England. Belcher was no more successful than his predecessors Shute and Burnet in disciplining the assembly.[61]

Why was patronage not more effective? Fragments of a Walpolean political system did take shape in Massachusetts by the middle of the eighteenth century. John Adams remarked in his 1787 defense of the American state constitutions that in New England villages "you will find that the office of justice of the peace, and even the place of representative, which has ever depended only on the freest election of the people, have generally descended from generation to generation, in three or four families at most."[62] A close study of forty-three Massa-

60. *Journals of the House*, VI, 458–459. John Murrin notes that over the fifty years from the confirmation of the Explanatory Charter to Independence, justices of the peace were much more likely to vote with the governor on nonfiscal questions than were other representatives. On the sensitive fiscal questions, there is no clear pattern. John H. Murrin, "Review Essay," *History and Theory*, XI (1972), 269. For an assertion that Gov. Dudley was able to control the House through patronage, see T. H. Breen, *The Character of the Good Ruler: A Study of Puritan Political Ideas in New England, 1630–1730* (New Haven, Conn., 1970), 225. See also Ellen E. Brennan, *Plural Office-Holding in Massachusetts, 1760–1780: Its Relation to the "Separation" of Departments of Government* (Chapel Hill, N.C., 1945), 20–21.

61. The administrations of Govs. Shute, Burnet, and Belcher in the 1720s and 1730s tested the governor's powers more strenuously than earlier or later. Before 1715 and after 1741, the governors' preoccupation with military expeditions inhibited their ability to confront the assembly on the explosive constitutional and fiscal questions. The failures of Shute, Burnet, and Belcher in contests with the assembly defined the limits of gubernatorial influence.

62. Charles Francis Adams, ed., *The Works of John Adams*, IV (Boston, 1851), 393.

chusetts towns confirmed the truth of Adams's observation for the middling range of towns between the poorest small towns and port towns like Boston and Salem. At the extremes, family made little difference in the likelihood of election to town office, but in the broad middle a few families or even a single family dominated. Three generations of Boardmans in Cambridge served a total of ninety-three terms as selectman, representative, and moderator as well as monopolized the offices of clerk and treasurer. Nine members of the Pynchon family served 24.5 percent of all leadership terms in Springfield. The Chandlers in Worcester, the Leonards in Norton, and the Partridges in Hatfield enjoyed the same confidence of the voters. These magnates owned land and mills, resided in the largest houses, and intermarried with each other and four or five other eminent families of the town. Lesser town leaders called themselves yeomen or husbandmen; these great families adopted the title of gentleman and worked as merchants, lawyers, or physicians.[63] One crucial element of the Walpolean system, a local aristocracy, was in place in Massachusetts.

Moreover, the local elites blended with the provincial elite. From the most prominent county leaders, the governor selected judges for the county courts, the superior courts, and the upper ranks of the military. The members of the Governor's Council emerged from this same integrated hierarchy of social and political positions. Forty-nine of the fifty-one councillors chosen in the eighteenth century from a sample of country towns served as major town leaders as well. Fifty-two of fifty-nine appointees to the Inferior Court of Common Pleas had similarly occupied major town offices.[64] In the colonies as in England, the natural local leaders had to be appointed to the courts at the risk of offending the political sensibilities of the populace. When governors disregarded local preferences, the locals complained. In 1759 eleven justices in Hampshire County resigned when the governor appointed a candidate whom they considered unqualified.[65] Though not always

63. Edward M. Cook, Jr., *The Fathers of the Towns: Leadership and Community Structure in Eighteenth-Century New England* (Baltimore, Md., 1976), 96–102, 89. For similar studies of Connecticut, see Bruce C. Daniels, "Family Dynasties in Connecticut's Largest Towns, 1700–1760," *Canadian Journal of History*, VIII (1973), 99–110; and "Large Town Officeholding in Eighteenth-Century Connecticut: The Growth of Oligarchy," *Journal of American Studies*, IX (1975), 1–12; and *The Connecticut Town: Growth and Development, 1635–1790* (Middletown, Conn., 1979), 198–199.
64. Cook, *Fathers of the Towns*, 149–150.
65. J. R. Western, *Monarchy and Revolution: The English State in the 1680s* (Totowa, N.J.,

pleased with the local favorites, in appointing them as provincial officials the governors did gain access to the power structure of the towns. The interwoven strands of leadership reached from the highest provincial offices through town and county elites to town meetings and ultimately to every village inhabitant.

Ideally the network should have given the governor control over the entire population and enabled him to govern through influence alone. But something went wrong. The towns were not compliant, and the legislature was unreliable. The breakdown came because of the size and independence of the electorate. Though deferential to the local magnates, most Massachusetts villagers were not beholden to them. There were simply too many independent voters for a handful of local leaders to patronize. The majority of adult males owned enough land to vote in town and provincial elections. In most English boroughs a select few exercised the franchise and could be influenced. Massachusetts towns were more like the English counties, which were notoriously difficult to influence. The towns presented unwieldy numbers of independent voters, far more than the magnates could encompass in their patronage.

John Adams contended that the rich men of the town "have many of the poor, in the various trades, manufactures, and other occupations in life, dependent upon them for their daily bread; many of smaller fortunes will be in their debt, and in many ways under obligations to them."[66] To Adams's list can be added licenses for public houses, ferries, stores, and the right to place weirs in rivers, all at the command of justices of the quorum in each county. The great could offer legal advice, lend oxen and plows, hand out work to sons of lesser landholders. Undoubtedly the magnates of the towns had a hundred favors to bestow in addition to their smiles, occasional meals, and simple kindness.

But the Massachusetts town aristocracies lacked the most powerful resources of their English counterparts, office and land. At most the town aristocracies controlled the lesser militia offices and a few clerkships, and these were few and the profits small. Office-seekers besieged English magnates in comparable positions with pleas for appointments. "The letter-bag of every M.P. with the slightest preten-

1972), 48; William R. Taylor, *Western Massachusetts in the Revolution* (Providence, R.I., 1954), 24.

66. C. F. Adams, ed., *Works of John Adams*, IV, 392.

sions to influence," J. H. Plumb has noted, "was stuffed with pleas and demands from voters for themselves, their relations or their dependents."[67] Except for an occasional letter, political correspondence of this kind does not exist in Massachusetts. The offices were too few, the rewards too slight. More important, in contrast to England, most villagers held their lands directly of the province with virtually a fee simple title, and rented only to supplement their own holdings. Local magnates could not threaten severity in rent collections or promise generosity. Except for the landless poor, who were not qualified to vote anyway, the people of Massachusetts existed as an independent force in politics.

On top of these social realities, the voting population had the advantage of annual elections for both town and colony offices. England's radical Whigs placed annual elections high on their agenda of reforms without coming close to achieving that goal in the eighteenth century. Massachusetts voters all along had the power to turn out unsatisfactory representatives to the assembly, and they used it. The electorate immediately purged individuals who displeased them. John Shepard of Stoughton, guardian of Indian lands, who stripped the property for his personal profit, was defeated in attempts to gain reelection to the assembly immediately after his maladministration was made known.[68] Boston voters rejected Thomas Hutchinson in 1749 for his part in restricting the currency. Forty-five other representatives suffered the same fate for supporting the controversial bill, as had thirty-six representatives in the land bank crisis of 1741.[69] Pamphlets warned voters to take particular care to avoid excisemen and other officeholders.[70] The electoral power of the people neutralized the influence of the town ar-

---

67. J. H. Plumb, "Political Man," in James L. Clifford, ed., *Man versus Society in Eighteenth-Century Britain: Six Points of View* (Cambridge, 1968), 6.

68. Stephen E. Patterson, *Political Parties in Revolutionary Massachusetts* (Madison, Wis., 1973), 49.

69. Malcolm Freiberg, "Thomas Hutchinson and the Province Currency," *New England Quarterly*, XXX (1957), 199–200; Robert Zemsky, *Merchants, Farmers, and River Gods: An Essay on Eighteenth-Century American Politics* (Boston, 1971), 125–126; Davis, *Currency and Banking*, II, 158–159.

70. [John Colman], *The Distressed State of the Town of Boston . . .* (Boston, 1720), in Davis, ed., *Colonial Currency Reprints*, I, 407; *A Letter from Mount Hope*, in *ibid.*, II, 263; Josiah Quincy, *A Municipal History of the Town and City of Boston, During Two Centuries, from September 17, 1630, to September 17, 1830* (Boston, 1852), 15; Breen, *Character of the Good Ruler*, 249.

istocracies, vitiating what strength there was in the frail dependency networks. Governor Joseph Dudley observed dispiritedly of his Council that they "do so absolutely depend for their stations upon the people that they dare not offend them, and so H.M. has no manner of service from them, nor countenance to H.M. affairs, which makes my station very difficult."[71]

Looking back after the Revolution, British observers easily detected the failings of British government in America. "The king and government of Great Britain held no patronage in the country," William Paley wrote, "which could create attachment and influence, sufficient to counteract that restless, arrogating spirit, which, in popular assemblies, when left to itself, will never brook an authority, that checks and interferes with its own."[72] William Gordon, the Scottish-born historian of the Revolution, specified more exactly where the miscalculation lay.

> The British ministry have been greatly mistaken, in supposing it is the same in *America* as in their own country. Do they gain over a gentleman of note and eminence in the colonies, they make no considerable acquisition. He takes few or none with him; and is rather despised, than admired to by former friends. He has not, as in Britain, dependants who must act in conformity to his nod. In *New England* especially, individuals are so independent of each other, that though there may be an inequality in rank and fortune, everyone can act freely according to his own judgment.[73]

The difficult point to grasp was that in America economic inequality did not entail dependence. The problem began with the first settlements, William Knox, a colonial bureaucrat, argued in 1779. "Lands were granted out in small tracts to each Individual in perpetuity." "This mode excluded all ideas of subordination and dependence. The relation between Landlord and Tenant could have no existence where every man held by the same tenure and all derived immediately from the Crown." The accumulation of property did not bring the social and political power customary in England.

71. Dec. 10, 1702, in Noel Sainsbury *et al.*, eds., *Calendar of State Papers, Colonial Series, America and West Indies* (London, 1860–), XXI, 39, cited hereafter as *Cal. St. Papers.*

72. William Paley, *The Principles of Moral and Political Philosophy*, 7th ed. (Philadelphia, 1788), 375.

73. William Gordon, *The History of the Rise, Progress, and Establishment, of the Independence of the United States of America . . .* (London, 1788), I, 143.

The superior industry or better fortune of some enabled them to extend their possessions by purchase, others become wealthy thro' successful trade, but their riches brought them little Influence for if they parcelled out their Lands it was upon the same tenure as they held it, only requiring a stated rent in addition to The King's Quit rent, or they sold the fee for a sum paid down. Influence with the people was therefore only to be acquired by becoming popular. And popularity was only to be obtained by following the humor or disposition of the People.[74]

Where rentals were common as in Maryland and Virginia, the relationship of owner and renter was contractual, financial, impersonal, without familial affection or associated obligations, not as lord of the soil and dependent. Where owners "sold the fee for a sum paid down," as in New England, the freeholders severed all ties and lost "all ideas of subordination and dependence." Enfeeblement of the lines of dependence reversed the normal flow of influence. Instead of the people's yielding to the magnates, Knox argued, the magnates followed "the humor and disposition of the People."[75]

The Massachusetts political system annoyed imperial administrators. More given to accusation than analysis, they attributed the assembly's contentiousness to excessive privileges or a rebellious spirit. "Massachusetts is a kind of commonwealth," the duke of Newcastle was told in 1740, "where the king is hardly a stadtholder."[76] "Many People think we are Disposed to rise in Rebellion against the King," a Massachusetts man wrote from London in 1723 when Governor Shute was entering his complaints, "and it's so Comonly talked of That I Scarse dare own my Self to be a New England Man." "Collo Blayden one of the Lords Commissioners Said That in any other Country than New England the Assembly would have been Esteemed Traitors and Rebellious and that by all he Could See we were Dancing to the Tune of 41."[77] Later in the colonial period, more dispassionate observers

---

74. Jack P. Greene, "William Knox's Explanation for the American Revolution," *William and Mary Quarterly*, 3d Ser., XXX (1973), 299–300.
75. *Ibid.*
76. Quoted in William H. Nelson, *The American Tory* (Oxford, 1962), 175.
77. Capt. Clark, London, to Edward Winslow, Sept. 9, 1723, forwarded by Winslow to William Dummer, Nov. 5, 1723, Massachusetts Archives, LI, 380, Archives Dept., State House, Boston. See also Henretta, "*Salutary Neglect*," 96; *Journals of the House*, VIII, 32–321; Palfrey, *History of New England*, IV, 525; *Cal. St. Papers*, XXXVI, 523–524.

conceived of New England as a different subspecies of English society, governed by a different spirit, and producing a distinctive personality type. Edmund Burke, reflecting on New England, noted the presence of gentlemen who let estates as in England:

> But the greater part of the people is composed of a substantial yeomanry, who cultivate their own freeholds, without a dependence upon any but providence and their own industry. . . . The people by their being generally freeholders, and by their form of government, have a very free, bold, and republican spirit. In no part of the world are the ordinary sort so independent, or possess so many of the conveniences of life.[78]

Adam Smith used the same word. "Their manners are more republican, and their governments, those of three of the provinces of New England in particular, have hitherto been more republican too."[79] Henry Hulton, reporting on a tour of backcountry Massachusetts in 1771, used another potent word. "The spirit of equality prevails throughout . . . and they have no notion of rank or distinction."[80] The presence of urban poor, of vagrants in the countryside, and of hardscrabble farmers struggling on tiny, depleted acres did not register with English observers who, of course, compared Massachusetts to the home country. In England by 1790, four hundred great landlords held one-fifth of all the farmland, and all landlords together owned three-quarters of all the cultivated land.[81] The prevalence of independent yeoman in New England, working their own freeholds, however small, distinguished Massachusetts society in English eyes and elicited the words "equal" and "republican."

Massachusetts, of course, was not republican in the technical sense of possessing a government of the people without a king. No one ever hinted at the need for such a change. The provincials themselves reaffirmed their loyalty to the crown of Great Britain on every possible

78. [Edmund Burke], *An Account of the European Settlements in America*, 6th ed. (London, 1777), 167.
79. Quoted in Gerald Stourzh, *Alexander Hamilton and the Idea of Republican Government* (Stanford, Calif., 1970), 66.
80. Quoted in Wallace Brown, *The King's Friends: The Composition and Motives of the American Loyalist Claimants* (Providence, R.I., 1965), 31.
81. G. E. Mingay, *English Landed Society in the Eighteenth Century* (London, 1963), 19–24.

occasion. Monarchical practices infused politics. The Massachusetts assembly bargained with the king for moral advantage according to the terms of the protection-and-allegiance covenant. In times of distress the assembly instinctively reverted to petitions in which they acknowledged their lowliness and need for royal protection. The assembly guarded its own tongue and hushed free-lance critics whose aspersions on government threatened to weaken allegiance. The culture of monarchy was everywhere evident in Massachusetts political practice.

But Massachusetts society was not monarchical. It was too flat, with too broad a base of independent yeomen. The chains of dependency reaching downward into society fell short of the broad mass of people. Particularly at the local level, the magnates exercised too little influence to assure royal governors of support. Monarchy in Massachusetts relied too heavily on the moral force of the king as symbol to eradicate the spirit of independence that perpetually troubled the colony's royal officials. Massachusetts partook of monarchical culture, but lacked a monarchical society.

iv. Consequences

The broad base of independent voters in Massachusetts set the tone of provincial society. The inhabitants of the grand Georgian houses, with their elegantly appointed rooms filled with fashionably dressed friends, could not, despite wealth and sophistication, disregard the ordinary people. Provincial gentlemen in pursuit of office might zealously cultivate those in power, but they had also to heed the power of their fellow townsmen to vote assemblymen in and out of office and indirectly, through the sway of opinion, affect all local appointments. The provincial gentry had to mind their manners with common farmers just as they observed the proprieties with the governor. The real political strength of the common people inhibited the flowering of aristocratic hauteur, as Dudley and Belcher exhibited it, and instilled instead that republican spirit which English observers consistently noted. Any who went too far toward aristocratic pretense put their political lives in jeopardy.

But manners were not all that the absence of monarchical society affected. Visitors and officials saw signs of political as well as social republicanism in Massachusetts. It was not uncommon for frustrated officers of the crown to accuse Massachusetts of striving for independence. The colonists themselves celebrated the monarch repeatedly, pledged their loyalty, and practiced politics by the rules of monarchical political culture. Notwithstanding, their critics gloomily predicted the demise of imperial rule if the colonists were not restrained.

Most critics blamed the liberal privileges in the charter for infecting Massachusetts with a republican spirit. But one observer offered an analysis based on the underlying contradiction of social structure and political form. Cato of the *Letters* offered an opinion on the fragility of a monarchical government that lacked a monarchical society to support it. Cato believed the two could exist in stable equilibrium for a time, but foresaw the eventual fall of the government. And he explained exactly what an acute eighteenth-century political observer believed would bring about that downfall.[82]

Cato had Dutch governments, not American, in mind, when he wrote in London in 1723, but similar conditions, mainly the wide distribution of property, made the analysis applicable to both places. The contradiction in the Dutch states, Cato said, was that the people held the property, or "natural Power," as he called it, while the provincial aristocracies had autocratic political power. The two forms of power, economic and political, which should have been in the same hands, were divided. "The natural Power being in the People, and the political in the Magistrates, it has all the Causes of Dissolution in its Contexture. Every Town is governed and subject to a little Aristocracy within itself, who have no Foundation of suitable Property to entitle them to their Dominion." So far, the contradiction had not disrupted government. The magistrates, Cato said, "judge so well of their own Weakness and the Power of the People, that they seldom or never give them just Cause of Provocation." By "not raising great Estates to themselves at the other's Expence, they make the Subjects easy," and so rule peaceably.

"But this is no steady and durable Dominion," Cato went on to say. There was one dangerous and disruptive factor. Universal "Appetites and Passions" will in time prevail, and when the magistrates lose their fear of France and Spain, "they will certainly think themselves at Lib-

---

82. The analysis that follows is from Trenchard and Gordon, *Cato's Letters*, II, 163–165.

erty to play their own Games at home: Those who are In Possession of Power will know what it is good for." The rich will pursue luxury, yield to extravagance, and fall at last into necessity. "When their Magistrates have impaired their Estates, or fancy that they want greater, they will plunder the Publick." The desire for gain will be too much for them, and they will use their political power for selfish purposes, with dire results. "The People will be impatient in continuing to pay large Taxes to such who pocket them, and will endeavour to right themselves, and have Power enough to do so." Property will enable the populace to stop the plundering. "Those who have Power [the magistrates], will endeavour to keep it; those who suffer under it, will endeavour to take it away; and the Event will be in the Will of Heaven alone, but in all Likelyhood will be some other Form of Government."

Had Cato turned his attention to New England, the critical point doubtless would have been the same: would the magistrates attempt to plunder the people? Frugality and honest government made the people easy in the Netherlands. In Cato's perception of political psychology, people bridled only when asked to pay taxes to "such who pocket them" to enlarge their own estates. In a more hierarchical society, patronage and large properties enabled magistrates to stifle protest. Among a population of freeholders, people were less compliant. Independent yeomen had the courage and the power to resist rulers. "These opposite Interests must raise Convulsions in the Body Politick," Cato speculated, and so end at last in a new constitution of government.

If Cato judged rightly, Massachusetts, in spite of its egalitarian society, could enjoy a secure future in the empire—unless magistrates tried to tax the public for private gain, or were thought to do so. Then a socially and economically independent people had the power to bring down the established order, and the contradiction of monarchical government without monarchical society would be resolved with the formation of a government more consistent with the condition of its people.

CHAPTER 3

The Rights of the People

Massachusetts lived under a king for nearly a century and a half with
scarcely a complaint about monarchy. The lack of a proper social order
to support royal authority did not prevent the king from holding the
allegiance of his colonial subjects. Provincial history bore out Cato's
observation that a society of independent freeholders could bear up, at
least for a time, under benevolent aristocratic rule.

But if loyalty to the king never wavered, opposition to the crown,
that is, to the royal bureaucracy, was also unremitting. The intrusion of
royal government in Massachusetts in 1691, after sixty years of virtual
independence, shocked the provincial political system. For fifty years
the colony struggled to adjust to an authority which was considered
alien and dangerous. The royal governor and the lower house seemed
perpetually in conflict, so much so that some claimed the province was
headed for independence. Amidst its pledges of allegiance to his majesty the king, the assembly constantly wrangled with the royal governor over the privileges of the representatives and the limits on royal
power.[1]

Here in the give-and-take of assembly politics, the other side of pro-

---

1. In *Order and Reason in Politics: Theories of Absolute and Limited Monarchy in Early Modern England* (Oxford, 1978), Robert Eccleshall argues that limited monarchy was an
outgrowth in the first place of the landed interests' attempt to control the king.

vincial political culture revealed itself, a side with a different focus and purpose. The moral center of talk in the assembly was the word "people," and the avowed purpose was defense of the people's rights. "People" gave strength to the opposition, as the symbol of the king was the basis of allegiance and submission. But the "people" were never set in opposition to the "king," even rhetorically. Popular rights were not antithetical to the principles of monarchy. To the contrary, the king's principal duty was to protect the people in their rights. The popular party, the men in the assembly who formed an alliance against the government when they thought it endangered the people, considered themselves loyal subjects of the crown. They simply turned the king's promise to protect the people against royal officials when it seemed as if they were abusing their power. Under that pretext, the popular party was entitled to be assertive, litigious, and suspicious.[2]

Unlike the ceremonies and formulas associated with the king, the language of popular rights was an instrument of practical politics. Politicians used this rhetoric to pursue their immediate ends day by day. Rather than merely shaping the framework of political activity as monarchy did, ideas of popular rights interacted continually with events. That difference reduced contact between the two great symbols. Functioning on different levels, the monarchical and the popular touched only now and then and confronted one another directly only at the end of the provincial period, in the Revolution.

The rhetoric of popular rights was in many respects different in tone and purpose from the words used to honor the king. The language of the popular party was legalistic and constitutional, not personal, and its purpose was to negotiate limits of power rather than to pay homage. The popular party most often spoke as lawyers in a court, referring to laws, precedents, grants of privileges, and customary rights. This language turned the struggle between governor and the lower house into an extended legal controversy rather than a raw contest for power. Dis-

2. Jack P. Greene discusses this tradition of opposition in "Political Mimesis: A Consideration of the Historical and Cultural Roots of Legislative Behavior in the British Colonies in the Eighteenth Century," *American Historical Review*, LXXV (1969–1970), 337–360. For a summary of the constitutional issues, see A. Berriedale Keith, *Constitutional History of the First British Empire* (Oxford, 1930). Randolph Greenfield Adams discusses the imperial constitution in the time of the Revolution, with particular attention to the vexed question of dominion and realm, in *Political Ideas of the American Revolution: Britannic-American Contributions to the Problem of Imperial Organization, 1765 to 1775* (Durham, N.C., 1922).

putes which seemed like factious turmoil were actually protracted legal negotiations.

Because controversy between governor and the lower house took this form, the conflicts could be resolved, and were. By mid-century, the constitutional conflicts between royal authority and popular rights were settled in the sense that the boundaries of rights and power had been agreed upon. By 1740, after a half-century of controversy, Massachusetts appeared to be integrated into the imperial political system, and the contest with royal power appeared to be ended. After that, for twenty years political controversy took the form of factional disputes among the colonists rather than controversies between royal authority and the people. The negotiations apparently succeeded.

But the calm at mid-century was misleading. There continued to be serious faults in the structure of government. Besides the contradiction of a monarchical government without a monarchical society, royal government suffered from another debilitating weakness. Below the surface of formal and polite argumentation lay an ineradicable suspicion. Rulers, according to the accepted political sociology, were governed by self-interest. Provincial politicians accepted as fact Cato's view of the Dutch rulers. Men in power would eventually use that power to exploit the people. The reason for insisting strictly on every iota of political privilege granted by charter was the conviction that officials could not be trusted. Their authority had to be held strictly within the bounds of the charter, or political power would be put to the service of greed. The popular party's suspicions were not meant as a reflection on the particular men chosen to govern the province; interest governed everyone. Men in power posed a greater danger only because they enjoyed greater opportunities. But power made them exceedingly dangerous. This belief was the driving force behind the half-century of controversy over the charter.

The strains began before 1691 with the crown's growing attention to the American colonies. Under the Lords of Trade and its various successors, a host of royal bureaucrats began filtering into the colonies, from the Restoration in 1660 on, largely to supervise the enforcement of trade regulations and to look after other crown economic interests. In addition, corporate and proprietary colonies were given royal governments, as happened in Massachusetts in 1691, bringing still more· royal appointees. Wherever they appeared, this corps of alien officials brought turmoil. There was the inevitable contest for power, but underlying all was the suspicion that they were to a man bent on managing the power for personal gain.

In the view of the colonists, the avarice of crown officials was all the more threatening because of the source of their appointments. They were beholden to their masters in England, not to the people in the colonies, and lacked all incentive to regard the people's interest. What was worse, many of them came from England, had no property or family in the colonies, and thus had nothing to lose from oppressive government. Unchecked by natural connections, royal appointees had every reason to plunder the colonies and return home with their ill-gotten gains.

The legalistic resolution of constitutional conflicts could not quench the fear of alien rulers. Even at mid-century when the royal governors complimented the colony on its loyal behavior, and no great constitutional issues disturbed politics for nearly a decade, the popular party's apprehensions were not laid to rest. Two contradictions remained as potential weaknesses in royal governance: the absence of a society of dependents to support formal government, and the provincial conviction that selfish interests controlled the men who were sent to govern.

i. Popular Rights and Official Avarice

Provincial politics, viewed as a whole, presents a scene of recurring conflict, mostly between the governor and the lower house of the assembly.[3] Many of the disputes involved the interpretation of the charter: the right to appoint the speaker of the House, the right of the House to adjourn itself, the right to audit accounts, the appropriation of a permanent salary for the governor. In one respect, as the governors pointed out, the posture of the House seemed contradictory. The Representatives avowed their loyalty to the king, and yet resisted his instructions and claimed powers that the governors believed were rightly the crown's. Moreover, the House held to its position year after year, unintimidated by letters and instructions from Westminster, and

3. Henry Russell Spencer, *Constitutional Conflict in Provincial Massachusetts: A Study of Some Phases of the Opposition between the Massachusetts Governor and the General Court in the Early Eighteenth Century* (Columbus, Ohio, 1905).

backed down, if ever, only under great pressure. The popular party in the House of Representatives was as adamant in its opposition to crown officials as it was fervent in its protestations of loyalty to the monarch.

Everyone understood how the House was able to take this apparently contradictory position. The language for defending popular rights was inherent in monarchical ideology itself. Rights and privileges, the mainstay of the popular party, were integral to monarchical political culture, not alien to it. The king's legitimacy rested on his success in protecting the people in their rights, and so did the governor's. God did not invest the king and his officials with might and glory for their own satisfaction. They were raised up to keep order in the world and to bless the people. On the advancement of William Shirley to the governorship in 1741, the House warned and congratulated him in the same breath. "Nothing could have more endear'd your Excellency to this People, than the Assurances you gave us of employing your Powers and Interest in Favour of the province, for the preservation of their religious and civil Rights and Interest."[4] The House did no more than rehearse the true principles of monarchy when it reminded the governor of his duty.

The proof of the king's regard for the rights of the people was the royal charter. The House understood the charter as representing the king's sober desire to grant political privileges to the people of Massachusetts, and the governor was never allowed to forget that. The House typically opened rejoinders to a governor with a reminder that "forasmuch as King WILLIAM and Queen MARY, of Blessed Memory; by their Royal Charter, were Graciously Pleased to Gratifie Their Subjects, the Inhabitants of this Province, with such Powers, Priviledges and Franchises, as in their Royal Wisdom was thought most conducing to the Interest and Happy State of the People here . . ." and then followed with the reasons for refusing to comply with the governor's wishes.[5] Even in flagrant disobedience, the House claimed to be on the king's errand.

4. *Boston Weekly News-Letter*, Aug. 13–20, 1741.
5. *Journals of the House of Representatives of Massachusetts* (Boston, 1919–), II, 219. See also *ibid.*, 246. After the attorney general had ruled on the right of the governor to veto the speaker of the House, the representatives told Gov. Shute that "notwithstanding what the Lords Commissioners of Trade and Plantations have wrote to your Excellency concerning your power of Non-concurring the Choice of a *Speaker*, and the opin-

There were two great social and political entities in monarchical political culture, king and people, whose relationship the charter regulated. The only moral force equal to the king was the people. Ideally the two were in balance and their interests in harmony. The "King's Prerogative when rightly used," a popular party leader wrote, "is for the good and benefit of the People, and the Liberties and Properties of the People are for the support of the Crown."[6] The design of government gave each a voice at the crucial points where laws were made and where they were enforced. In law enforcement, the jury spoke for the people, the judge for the king; in lawmaking, the governor for the king, and the Representatives for the people. The Council moderated the disagreements between the two great estates.[7] Conflict was taken as a sign of party or private interests at work. When purged, the political system was expected to return to its normal condition of harmonious balance.

The main question for the two parties was which side of the scale weighed too heavily. The governors complained that the House of

---

ion of the Attorney General in *England* thereon; We beg leave in all defference to that Board of Mr. Attorney's Opinion, to esteem it our duty to maintain and enjoy all the Rights and Liberties which we claim, or ought to claim by the Royal Charter." *Ibid.*, III, 107. See also *ibid.*, 65; XI, 68. The assembly thought of itself as claiming English rights, natural rights, and charter rights imperceptibly blended. Often they were mentioned in the same sentence: "Our Charter is the great Hedge which Providence has planted round our natural Rights, to guard us from an Invasion"; or, "AS THE Royal Charter *granted Us by King WILLIAM and Queen MARY of glorious Memory, has vested in the General Court a Power to impose and levy proportionable and reasonable Rates and Taxes, and to apply and dispose of the same pursuant to the Rights and Priviledges inherent in Us in common with other His Majesties Freeborn Natural Subjects which are in said Royal Grant particularly so declared and asserted. . ."* New-England Weekly Journal* (Boston), Mar. 18, 1728; *Journals of the House*, VIII, 269; see also III, 219.

6. Elisha Cooke, Jr., *Mr. Cooke's Just and Seasonable Vindication: Respecting some Affairs transacted in the late General Assembly at Boston* ([Boston, 1720]), 18.

7. Fritz Kern points out that in the acclamation the king was symbolically elected, thus giving the people a voice in his selection. *Kingship and Law in the Middle Ages*, trans. S. B. Chrimes (Oxford, 1939), 77. For the conflicting views of kingship in seventeenth-century England, see Corinne Comstock Weston and Janelle Renfrow Greenberg, *Subjects and Sovereigns: The Grand Controversy over Legal Sovereignty in Stuart England* (Cambridge and New York, 1981); J. R. Pole, *Political Representation in England and the Origins of the American Republic* (New York, 1966); Betty Kemp, *King and Commons, 1660–1832* (London, 1957); and Margaret Atwood Judson, *The Crisis of the Constitution: An Essay in Constitutional and Political Thought in England, 1603–1645* (New York, 1964).

Representatives invaded the king's authority, and the House the reverse. During the controversy over approval of treasury warrants in 1732, Governor Belcher wrote the duke of Newcastle that the question was "whether the King shall appoint his own Governour, or whether the House of Representatives shall be Governour of the Province."[8] Their presumption was intolerable, Belcher told the Board of Trade in typical flamboyant dismay. They would easily perceive, he said, "that the House of Representatives are continually running wild, nor are their attempts for assuming (in a manner) the whole Legislative, as well as the executive part of the Government into their own hands to be endur'd with honour to his Majesty."[9] Earlier Burnet had told the House, "You seem to allow the Governour's powers only so far as he uses them according to your Pleasure: But in using your own Powers you take it very ill to be directed by any body."[10] Burnet told Newcastle that Elisha Cooke, Jr., a leader of the popular party, was a professed enemy to the king's lawful authority.[11] In that manner, governor and House seesawed over warrants, salary, speakers, adjournment.

The force of the word "people" in the political value system gave the House its determination. The refrain in every conflict was that the Representatives were "constrained in faithfulness to the People of this Province" to refuse a fixed salary, or to insist on their right to elect their speaker.[12] As the governor guarded the prerogatives of the crown, so the House was keeper of the people's liberties. "Your Excellency may be as well assured," they told Belcher in 1732, "(what is now offered comes from our Mind and Soul) that as long as this Assembly retain any regard to the great trust and confidence our Electors have put in us, all efforts to perswade and induce us to forsake their true Interst" are in vain.[13] The "Principal Article Expected from us," they said, was to defend liberties.[14] They were "strictly bound to advance, and not pull down," the rights of the people. Were they ever to falter or fail to speak out, they would "thereby render themselves unworthy

8. Gov. Belcher to Newcastle, Dec. 26, 1732, in Noel Sainsbury *et al.*, eds., *Calendar of State Papers, Colonial Series, America and West Indies* (London, 1860–), XXXIX, 286, cited hereafter as *Cal. St. Papers.*
9. Jan. 5, 1733, *ibid.*, XL, 6.
10. *Journals of the House*, VIII, 309.
11. Gov. Burnet to Newcastle, Jan. 23, 1729, *Cal. St. Papers*, XXXVI, 306.
12. *Journals of the House*, VIII, 281. See also *ibid.*, 269, 298.
13. *Ibid.*, XI, 112. See also *ibid.*, VIII, 302.
14. *Ibid.*, VIII, 56.

ever after to sustain from the People any such Trust again."[15] That office of trust was the rock on which gubernatorial pique and royal instructions broke.

From that ideology emerged a role for the men elected to the House and especially for those who conducted the debates and drafted replies to the governors. The major prescription for that role was resistance. In its great moments the House dug in its heels and refused to budge, whether Governors Dudley and Shute threatened the king's wrath, or Burnet held them in prolonged session, or Belcher starved the province while he refused to sign a money bill which included House scrutiny of treasury warrants. The House made notable compromises in the 1720s and 1730s. It accepted the Explanatory Charter, which granted the governor the right to veto the speaker, and it backed down entirely on the advance approval of treasury warrants. But these were never celebrated in song and story. The House knew no language to honor compromise. It chose, rather, to depict itself as steadfastly resisting invasions of the people's rights at whatever personal cost to themselves. That was the natural outgrowth of their ideology.

The people at large recognized and honored the defenders of their liberties. No quality more endeared a man to the populace than stubborn resistance to arbitrary power. Popular favor invariably compensated the popular leaders for the displeasure of the governor. An exasperated Shute complained to the Board of Trade, "The common people of this Province are so perverse, that when I remove any person from the Council, for not behaving himself with duty towards H. M. or His orders, or for treating me H. M. Govr. ill, that he becomes their favourite, and is chose a Representative."[16] Huge majorities rallied behind the leaders of the popular party. It won in the House by margins of fifty-four to eighteen, and fifty-six to one. Unanimous votes were not unknown.[17] Governor Burnet said that men "attack the prerogative only to gain more power into their own hands."[18] Ironically, monarchical principles justified a defense of rights and privileges, which in

15. *Ibid.*, III, 97. For a similar rhetorical strategy in England, see Archibald S. Foord, *His Majesty's Opposition, 1714–1830* (Oxford, 1964), 151.

16. Shute to the Council of Trade and Plantations, June 1, 1720, *Cal. St. Papers*, XXXII, 45.

17. *Journals of the House*, II, 233, 370; III, 40, 74, 100; XI, 93, 221; Lt. Gov. Dummer to Newcastle, Sept. 15, 1729, *Cal. St. Papers*, XXXVI, 481; Cooke, *Just and Seasonable Vindication*, 4.

18. Burnet to Newcastle, Jan. 23, 1729, *Cal. St. Papers*, XXXVI, 306.

turn brought forward popular leaders dedicated to resistance of royal government.[19]

But a puzzle remains. The reasons for the broad public support are not immediately evident. It is one thing to understand that monarchical ideology permitted the defense of popular rights; it is another to explain the motive. The popular party's zeal appears out of proportion to the issues. The rights to select a speaker, dismiss an assembly, or pay the royal governor annually seem like remote and bloodless matters, unworthy of the furor they provoked.[20]

The record of political conflict in the first half of the eighteenth century to some extent waylays doubt. The popular party relentlessly argued for its privileges year after year, as if the safety and happiness of the colony depended on them. Consistency and zeal make their words more believable. But the very structure of the rhetoric leads us to question it as a complete explanation. Politicians frequently used the word "safety" and described rights as a "bulwark," as if the people were under attack. A sense of danger is required for the talk of rights to have meaning. The rhetoric assumes the presence of an unnamed enemy.

Occasional comments in the exchanges with governors hint that there was more below the surface. The proprieties of politics required assemblies to treat governors with respect, and even in the extended controversy with Governor Burnet over the salary, the lower house held to the rule. But as their patience ran out, the Representatives observed to Burnet, "We have always been careful that our Consultations and Conclusions thereabout, might be managed in the most decent and

19. It was proper for the young Benjamin Franklin to have his Do Good persona say that "the least appearance of an Incroachment on those invaluable Priviledges, is apt to make my Blood boil exceedingly." In such a cause anger was manly, even in a woman. One proudly presented oneself as "a mortal Enemy to arbitrary Government." Acquiescence to power out of self-regard, submissiveness, or passivity was shameful and weak. Had the House "given up the Cause," Elisha Cooke said at one point, "ages to come would [have] justly said, they had . . . deprived the People whom they Represented of their Proper Rights, which would have been a Reproach to them when in their Graves," and ranked them "among those despicable Wretches that would Sacrifice their Country to serve themselves." *New-England Courant* (Boston), Apr. 9–16, 1722; Cooke, *Just and Seasonable Vindication*, 12, 13.

20. For an analysis of the nature and the social causes of struggle in the southern assemblies, see Jack P. Greene, *The Quest for Power: The Lower Houses of Assembly in the Southern Royal Colonies, 1689–1776* (Chapel Hill, N.C., 1963).

respectful manner; chusing to say less than the subject would bear, and no more than what the Nature of the thing and Faithfulness to the People required."[21] Had they chosen not to manage the controversy in the "most decent and respectful manner," the assembly suggested, they could have said more. While a governor was in office, criticism rarely rose above a whisper. Only in occasional crises or after a governor left did the dark suspicions underlying popular party actions break through to reveal the fears that drove the endless talk of rights and privileges.

Attached to the underside of popular party ideology, with its legalistic discourse for public occasions, was a sociology of oppression, a description of malevolent forces operating below the surface of public events. In this view of politics, the primary danger, surpassing all others, was official avarice. Puritan pastors called it covetousness and saw it working everywhere. "*Covetousness is a distemper of the Soul, which manifests it self in a constant, greedy, insatiable desire after Riches, and employeth* the *whole man in various methods to gratifie that desire.*"[22] "Among all the vicious Qualities which have tainted the Humane race, there is none which seems to look with a more Malignant Aspect upon the Publick, than this of Covetousness, especially when it is found in the exalted Stations of Life."[23] Every colony had to combat that insatiable desire. In New York, it was said of Governor Benjamin Fletcher that he was "a poor beggar, and seeks nothing but money, and not the good of the country,"[24] South Carolina accused their governor in 1686 of "extreme Avarice" and said he "would leave no money in any mans pocket in Carolina but his owne."[25] Maryland complained in 1739 that the government "pursued its own profit and benefit." "This house have so many recent instances of the people of this province being made a property to his lordship's officers and the many evils that proceed therefrom, that they are under the greatest apprehension of every act

21. *Journals of the House*, VIII, 322; see also 412.
22. Thomas Bridge, *Jethro's Advice Recommended To The Inhabitants of Boston, in New-England, Viz. To Chuse Well-qualified Men, and Haters of Covetousness For Town Officers* (Boston, 1710), 13.
23. *New-Eng. Weekly Jour.*, May 29, 1727.
24. Quoted in John Gorham Palfrey, *History of New England* (Boston, 1858–1890), IV, 149.
25. Quoted in M. Eugene Sirmans, *Colonial South Carolina: A Political History, 1663–1763* (Chapel Hill, N.C., 1966), 45.

that may put them into their power or mercy, the effects of which hath too often and daily doth demonstrate itself in the ruin and oppression of many."[26] An anonymous versifier wrote of Governor Robert Dinwiddie in Virginia:

> You promis'd, to relieve our woes,
> and with great kindness treat us.
> but whoof, Awaw! each Infant knows
> your whole design's *to cheat* us.
>
> To turn like Midas, all to pelf,
> (Regardless of our tears.
> to make it center in your self,
> you'd not disdain his *Ears.*[27]

When a Virginian in 1701 attempted to generalize about the needs and problems of the colonies as a group, his major concern was that "the chief End of many Governours coming to the Plantations, having been to get Estates for themselves, very unwarrantable Methods have sometimes been made use of to compass those Ends." Governors sought added powers, above the powers of government in England, not to enhance the king's interests, but "to gripe and squeeze the People."[28] In various colonies it was noted that "an empty Treasury is very much our Security."[29] Governor William Keith said of Pennsylvania in 1726 that "the Publick there is generally in Debt, because they are extreamly jealous of Attempts upon their Liberties; and apprehensive, that if at any Time their publick Treasury was rich, it might prove too great a Temptation for an artful Governor, perhaps in Concert with their own Representatives, to divide the Spoil amongst them."[30]

26. Quoted in Charles A. Barker, *The Background of the Revolution in Maryland* (New Haven, Conn., 1940), 224.
27. Quoted in Richard Beale Davis, "The Colonial Virginia Satirist: Mid-Eighteenth Century Commentaries on Politics, Religion, and Society," American Philosophical Society, *Transactions*, N.S., LVII (1967), Pt. i, 18. See also Gary B. Nash, *Quakers and Politics: Pennsylvania, 1681–1726* (Princeton, N.J., 1968), 93–94.
28. Louis B. Wright, ed., *An Essay upon the Government of the English Plantations on the Continent of America (1701): An Anonymous Virginian's Proposals for Liberty under the British Crown, with Two Memoranda by William Byrd* (San Marino, Calif., 1945), 24, 20.
29. *A Letter, From One in Boston, To his Friend in the Country . . .* ([Boston], 1714), in Andrew McFarland Davis, ed., *Colonial Currency Reprints, 1682–1751* (Boston, 1910–1911), I, 279.
30. Quoted in Jack P. Greene, ed., *Great Britain and the American Colonies, 1606–1763* (New York, 1970), 193.

To stop that spoliation, to prevent the governors' making "a gainful Trade" of their offices, and to check the plunder of the people's wealth were the main purpose of the popular party.[31] The party valued the rights of the people, the privileges of the House, and the charter itself chiefly as barriers against official avarice. Jeremiah Dummer, Massachusetts' London agent, argued for the charter's continuation basically because experience showed "That Governours are apt to abuse their Power and grow rich by Oppression." "To enlarge their powers," as charterless government doubtlessly would, "is to give them greater Power to oppress." "We have had more than one flagrant Instance of this very lately, where Governours have bin convicted and censur'd not so properly for oppressing as for a direct plundering their People."[32] The excessive caution of the popular party about its privileges can be accounted for only by the depth and prevalence of the assumption that "the chief End of many Governours coming to the Plantations" was "to get Estates for themselves."[33]

ii. The Invasion of Royal Power

The apprehension of official abuse arose early in the seventeenth century. From the first years of settlement, people in Massachusetts had recognized the danger. Emmanuel Downing congratulated John Winthrop for remaining poor. That was better, Downing said, "then if

31. *Boston Gazette, or, Weekly Journal*, May 12, 1755.
32. Jeremiah Dummer, *A Defence of the New-England Charters* (London, 1721), 70. William Byrd believed that the Virginia assembly was so skilled in the use of their privileges that not even a tyrannical or needy governor could rob the people or interfere with justice. Richard L. Morton, *Colonial Virginia* (Chapel Hill, N.C., 1960), II, 484. Cotton Mather thought that the right to consent embodied in the assembly was an adequate control of gubernatorial greed. "Political Fables," in William H. Whitmore, ed., *The Andros Tracts: Being a Collection of Pamphlets and Official Papers Issued during the Period between the Overthrow of the Andros Government and the Establishment of the Second Charter of Massachusetts* . . . (The Prince Society, *Publications*, V–VII [New York, 1868–1874]), II, 327–328.
33. Wright, ed., *An Essay upon the Government of the English Plantations*, 23. Charles I himself confessed in 1642, under pressure, of course, that the reason for entrusting the Commons with the levy of money was so that "the prince may not make use of this high and perpetual power to the hurt of those for whose good he hath it, and make use of the name of public necessity for the gain of his private favourites." Quoted in J. P.

you had gayned riches as other Governours doe, both in Virginea and elswhere."[34] The dimensions of the problem mushroomed after the Restoration of Charles II in 1660, when the crown attempted to reassert its authority in the colonies and sent royal commissioners to set government in order. Massachusetts complained to the king about such men. "Instead of being governed by rulers of our owne choosing, we are like to be subjected to the arbitrary power of strangers, proceeding not by any established lawe, but by their owne discretions."[35] Every new emissary from London set off the same suspicions. Edward Randolph, who first came as a messenger in 1676 and then as commissioner of customs, epitomized what the colonists most feared. Though Randolph gave little evidence of venality, a versifier wrote that he came "To play the horse-leach; robb us of our Fleeces, / To rend our land, and teare it all to pieces."[36] Popular leaders foresaw a multiplication of Randolphs if royal authority obtained a purchase in Massachusetts.

The colony was aware that up and down the continent in the 1670s royal officials were filtering into America to occupy positions of power beyond the control of the people. Though few, they had authority as governors, secretaries, or customs officials to siphon off profits for personal gain. Edward Cranfield's career as royal governor in New Hampshire from 1682 to 1685 was observed with horror from Massachusetts. A down-at-the-heels courtier, with unusually crass schemes for profiteering, Cranfield set about at once to get the governorship of Massachusetts as soon as the charter fell. He confided to William Blathwayt that three thousand pounds was to be made from the settle-

---

Kenyon, ed., *The Stuart Constitution, 1603–1688: Documents and Commentary* (Cambridge, 1966), 21. The fear of corruption was the staple of England's country party as well, and official avarice was almost hackneyed material for its satirists. See, for example, Sir Robert Howard and George Villiers, 2d duke of Buckingham, *The Country Gentleman* (1669), ed. Arthur H. Scouten and Robert D. Hume (Philadelphia, 1976).

34. Quoted in T. H. Breen, *The Character of the Good Ruler: A Study of Puritan Political Ideas in New England, 1630–1730* (New Haven, Conn., 1970), 69.

35. Nathaniel B. Shurtleff, ed., *Records of the Governor and Company of the Massachusetts Bay in New England* (Boston, 1853–1854), IV, Pt. ii, 130.

36. Quoted in Michael Garibaldi Hall, *Edward Randolph and the American Colonies, 1676–1703* (Chapel Hill, N.C., 1960), 69. See also Bernard Bailyn, *The New England Merchants in the Seventeenth Century* (Cambridge, Mass., 1955), 162. On the events of this period in an imperial setting, see J. M. Sosin, *English America and the Restoration Monarchy of Charles II: Transatlantic Politics, Commerce, and Kinship* (Lincoln, Nebr., 1980).

ment of Maine, and ten thousand pounds from pardons and the management of Massachusetts' Indian missionary lands. Randolph told the Lords of Trade that Cranfield's oppression was the main reason for Massachusetts' refusal to accept enlarged royal control.[37]

The Dominion of New England, organized in 1686 after the loss of the first charter, was the realization of all of Massachusetts' nightmares of oppression and avarice. Governor Andros not only governed without an assembly as his commission authorized him to do but paid little heed to the New England men in his Council, relying more on New York members with whom he was familiar from his term as governor there. Through two and a half years the colony endured imposed excise taxes, excessive fees for licenses and deed registrations, a requirement to register their lands under the crown in place of questionable titles from the town corporations, and the fear of an Anglican or perhaps even a Roman ecclesiastical establishment.[38] One pamphlet written after Andros's downfall asked "whether the whole Government was not become a meer *Engine*, a sort of *Machin* contriv'd only to enrich a crew of Abject Strangers, upon the Ruines of a miserable people."[39] The governor's swollen powers licensed him and his creatures to enrich themselves at the public expense. They could, for example, extort intolerable fees because they were unrestrained by "any Rules but those of their own insatiable Avarice and Beggary." The governor challenged land titles, wrested them from the rightful owners, and measured them out "for his Creatures." Throughout the Andros administration, New England was "*squeez'd* by a Crew of abject Persons fetched from *New York*, to be the Tools of the Adversary."[40] "All that we counted dear was made a Prize to th' raging Lust and hungry Avarice of a few tatter'd Rascals from New York."[41] The Andros admin-

37. David S. Lovejoy, *The Glorious Revolution in America* (New York, 1972), 151–153; Hall, *Edward Randolph*, 80–81; Palfrey, *History of New England*, III, 388n.
38. For the issues in contention during the dominion period, see Viola Florence Barnes, *The Dominion of New England: A Study in British Colonial Policy* (New York, 1960 [orig. publ. New Haven, Conn., 1923]).
39. Whitmore, ed., *Andros Tracts*, II, 192.
40. *Ibid.*, I, 13–14, 16. On land titles, see Richard L. Bushman, "Massachusetts Farmers and the Revolution," in Richard M. Jellison, ed., *Society, Freedom, and Conscience: The American Revolution in Virginia, Massachusetts, and New York* (New York, 1976), 104–108.
41. *The Plain Case Stated Of Old—but especially of New England* . . . (Boston, 1688). (The broadside is dated 1688, but tells of events that occurred in 1689.) For additional indictments of avarice in the Andros administration, see Whitmore, ed., *Andros Tracts*,

istration showed what destruction a few officials could accomplish, given the chance.[42]

The second charter, granted after the overthrow of Governor Andros in 1689, was of course, an improvement over the Dominion of New England. An elected House of Representatives was once again authorized, and this House could nominate the members of the upper house. But a place was made for alien officials with extensive powers. The king appointed the governor; he selected the Council from the Representatives' list of nominees; and he had other large powers of appointment. No enactment became law without his signature.[43] Cot-

---

I, 80, 87, 98, 114–116, 124–125, 137–138, 145; II, 6–7, 36, 56, 128, 192, 254–255; III, 195, 197–198.

42. English country party publicists reinforced the popular party's assessment of the colonial placemen. Although the actual connections of country party writers with American leaders cannot be pinned down for this period, English tracts addressed to American themes likely had influence in the colonies. One essay on the Dominion of New England published in 1691 put the campaign for greater royal control in an alarming perspective. *The Humble Address of the Publicans of New-England, to which King you please; with some Remarks Upon it* identified the influence of royal officials, labeled publicans, with a class of marginal English gentlemen of limited means, driven by greed and desperation to schemes for obtaining office and money. These desperadoes practiced their craft in England, according to *The Humble Address*, until offices were exhausted, and then fixed their ambitions on New England. They liked New England because "*they understood, That the People of* New-England *were grown exceeding Rich, and that, without doubt, they had been so imploy'd in improving themselves, as to have little or no leisure to study Court-Juggles, and little Tricks.*" These placemen, of course, brought ruin wherever they went. The officials constituted "a sort of an Army, who not only Ruin'd the Countrey, but spent the King's Money into the bargain: and this was all brought about, only to bring a few poor Distressed *Publicans* into Imployment."

The Humble Address put forward an explanation of revolutions comparable to Cato's in 1722. The publicans accused everyone else of desiring a republic, but the oppressive officials themselves were the actual cause of revolution. People turned on their rulers "by reason of oppression and hard usage" from the officials. The truth was that "Publicans *make Common-wealths, as Malefactors make Laws*; for were there no Malefactors, there would be no need for Laws: *and were there no* Publicans, *there need be* no Republicks." "There never was any Rebellion or Revolt of People upon earth, but what has been caused directly or indirectly by the *Publicans*." It was oppressing, fleecing, robbing that drove people to bring down kings and take government into their own hands. In Whitmore, ed., *Andros Tracts*, II, 233, 241, 243, 245, 246.

43. For a clear, brief description of government under the second charter, see the introduction to L. Kinvin Wroth *et al.*, eds., *Province in Rebellion: A Documentary History of the Founding of the Commonwealth of Massachusetts, 1774–1775* (Cambridge, Mass., 1975), 4–8.

ton Mather tried to sweeten the bitter taste of the new charter by recollecting the miseries of the dominion, which allowed "harpies to commit as much rapine as they pleased," and arguing that such depredations could not occur under the new regime.[44] Mather admitted that the new charter "makes the Civil Government of New-England more Monarchial and less Democratical than in former Times."[45] But the charter granted enough power to the people, Cotton said, to "Discourage any ill Governour" from accepting a post in Massachusetts. The first royal governor, Sir William Phips, was unlike the "vast number of Governours" of the Roman Empire, "who were Infamous for Infinite Avarice and Villany." Phips's purpose, Mather said, was to enact "such a Body of good Laws, that no Person coming after me may make you uneasie."[46]

Massachusetts could not be expected to react supinely to the invasion of this alien and threatening system of governance. The new charter resolved into one the two constitutional issues that had most troubled Massachusetts in the seventeenth century: the limits of gubernatorial power under Winthrop and the intervention of royal power after 1660. Anxieties, anger, and resistance previously divided between two dangers now focused on one person, the royal governor. Except for the dominion interlude, no governor since 1634 held so much power as Phips, and never before 1684 had the royal bureaucracy so much control over the lives of individual colonists. The effort to neutralize this new force in the political system, with its constant threat of oppression by avaricious officials, was the central theme of Massachusetts political history for the next fifty years.

The popular party, a loose coalition that came into being almost immediately after the arrival of the second charter, had as its primary purpose the containment of the royal governor. Among all the issues in the assembly in the half-century after 1691, the ones to attract the largest majorities and the most strenuous rhetoric were those associated with the privileges of the House over against the power of the governor. Seemingly abstract matters involving technical interpretations of the charter, the constitutional issues were the ones to arouse the deputies and rally the largest majorities. Questions of rights and

44. Cotton Mather, "Political Fables," in Whitmore, ed., *Andros Tracts*, II, 326.
45. Whitmore, ed., *Andros Tracts*, II, 290.
46. Cotton Mather, *Magnalia Christi Americana, Books I and II*, ed. Kenneth B. Murdock (Cambridge, Mass., 1977, [orig. publ. London, 1702]), 321, 324, 323.

powers had that effect because everyone knew the charter was the colony's defense against the self-interested exercise of the governor's great powers.

Two of the men to take the leadership of the popular party, Elisha Cooke and Thomas Oakes, had accompanied Increase Mather to England to request a renewal of the old charter from William III. Mather had compromised when the king refused and had gratefully accepted the new charter instead. Cooke and Oakes repudiated the document before it passed the seals and declared that they preferred no charter to the one granted. They returned to Massachusetts unreconciled, and men of similar humor gathered about them.[47] Although required to live with the new charter eventually, the popular party was dedicated above all to reducing the powers of the royal governor and enlarging the powers of the elected House, in conformity with the spirit of their first government.

The leading figures in the party were not drawn from the ranks of ordinary people. The two Cookes, for example, who took leading roles in the first three decades of the eighteenth century, were men of wealth, education, and standing.[48] Elisha Cooke, Sr. (1637–1715), the son of a Boston selectman and deputy, graduated from Harvard in the class of 1657 and went on to practice medicine and politics. Boston chose him as its deputy, and the House later nominated him to the Council. His marriage to the daughter of Governor John Leverett in 1668 brought Cooke to the top of Massachusetts society. He died one of the city's wealthiest men.[49]

His son, Elisha Cooke, Jr. (1678–1737), ranked first socially in the Harvard class of 1697. He followed his father into medicine and involved himself in various business enterprises. He owned thousands of acres of Maine timberland and headed the Muscongus Company, which held title to thirty square miles in Maine. Cooke's estate in-

47. Six old charter men in all were left off Mather's list. His selection of North End neighbors did not endear Mather to his enemies. Kenneth Ballard Murdock, *Increase Mather, The Foremost American Puritan* (Cambridge, Mass., 1925), 252; G. B. Warden, *Boston, 1689–1776* (Boston, 1970), 37; Breen, *The Character of the Good Ruler*, 188–189.
48. Although prominent, Elisha Cooke, Sr., was not necessarily the dominant figure in the popular party. Richard R. Johnson, *Adjustment to Empire: The New England Colonies in the Era of the Glorious Revolution, 1675–1715* (New Brunswick, N.J., 1981), 402.
49. For information on Cooke, see *Dictionary of American Biography*; and John Langdon Sibley, *Biographical Sketches of Graduates of Harvard University . . .* (Boston, 1873–1885), I, 520–525.

cluded twelve houses and three warehouses. In the ten years previous to his death he divested himself of an additional three ropewalks and thirty-three parcels of land. The total value of his estate at death amounted to sixty-three thousand pounds, making him one of the wealthiest men in the province.[50]

Both Cookes held a place among the small pool of persons from which the highest positions in the province were filled. Elisha Senior was councillor for twelve years, and his son was for six. They would have held seats for many more years except for the governor's veto. Elisha Senior was justice of the Superior Court; his son received an appointment as clerk the year after his graduation from Harvard and later was made judge of the Court of Common Pleas for Suffolk County. Elisha Senior was also commissary of the province in 1709.[51] Neither father nor son appeared eccentric, extravagant, or radical. The moderate Samuel Sewall told Mrs. Cooke after Dudley's veto of Elisha Senior's nomination to the Council that they would miss his "Caution, Discretion, and Constancy."[52] Thomas Hutchinson said Elisha Junior had the reputation of being "a fair and open enemy."[53]

The wealth and eminence of the Cookes did not prevent them from being popular. The lower house showed its confidence in Cooke Senior soon after he returned from England. Mather and the king omitted Cooke's name from the first Council as one who opposed the charter. On the first occasion, when the representatives nominated the Council, Cooke's name was on the list. Governor Phips also refused to make the appointment, but Cooke was nominated again the following year. For the next twenty years, the House of Representatives chose him for the Council in spite of frequent rejections.[54] Elisha Cooke, Jr., enjoyed

50. Clifford K. Shipton, *Sibley's Harvard Graduates: Biographical Sketches of Those Who Attended Harvard College,* IV (Cambridge, Mass., 1933), 349–356; Warden, *Boston,* 95–96.

51. William H. Whitmore, *The Massachusetts Civil List for the Colonial and Provincial Periods, 1630–1774* . . . (Baltimore, Md., 1969 [orig. publ. Albany, N.Y., 1870]), 46, 47, 50–53; Palfrey, *History of New England,* IV, 140, 540; Massachusetts Council Records, V, 48, Archives Dept., State House, Boston.

52. Samuel Sewall, *Diary of Samuel Sewall, 1674–1729* (Massachusetts Historical Society, *Collections,* 5th Ser., V–VII [Boston, 1878–1882]), II, 64, cited hereafter as Sewall, *Diary.*

53. Thomas Hutchinson, *History of the Colony and Province of Massachusetts-Bay,* ed. Lawrence Shaw Mayo (Cambridge, Mass., 1936), II, 333.

54. Warden, *Boston,* 35.

similar popular support. His funeral in 1737 was the greatest ever given a private citizen in Boston. Every church in town tolled its bell, and with flags at half-mast on the ships, cannon roared their respect from a specially erected battery. Despite the Cookes' high places in society, the people loved them for their valiance in leading the opposition.[55]

The support of Cooke Senior after his return from England suggests the nature of popular sentiments in the assembly. His repudiation of the new charter was the wish of the majority.[56] Failing that, the representatives attempted to encase the governor in protective legislation that would render him harmless. They had three general aims in mind. The first was to establish the privileges of the House of Representatives, the one agency in the government wholly responsible to the people and hence in their interest. The second aim was to regulate expenditures to prevent extravagance and graft. And the third was to secure the courts of law in the people's interest.

From 1692 to 1694 the assembly passed a series of resolves and legislation to achieve these ends. The speaker elected by the first House under the new charter asked the governor for all the privileges of the House of Commons, mentioning liberty of debate, security from arrest, and access to the governor. In 1694 the assembly resolved that only the Massachusettts assembly—the House, the Council, and the governor—could tax the colony. King and Parliament were no exception. The assembly further claimed the right to fix salaries for provincial officials and to know the intended use of tax money before it was granted. To restrict the jurisdiction of governor-appointed justices of the peace, cases to be heard before the justices were limited to forty shillings. In the Court of Common Pleas, where more substantial cases were heard, the juries were to be elected by the towns.[57]

---

55. *Boston Evening-Post*, Aug. 27, 1737.

56. After the overthrow of Andros, delegates from fifty-four towns gathered in convention. Forty of them favored resumption of the old charter without royal approval. Palfrey, *History of New England*, III, 589. In the Revolutionary era, there were many complaints against the 1691 charter. Richard D. Brown, *Revolutionary Politics in Massachusetts: The Boston Committee of Correspondence and the Towns, 1772–1774* (Cambridge, Mass., 1970), 116; John M. Murrin, "Review Essay," *History and Theory*, XI (1972), 258–259.

57. Palfrey, *History of New England*, III, 49; IV, 137–139, 161; Warden, *Boston*, 43, 44. In 1694 the House claimed to have the same rights of debate and suffrage as the Commons of England. E. Ames and A. C. Goodell, eds., *The Acts and Resolves, Public and*

This legislation passed between 1692 and 1694, while Phips occupied the governor's chair. The charter gave the Privy Council three years to review and disallow if they chose. Less than three months before the three years expired, the Privy Council acted. In 1695 and 1696, fifteen of forty-five pieces of legislation were disallowed, including many of the critical safeguards: the right to specify how money was to be spent, the sole right to raise taxes, the Judiciary Act, and many other valued laws, including the incorporation of Harvard College, which was disallowed because his majesty was not permitted to appoint a visitor. In desperation, the House for a time in 1696 considered a campaign to recover the old charter.[58]

The disallowances served notice that Massachusetts and the colonial administration differed fundamentally on the interpretation of the charter and that constitutional issues were going to trouble the waters in Massachusetts, but it was also apparent that the differences were not beyond resolution. In the give-and-take of the first decade under the new charter, quite a number of the issues were laid to rest. At least one was a bogeyman. Anxieties over the appointed justices of the peace dissipated when it became apparent that the governor had little choice in most instances but to select the individual of highest standing in the community. More often than not, the governor picked the same man whom the people chose as their representative to the General Court.

On another point the assembly had to back down when it found the crown fixed in its purpose. In three successive acts, the assembly curtailed the right of appeal from Massachusetts to England. The Privy Council disallowed each one in turn. Finally, in 1699, on the advice of

---

Private, of the Province of the Massachusetts Bay . . . (Boston, 1869–1922), VII, 393. One of the first acts of the House in 1692 was to request of the governor "the Accustomed Priviledges of an English Assembly," by which they meant free and open debate, access to the governor, and freedom from arrest. June 8, 1692, Massachusetts Archives, VI, 223, Archives Dept., State House, Boston. See Mary Patterson Clarke, *Parliamentary Privilege in the American Colonies* (New Haven, Conn., 1943). Phips allowed the Council to select civil officers, contrary to the charter. His successor quickly reversed this practice. The House claimed the right to appoint all officials not put in the governor's patronage by the charter. Palfrey, *History of New England*, IV, 138–140; Breen, *Character of the Good Ruler*, 199.

58. Palfrey, *History of New England*, IV, 160–162; Leonard Woods Labaree, *Royal Government in America: A Study of the British Colonial System before 1783* (New Haven, Conn., 1930), 376; Murrin, "Review Essay," *History and Theory*, XI (1972), 258.

Governor Bellomont, a Judicatory Act was passed without reference to appeals and accepted in England.[59]

In two instances, Massachusetts had its way. It successfully claimed the right to fix salaries, and it put the selection of juries in the hands of the towns. The Privy Council had objected in the 1690s to provisions in the judiciary acts which put all cases over a certain value before jury courts. They wished to reserve the right to enter customs suits in Admiralty, where there were no juries to protect the offender. Having allowed for that exception, the General Court was able to provide for the election of juries to the Court of Common Pleas. Appointed sheriffs were deprived of the right exercised in England of appointing and hence of packing juries. The governor never achieved the control over the towns of New England that the offices of sheriff and justice of the peace gave the crown in England, and probably for that reason constitutional disputes never arose in the towns.[60]

Although these accommodations were reached in the first decade of provincial government, the popular party still entertained suspicions. The assembly watched its governors with an eagle eye. The slightest misstep brought immediate recriminations. No one suffered more from such scrutiny than Joseph Dudley, who came to the governorship in 1702 defiled by his collusion with Andros. When he left New England in 1689, he was "the object of the peoples displeasure" for "his extream covetousness; getting to himself so many bags of money, to the ruinating of trade."[61] Wait Winthrop interpreted Dudley's machinations for the governorship as the design of a small party of former Andros judges who hoped "to get their comrade Mr. D. to be Govr here and so drive on their private interest with the ruine of this people's libertyes."[62] A memorial sent from New England shortly after his arrival urged the queen to appoint a new governor, charging, "One Prin-

59. Labaree, *Royal Government*, 376–377; Palfrey, *History of New England*, IV, 172–173.
60. Labaree, *Royal Government*, 376; Palfrey, *History of New England*, IV, 172–173; Warden, *Boston*, 44. William Douglass considered the practice of electing juries an egregious invasion of prerogative rights. *A Summary, Historical and Political, of the First Planting, Progressive Improvements, and Present State of the British Settlements in North-America* (Boston, 1747–1752), I, 519–520.
61. Thomas Danforth, quoted in Breen, *Character of the Good Ruler*, 144.
62. Wait Winthrop to Henry Ashurst, Aug. or Sept. 1699, Mass. Hist. Soc., *Collections*, 6th Ser., V (Boston, 1892), 47.

cipal Grievance, which Comprehends many under it, is, The Course of *Bribery*, which runs thro' the Governour's Administration."[63]

The most serious accusation against any Massachusetts governor between 1692 and 1760 was the charge that Dudley had traded illicitly with the French in Nova Scotia in 1707 under the guise of a prisoner exchange. Increase Mather bluntly told the governor, "I am afraid you cannot clear yourself from the guilt of bribery and unrighteousness."[64] Under duress, House and Council cleared the governor, but Cotton Mather nonetheless wrote Dudley: "Sir, your *snare* has been that thing, the *hatred* whereof is most expressly required of the *ruler*, namely COVETOUSNESS. . . . The main channel of that COVETOUSNESS has been the *reign of bribery*, which you, Sir, have set up in the land, where it was hardly known, till you brought it in fashion."[65] Samuel Sewall of the Council thought the governor cynically tolerated bribery. In a dramatic encounter in the council chamber, Sewall withdrew his vote from a declaration clearing Dudley of suspicion. His brother afterwards told him "the generality of thoughtfull people" approved his "Mount Etna Eruption." In the next nomination of councillors, Sewall received ninety-eight of ninety-nine possible votes, more than any other councillor. Sewall's rebuke probably spoke the true feelings of the House.[66] A memorial sold in Boston in 1707 accused the governor and his son Paul of "not being Content with what Money they come fairly by, and over greedy of Gain" and of being "very Screwing and Exacting upon the People." "They are so Mercenary, there is no Justice to be had without Money."[67] To the end of his administration, Dudley was suspected of pursuing his "mercenary interest" before the public good. Near the close of his administration, the deputies struck from an address to the queen an expression of satisfaction with Dudley's disposition of the colony's money.[68]

---

63. *The Deplorable State of New England By Reason of a Covetous and Treacherous Governour* . . . (London, 1708) (Mass. Hist. Soc., *Colls.*, 5th Ser., VI [Boston, 1879]), 107.

64. Increase Mather to Gov. Dudley, Jan. 20, 1708, Mass. Hist. Soc., *Colls.*, 1st Ser., III (Boston, 1810), 126–127.

65. Cotton Mather to Gov. Dudley, Jan. 21, 1708, *ibid.*, 130.

66. Sewall, *Diary*, VI, 208, 213–214, 224, 228. See also *Bost. News-Letter*, Dec. 1, 1707.

67. *A Memorial of the Present Deplorable State of New-England with the many Disadvantaages it lyes under in the Male-Administration of their Present Governour, Joseph Dudley* . . . (Boston, 1707) (Mass. Hist. Soc., *Colls.*, 5th Ser., VI [Boston, 1879]), 39, 42.

68. Sewall, *Diary*, VI, 353; Palfrey, *History of New England*, IV, 322.

It was the same with every governor to a greater or lesser degree. A 1729 petition to the king said Burnet made "the general good and welfare of the whole Province subservient to his own private particular interest" and seemed "by his words and actions to have no other end or view in coming to preside over them but to consult his own advantage."[69] He was specifically accused of collecting twelve shillings for let passes to permit vessels to clear the port and of raising the registration fee from six shillings to twenty shillings.[70] Cooke suspected the surveyors of the woods of similar malfeasance. He learned that John Bridger sold licenses to cut logs reserved for the king, thus betraying the crown "by daily Selling and Bartering these very Trees and Timber, which he gave out was the King's his Masters." "Mr. Bridger had Perverted the True Intent of his Commission, and far exceeded the Powers therein granted him in his boundless and unwarrantable wresting Monies from the poor People to inrich himself."[71] Belcher said of one of Bridger's successors that he would "betray his own father if he might reap an advantage by it." "I don't believe he would stick at any thing to extricate himself out of his poverty and wretched circumstances."[72]

Means had to be found to check oppression, and for fifty years, Massachusetts strove to set the limits. The popular party reacted differently from its counterpart in England. Similarly concerned about malfeasance in office, the English country party vented its wrath in newspapers, pamphlets, the theater, and coffeehouse fulminations. The

69. Francis Wilks and Jonathan Belcher, agents for the House, to the king, 1729, *Cal. St. Papers*, XXXVI, 489.

70. *Ibid.*, 513; Palfrey, *History of New England*, IV, 533.

71. Elisha Cooke, *Letter to Mr. Speaker Burrill and Mr. Bridger* (Boston, 1719), 4, 9. See also Mass. Arch., X, 251–252; Cooke, *Just and Seasonable Vindication*, 6; *Journals of the House*, II, 220.

72. Jonathan Belcher to Sir Charles Wager, Oct. 28, 1739, *Belcher Papers* (Mass. Hist. Soc., *Colls.*, 6th Ser., VI–VII [Boston, 1893–1894]), Part II, 288, cited hereafter as *Belcher Papers*. For suspicions of forest officials, see Breen, *Character of the Good Ruler*, 148; Robert G. Albion, *Forests and Sea Power: The Timber Problem of the Royal Navy, 1652–1862* (Cambridge, Mass., 1926), 252–253; Joseph J. Malone, *Pine Trees and Politics: The Naval Stores and Forest Policy in Colonial New England, 1691–1775* (Seattle, Wash., 1964), 87; *Cal. St. Papers*, XXXII, 478. For accusations against Thomas Pownall, in general a popular governor, see John A. Schutz, *Thomas Pownall: British Defender of American Liberty: A Study of Anglo-American Relations in the Eighteenth Century* (Glendale, Calif., 1951), 178.

party's lack of power in Parliament left no alternative. It was a party of many words and little action. The Massachusetts popular party, fully in control in the assembly, reversed the order. The words of opposition politicians in Massachusetts were moderate, disciplined, and designed for use in the courts, not in the streets. The Cookes used a legalistic language of rights, not the accusatory language of corruption. The party's aim was to rally the majorities in the assembly and thus control legislation, not to arouse the public. The provincials channeled their anxieties about marauding officials into the endless battles over the interpretation of the charter rather than into inflammatory tracts and books. The popular party believed that by construing the governors' powers as strictly limited and the assembly's as ever more generous, they could contain the alien power introduced by the royal charter in 1691.

By forgoing accusations against officials and restricting themselves primarily to legal and constitutional issues, the popular party made compromise possible. Legal rights could be discussed and adjudicated. And over the fifty-year period following the issuance of the second charter, accommodations were reached. The history of politics between 1691 and the settlement of the salary question in 1736 appears as a narrative of incessant conflict, but it was in fact a history of negotiation and ultimate resolution.[73]

iii. The Resolution of Differences

Four constitutional issues divided the province and the home government between 1700 and 1736: the appointment of a speaker, adjournment of the assembly, auditing of expenditures, and the permanent salary. All four were first raised in 1693 and 1694 when the Court was testing the bounds of the charter, but they caused no trouble until later. One reason was that between 1692 and 1713 the colonial governors were at a severe disadvantage in negotiating with the Representatives. For all but five years of that time, England was at war with France, and during those five years a renewal of hostilities was expected momen-

---

73. For the impact of the second charter and all it entailed with regard to Massachusetts in the empire, see Johnson, *Adjustment to Empire*.

tarily. Nothing was more important to the governor than successful prosecution of wartime assignments. Every hope of advancement in the colonial system and for favor at home depended on a quick response to military exigencies. Nothing could discredit a governor faster than lethargy or ineffectiveness in wartime. In these crucial enterprises, the governor required the active assistance of the assembly. The governor could not raise a penny for provisions, salaries, or arms without a tax bill initiated and approved in the House of Representatives. He was in no position to demand a permanent salary or to veto a speaker so long as a miffed House could retaliate against his vital interests. Consequently the administration of the wartime governors suffered from less popular opposition simply because they could not raise the constitutional issues that most nettled the popular party. Peace in the assembly was necessary to the conduct of war abroad.[74]

After the Peace of Utrecht in 1713, the governors could not plead wartime necessity as an excuse for compromise on constitutional matters. Samuel Shute, who came to Massachusetts as governor in 1716, felt obliged to stand firm in accord with royal expectations. Shute's family were distinguished dissenters in England and Ireland, and Cotton Mather extravagantly welcomed him in a published speech, but the auspicious opening did not foretell a happy administration. The coming of peace brought a series of issues to the fore that made his time in office one of the most turbulent periods in the province's history. Temporary relief from Indian pressure revived the masting trade in Maine, and the surveyor of the woods demanded prosecution of trespassing lumbermen. The stoppage of wartime bills of credit and constriction of the money supply built pressure for a bank and for currency issues. In the midst of all this Shute asked the assembly to grant a permanent salary as the crown had long desired, and the assembly, suddenly wary of excessive military expenditures, insisted on auditing the governor's warrants on the treasury. Meanwhile, with French harassment of New England's northern settlements starting up again, Shute had the delicate task of extricating a wartime budget from an irascible assembly.

It was no time to veto the speaker elected by the House, and Shute

---

74. For examples, Palfrey, *History of New England*, IV, 388–389, 324–325; V, 57; Labaree, *Royal Government*, 180–181. William Pencak argues that governors suffered from less political strife in periods of wartime for other reasons, in *War, Politics, and Revolution in Provincial Massachusetts* (Boston, 1981).

had ample precedent for backing down when he met resistance. Previous governors had made little of the matter. Governor Phips raised the question of his right in 1693, and the Board of Trade had put it aside without settling it.[75] But the nomination of Elisha Cooke, Jr., put Shute in a corner. Besides leading the opposition in the assembly, Cooke had personal disagreements with Shute. Cooke's nomination in 1720 appeared as a calculated affront. The governor had little choice but to reject Cooke, even though Shute needed the House's cooperation. The assembly protested on principle and refused to elect another speaker.[76]

While this issue was simmering, the question of the right to dismiss the House of Representatives came into debate. One form of discipline available to the governor was to hold the House in session beyond the appointed time, while fields went to weed and crops rotted on the ground.[77] By the same token, the House could block the executive body by adjourning prematurely. In its absence, no taxes could be raised, and legislation was held in suspension. A House that could adjourn itself was much more independent of the governor than one he could hold in session or dissolve as he chose. In the midst of his troubles Governor Shute could not disregard the assembly's six-day adjournment in July 1721 for the apparently innocent purpose of honoring a colony-wide fast day, especially after he had previously refused their request. The assembly admitted that the charter gave the governor the power to adjourn. It merely argued that the House in addition had the right to adjourn itself for short periods as was the custom in the House of Commons. Two days was considered a normal brief adjournment, and the House deducted the fast day and the sabbath from their six days and counted it a mere four-day adjournment.[78]

75. Gov. Dudley objected to the election of Thomas Oakes, an enemy of the new charter and "a known Commonwealth's man," as Dudley put it. He directed the House to a new election, but they disregarded his request and proceeded to business with Oakes in the chair. Reluctant to stop them when the war effort depended on a large, immediate appropriation, Dudley acquiesced. Palfrey, *History of New England*, IV, 295; Dudley to the House, May 31, 1705, Mass. Arch., VIII, 115–118; Sewall, *Diary*, II, 131; Dudley to the Board of Trade, Oct. 23, 1706, *Cal. St. Papers*, XXIII, 234.

76. Palfrey, *History of New England*, IV, 408–411, 433–434; *Journals of the House*, II, 229, 233, 245–246; *Cal. St. Papers*, XXXII, 45, 259, 270.

77. Shute's successor, William Burnet, held the House in session six months to force compliance on the salary issue. *Journals of the House*, VIII, 298, 303–304, 338, 367, 376–377, 381–382, 430; House of Representatives to the king, Nov. 28, 1729, *Cal. St. Papers*, XXXVI, 312–313. The House remained sensitive to prolonged sessions long after the king settled the question of adjournment. *Journals of the House*, XXXI, 287.

78. *Journals of the House*, III, 74–76, 78, 89–90, 100.

With this and all the other issues weighing on him, Shute sailed for England in January 1723. The obstructionist tactics of the assembly caused him to despair of governing the province successfully. In two memorials to the king, he presented his complaints and included the House's choice of a speaker contrary to his wishes and its claim to the right to adjourn. Neither loomed large in the governor's mind compared to other usurpations, but they happened to be something the king could deal with. In 1725 the Privy Council recommended that the crown issue an explanatory charter as an amendment to the charter of 1691. The addition made explicit the governor's right to approve the speaker and forbade the House to adjourn for more than two days.[79]

Like any contract, the royal charter could not be amended without the concurrence of both parties. The people of Massachusetts, acting through their representatives, had to accept the Explanatory Charter before it went into effect. Although the House had previously taken a stand, in 1726 it was under the apprehension that a refusal would bring the entire charter into court as in 1683, with the threat of a further loss of privileges.[80] With that in mind the House accepted the Explanatory Charter forty-eight to thirty-two in a roll call vote. Considering the risk and that the choice of speaker and adjournment had to that point small practical effect on provincial politics, the size of the opposition measures the commitment to the assembly's liberties. At the same time, the much larger size of the supporting majority showed the capacity for compromise. The accompanying address to the king said acceptance was meant "to signallize Our Duty and Obedience, which we at all times Owe to His Most Excellent Majesty," and prayed their compliance would "recommend His Majesty's Loyal and Faithful Subjects the Inhabitants of this Province to His further most Gracious Favour and Protection."[81]

By 1726 the lesser constitutional issues surrounding the power of the royal governor and the privileges of the lower house had been resolved.[82] Both sides yielded here while gaining there, and step by step

79. Palfrey, *History of New England,* IV, 428, 446–452.
80. *Ibid.,* 52.
81. *Journals of the House,* VI, 460. Significantly, just 6 of the representatives in the opposition held judicial or military appointments, while 30 of the supporters did. *Ibid.,* 458–459.
82. Old issues flared up from time to time, but precedent sufficed to put them down. In

the distribution of power was more precisely defined. Only two questions remained, the hardest ones of all: the House's right to monitor government expenditures, and the grant of a permanent salary. It took another decade to hammer out the necessary compromises before the province could at last enjoy a respite from constitutional conflict.[83]

The assembly's purpose in monitoring expenditures was to prevent the governor from spending public money for his own benefit. The appropriation bills specified what the tax moneys were for, and the House wanted expenditures limited to those ends. The first generation of post-Andros politicians saw the danger of a royal governor with free access to the treasury.[84] In 1694 the assembly passed an act declaring that "no public money be or ought to be disposed of by his excellency the governour, and council, but for the uses and intents" specified in acts of the entire Court.[85] The Privy Council disallowed this act along with so many others, but the principle was not forgotten.

The Representatives' tactical problem, once money was in the treasury, was how to prevent the governor from drawing it out for purposes of his own. The House audited his accounts annually after the money was spent, but by then the cows were in the corn. What the House wanted, as they told Governor Dudley, was "the undoubted Privilege" of concurring in "the particular Application and Disposal of all and every Sum and Sums that are put into the Treasury."[86] They

---

1731 the House adjourned itself for three days instead of the allotted two, but backed down when challenged. Palfrey, *History of New England*, IV, 541.

83. One other constitutional issue occasionally occupied the House. In 1716 it successfully asserted the right to appoint the attorney general. Lt. Gov. Tailer acquiesced, as Gov. Shute did later, albeit under protest. Burnet in his resolve to bring the House to heel, refused, and the Council backed him. Apparently the House's legal right to the appointment was weak, for they yielded. They asserted the right again under Belcher and appointed the attorney general jointly with the Council until 1752, when the Council got cold feet. Thereafter the governor appointed the attorney general with the advice and consent of the Council. Palfrey, *History of New England*, IV, 523–524; V, 115–116; *Cal. St. Papers*, XXXII, 407; XXXVI, 556, 572; *Journals of the House*, XII, 38; Douglass, *A Summary*, I, 515.

84. Cooke Senior wrote from England in 1691 to warn against allowing the new royal governor any permanent revenues. Johnson, *Adjustment to Empire*, 277.

85. Ames and Goodell, eds., *Acts and Resolves*, I, 170. See also Palfrey, *History of New England*, IV, 161n.; Breen, *Character of the Good Ruler*, 199.

86. The House to Dudley, July 16, 22, 23, 1703, Court Records, VII, 418, Archives Dept., State House, Boston.

wished to protect that privilege by requiring that every warrant from the governor and Council indicate from which account in the original appropriation the money was to be withdrawn and by approving the warrants themselves before the treasurer honored them. In effect the House desired an equal part in the executive's traditional right to dispose of public money. The House could see no other way of guaranteeing that tax funds would not be misapplied.

In 1721, amidst a House investigation into manipulations of the muster rolls submitted by militia officers with their requests for reimbursements, the House achieved the control they had sought since 1694. The Council and, for some unknown reason, the governor approved a tax bill which required that every warrant specify the particular account on which it drew and which gave the House the right to approve each warrant before the treasurer paid out the money. Two years later, when the Council belatedly recognized how annoyingly scrupulous the House intended to be, the board protested the loss of executive autonomy and asked for a return to the former method of managing the treasury. By then it was too late to go back. For eight years the House exercised its extraordinary powers with little hindrance, until Governor Burnet in 1729, in the middle of his do-or-die attempt to wring a permanent salary from the assembly, objected to the form of the tax bill as well. Burnet died before the issue was resolved, and Lieutenant Governor William Dummer, Burnet's temporary replacement, acquiesced in the House's demand, but by then the issue was in England. In 1730 the thirtieth instruction in the governor's commission forbade the House to audit accounts before payment. Governor Belcher arrived in that year committed to renewing the controversy Burnet had begun. Unabashed by the pronouncement of the king's will and pleasure, the assembly, now with the Council's backing, refused by a vote of fifty-seven to one to alter the form of appropriation. "Your Excellency may be as well assured," the House told Belcher,

> that as long as this Assembly retain any regard to the great trust and confidence our Electors have put in us, all efforts to perswade and induce us to forsake their true Interest and bring them and their Posterity under the weight and burden of such innumerable and inconceivable inconveniencies as the House firmly believe may soon be their lot and portion, should the House give into the aforesaid Instruction,

would fail. "Such a concession would be to act against the light of our own Reason and Conscience."[87] While appealing to both the king and the House of Commons for a withdrawal of the thirtieth instruction, the House refused for two years to refill the province's treasury.

Ultimately the assembly had to give way. The king in council and the Commons turned their plea aside and confirmed the right of the governor and the Council to make withdrawals. The Commons, despite a similar concern about misappropriations, could not endorse the assembly's claim to audit accounts before payment, because the Commons itself did not enjoy that privilege. As a committee of the Privy Council reported, "If your Majesty should withdraw Your Instruction on this Head, the Assembly of Massachusetts-Bay would be left in possession of a Power superiour to any which the British House of Commons lay Claim to in Cases of the same Nature." Parliament was permitted exactly what the thirtieth instruction allowed to Massachusetts: the right to examine accounts annually after payment.[88]

When the bad news arrived from London, the creditors of the province had not been paid for over a year. The hurt to the representatives' constituents was nearly as great as to the governor. In 1733, with no

---

87. *Journals of the House*, XI, 112. For the muster rolls controversy and the contest over audits: *The Case of the Muster Rolls of His Majesty's Castle William . . .* (Boston, 1720); *Journals of the House*, III, 77, 188; IV, 161, 179; V, 46, 62, 69, 75–76, 82, 84, 90–93, 177, 282, 294, 328–329; VI, 39, 58, 319–320, 330, 331, 334, 436–438; XI, 43, 50–52, 84–88, 121, 129, 142, 143, 171–172; Ames and Goodell, eds., *Acts and Resolves*, X, 61–62, 96, 134, 191, 263–264, 271, 323, 418, 454, 528; William Dummer to Newcastle, Oct. 7, 1729, *Cal. St. Papers*, XXXVI, 495; Francis Wilks and Jonathan Belcher to the king, Oct. 3, 1729, *Cal. St. Papers*, XXXVI, 491; William Burnet to the Council of Trade and Plantations, Mar. 31, 1729, *Cal. St. Papers*, XXXVI, 341; Order of Privy Council, Oct. 23, 1729, *Cal. St. Papers*, XXXVI, 512–513; Draught of additional instructions to William Dummer, Nov. 12, 1729, *Cal. St. Papers*, XXXVI, 524–525; Palfrey, *History of New England*, IV, 541, 543, 545; *Weekly Rehearsal* (Boston), Feb. 5, 1733.
88. *Journals of the House*, XI, 169. See also *ibid.*, 24–25, 43–44, 170–171, 277. William Shirley to Newcastle, July 1, 1733, Charles Henry Lincoln, ed., *Correspondence of William Shirley, Governor of Massachusetts and Military Commander in America, 1731–1760* (New York, 1912), I, 4. The right to state the purpose of taxes was regularized in King William's parliaments. Kemp, *King and Commons*, 72. After the Glorious Revolution most expenditures were authorized individually each year. The country party favored expansion of the powers of the parliamentary commission of accounts. Sir William S. Holdsworth, *A History of English Law*, X (Boston, 1938), 521–524, 586–588; Henry Horwitz, "The Structure of Parliamentary Politics," in Geoffrey Holmes, ed., *Britain after the Glorious Revolution, 1689–1714* (London, 1969), 106–107.

further recourse, the House passed an acceptable tax bill. The attorney general permitted the House to appropriate taxes for particular uses, but after 1733 it never again audited accounts before payment. The House occasionally carped about a misappropriation or asked for a place on committees on expenditures, but on the principle of monitoring treasury warrants which they had said they would never give up, the House yielded. In the developing provincial constitution, the governor and Council retained the power to spend.[89]

Thus in three of the four primary constitutional issues, veto of the speaker, adjournment, and approval of warrants, the popular party yielded. The assembly had better luck with the permanent salary. From the very start the Privy Council wanted the House to grant a fixed salary which the governor could claim automatically without further legislative action and which the House could not delay, cut back, or withhold.[90] Governors of the Caribbean islands and royal colonies in the south received their salaries from funds that were beyond the control of the assemblies, such as quitrents, the 4.5 percent export duty in Barbados and the Leeward Islands, and the two-shilling export duty on hogsheads of tobacco in Virginia and Maryland.[91] The Board of Trade expected Massachusetts to make a similar provision. At the very least, the crown wanted the assembly to state the governor's salary at the beginning of his administration and not tamper with it again until a new governor was appointed. The House of Commons granted each monarch a civil list at the beginning of the reign, which included salaries for a great number of officials, and did not review it until the accession of a new king or queen. The board insisted that the governor,

89. *Journals of the House,* XI, 278; XII, 170; XVII, 81; Palfrey, *History of New England,* IV, 553. The issue of treasury warrants was not forgotten in Massachusetts. In 1757 the House requested a renewal of the privilege of audit before expenditure, and Gov. Pownall agreed. In his later work, Pownall recognized the widespread suspicion of avaricious governors. Palfrey, *History of New England,* V, 156; Thomas Pownall, *The Administration of the British Colonies,* 5th ed. (London, 1774), I, 80–86.

90. In 1708 when Gov. Dudley was suspected of underhanded dealings with the French, the House cut back his salary with the lame explanation that they must alter the salary occasionally to show it was not a fixed grant. Dudley to the Board of Trade, July 10, 1708, *Cal. St. Papers,* XXIII, 32; Sewall, *Diary,* II, 22. In 1720 and 1721 Shute received £500 for six months rather than the usual £600. Palfrey, *History of New England,* IV, 411, 415.

91. New York, New Jersey, and New Hampshire battled the crown over salaries along with Massachusetts. On the eve of the Revolution, governors in 18 royal provinces received permanent salaries. Labaree, *Royal Government,* chap. 8.

and preferably the lieutenant governor and judges, receive the same treatment.[92]

In 1693 Governor Phips had asked the board to settle a permanent salary on him. The next year the House claimed for itself the right to fix salaries, including by implication the governor's. The Privy Council disallowed the act in which the claim was stated and soon thereafter made clear its position. From 1702 on, royal instructions directed the governor to require a permanent salary of the assembly. Thereafter, each governor dutifully made the request, and each House humbly replied that it could not in good conscience jeopardize the people's rights. Not until the arrival of Shute's successor, William Burnet, in 1728 did the Massachusetts House confront a governor determined to break its will.[93]

Burnet's strategy was to hold the House in session until a bill for granting a permanent salary was brought up, and hold it he did, week after week, month after month, while the House repeatedly reported no business and pleaded for dismissal. When the representatives bull-headedly held on, he adjourned the House to Salem, where Boston men could not conduct business after hours and it was harder for the representatives to escape to their farms.[94] The assembly was in session for six months. Tempers frayed, the governor was in a rage, speeches and replies shot back and forth, letters of appeal and indignation plied the Atlantic. In late December the House moved to appoint agents to carry its case to England. Burnet dismissed the House and called it back only briefly thereafter to discover that neither side had budged.[95] In the middle of the crisis, Burnet died. Spilled from his carriage into the water, he came down with a fatal fever. The province dutifully mourned his passing and awaited the arrival of the new governor.

Jonathan Belcher as agent for the Massachusetts House was plead-

92. Newcastle to Burnet, June 26, 1729, *Cal. St. Papers*, XXXVI, 413–414; Palfrey, *History of New England*, IV, 392, 458, 537.

93. Palfrey, *History of New England*, IV, 141, 519n; Labaree, *Royal Government*, 352; Ames and Goodell, eds., *Acts and Resolves*, VII, 292; Mass. Arch., VII, 291–292, 312; VIII, 1; Dudley to Board of Trade, Oct. 2, 1706, *Cal. St. Papers*, XXIII, 233; Dudley to Popple, May 2, 1706, *Cal. St. Papers*, XXIII, 128. See Palfrey, *History of New England*, IV, 539n, for Belcher's hope for a salary from an independent source.

94. The governor also refused to sign warrants for the representatives' salaries. *Journals of the House*, VIII, 435.

95. *Ibid.*, VIII, 316–318; Board of Trade to the king, Mar. 27, 1729, *Cal. St. Papers*, XXXVI, 338–340. Privately Burnet offered to accept a stated salary for three years. Board of Trade to the Privy Council, Nov. 12, 1729, *Cal. St. Papers*, XXXVI, 521–523.

ing for a withdrawal of the instruction on the salary when news came
of Burnet's death. Belcher quickly changed his tune and returned to
Massachusetts in 1730 with the governor's commission and instructions to require a permanent salary. It fell to him to oppose the House
on both major constitutional issues: the monitoring of treasury warrants and the permanent salary. Once again the long waiting game ensued. Belcher did not hold the legislature in session all the while he
was refusing appropriations bills with prepayment audit provisions.
He relied on a combination of threats, pleas, and dissolution to pressure the assembly.

Belcher was less convinced about the merits of a permanent salary
than were his predecessors. While showing one face to the assembly,
he pleaded with the Board of Trade to permit him to back down. From
1731 through 1734 the Council allowed him to accept a temporary salary while demanding a permanent one. In 1735 the Privy Council gave
way and permitted Belcher to accept an annual salary if it were granted
at the beginning of the legislative session. The request for a permanent
salary was simply dropped. The guarantee of an early salary grant
partly achieved the crown's purposes: the House was less able to pressure the governor into backing down on a contested point. Though
actually a compromise, the House took the concession as a victory and
agreed. Subsequent governors brought up the permanent salary now
and then only to let the issue pass. The assembly almost without exception voted the governor his salary at the beginning of the session.
The salary issue was peacefully buried, the last of the constitutional
issues.[96]

With the settlement of the salary question, the popular party went
into decline. Currency kept the province in a furor until 1750, but except for the general principle of continued emissions, currency divided
the towns more than it united them. After the dissolution of the land
bank in 1741, the Representatives split on what to do about printing
money. In the late 1740s, James Allen, a Boston merchant, who laid
claim to the mantle of Cooke as popular leader, wanted to continue
easy money policies, but could not win a majority in the House when
he needed it. Anti-inflationists wished to use a hard-cash reimburse-

96. Palfrey, *History of New England*, IV, 539; V, 54–57; Labaree, *Royal Government*,
365–366. In 1739 the House delayed the salary until the supply bill was passed, and
Belcher did not protest. With the currency issue inflaming the province, he was in no
position to revive the old controversy. *Journals of the House*, XVII, vii, 37.

ment for Massachusetts' part in the Louisburg expedition to redeem the colony's paper money. Notwithstanding Allen's opposition, the House passed a resolve to accomplish the redemption. Allen denounced the measure so ferociously that he was expelled. His reelection from Boston did not win him his place back until he apologized.[97] He certainly was no popular leader in the sense of commanding support in the House of Representatives. Neither Allen nor anyone else could lead a party in disagreement on basic questions. Without a clearly defined constitutional issue to rally large majorities, the popular forces could not coalesce.

Allen's expulsion epitomized the condition of Massachusetts politics between 1741 and 1760. The controversial issues turned colonist against colonist, rather than uniting them against the royal governor. When the House imposed an excise tax on tea and carriages which would hurt city people most, Boston chose an agent to represent the town in London—not to lay charges against the governor, but to protest the actions of the House. During the province's embittered flight over an excise tax on liquor in 1754, the governor stood by as arbiter, while Boston and the country towns did battle.[98] Nothing came before the House that united the representatives against executive encroachments. Moved mostly by desire for the power and profit of office, opposition took the form of shifting coalitions rather than a united front based on constitutional principles.[99]

In 1760, Samuel Adams was thirty-eight and James Otis thirty-five. They had been in politics nearly a decade and were never able to call the old popular party into being for a sustained period. In that year

97. Warden, *Boston*, 130, 139.

98. *Ibid.*, 142; *Journals of the House*, XXXI, 45–47; Paul S. Boyer, "Borrowed Rhetoric: The Massachusetts Excise Controversy of 1754," *William and Mary Quarterly*, 3d Ser., XXI (1964), 328–351; Hutchinson, *History of the Colony*, II, 41–42.

99. John A. Schutz tells the story of patronage politics exceedingly well in *William Shirley: King's Governor of Massachusetts* (Chapel Hill, N.C., 1961). For an analysis of partisan politics in the period 1740–1763 based on social and economic factors, see Stephen E. Patterson, *Political Parties in Revolutionary Massachusetts* (Madison, Wis., 1973). See also Joel A. Shufro, "Boston in Massachusetts Politics, 1730–1760" (Ph.D. diss., University of Wisconsin, 1976).

The only constitutional issue of note to come before the assembly in Shirley's administration was the Albany Plan of Union in 1754. Because it raised the old issue of an invasion of external power, Boston and the country towns united in opposition, but votes such as 41 to 37, and 48 to 31 did not compare to the old majorities. Warden, *Boston*, 145; Schutz, *Shirley*, 183.

Otis won a majority in the assembly on establishing gold as legal tender, and Thomas Hutchinson, an opponent of the measure, observed that the country party took sides "as if it had been a controversy between popular privilege and prerogative."[100] But it was not; rather than opposing Otis, Governor Bernard signed the bill into law. He was an observer, not a contestant.[101] Despite the economic turmoil of the preceding twenty years, without a constitutional issue to arouse the delegates, the popular party was more a faction than the voice of a united people.

iv. The Alignment of Interests

It took the colony fifty years to accommodate the traumatic invasion of royal power in 1691, but the accommodations were made. The resolution of the constitutional issues showed the capacity of the popular party and the crown to compromise. The legalistic language of rights and privileges afforded a means for negotiating the differences while providing assurances to both parties. Though neither side was entirely satisfied, the popular party felt some confidence that the governors' powers were in check, while the crown acquiesced in the limits on its authority. When Governor Bernard arrived in Massachusetts in 1760, he reported to the Board of Trade that he found no points of government in dispute and expressed satisfaction with the colonists. "This people are better disposed to observe their contract with the Crown than any other on the continent I have known." He told William Pitt that "there is most perfect harmony in the government of this Province."[102] By 1760 the opposing forces of monarchical government and an electorate of independent freeholders were in equilibrium.

That equilibrium did not imply the absence of tension. Although the particular points of friction in the interpretation of the charter were smoothed over, the suspicions underlying the disputes did not dissolve. Officials were still thought to pursue their own interests at whatever cost to the public. It was assumed without question that power

100. Hutchinson, *History of the Colony*, III, 72.
101. Hugh F. Bell, "'A Personal Challenge': The Otis-Hutchinson Currency Controversy of 1761–1762," Essex Institute, *Historical Collections*, CVI (1970), 297–323.
102. Quoted in Palfrey, *History of New England*, V, 225.

would serve greed at every opportunity. The colonists always suspected the governors of profiteering when men and supplies were raised for military campaigns, for example, and that problem was never resolved.[103] Governor Dudley was accused of making a trade of the military expeditions.[104] The House discovered padded muster rolls in Shute's administration and was convinced that "the lucre of gain" had corrupted the militia.[105] In the midst of the French war in 1756, the House ordered an investigation which it was expected "May possibly bring to Light some hidden Things of Darkness."[106] Benjamin Franklin summarized the feelings of the popular party when he wrote Governor Shirley that, because "Governors often come to the Colonies merely to make Fortunes," they "might possibly be sometimes fond of raising and keeping up more Forces than necessary, from the Profits accruing to themselves and to make Provision for their Friends and Dependents."[107] Unable to remove that doubt, the governors found the assemblies ever zealous *"to wrest the sword out of the Royal Hand."*[108]

The suspicions sprang from a deeper well than a jaundiced view of human nature. Besides the simple belief that humans were by nature self-interested, the provincials believed that self-interest formed people

103. In wartime, defense was the largest single item in the provincial budget and a natural target for a money-conscious assembly. During Queen Anne's War in the first decade of the century, Gov. Dudley estimated that military expenditures added £30,000 annually to the budget. In 1721 the Board of Trade estimated that the cost of defense in Massachusetts was £17,000 annually against £11,000 for the remainder of the budget. Dudley to Popple, July 22, 1706, *Cal. St. Papers*, XXIII, 178–179; Dudley to the Board of Trade, Mar. 1, 1709, and Oct. 24, 1709, *Cal. St. Papers*, XXIV, 235, 493; Board of Trade to the king, Sept. 8, 1721, *Cal. St. Papers*, XXXII, 415; Palfrey, *History of New England*, IV, 278n, 333, 290; Mass. Arch., VIII, 15.

104. Sewall, *Diary*, II, 351, 228.

105. *Journals of the House*, IV, 161, 179; VI, 436–438; VII, 345; VIII, 419, 86, 129, 169, 186, 187, 281, 329, 345; XI, 151, 381, 383–384, 396–399, 407–408; XVII, 81; Palfrey, *History of New England*, IV, 199, 205–206, 415; Mass. Arch., VI, 325; VIII, 8; Dummer, *Defence of the New-England Charters*, 24–25.

106. *Bost. Gaz.*, Feb. 9, 1756. See also Palfrey, *History of New England*, V, 546, 553; *Journals of the House*, XVII, 125–128.

107. Dec. 4, 1754, in Lincoln, ed., *Correspondence of William Shirley*, II, 103–104. See also Fitz-John Winthrop's suspicions of Gov. Fletcher, in Richard S. Dunn, *Puritans and Yankees: The Winthrop Dynasty of New England, 1630–1717* (Princeton, N.J., 1962), 305–306.

108. Mar. 31, 1729, *Cal. St. Papers*, XXXVI, 341. See also Douglas Edward Leach, *Arms for Empire: A Military History of the British Colonies in North America, 1607–1763* (New York, 1973), 275–279; Schutz, *William Shirley*, 81, and *Thomas Pownall*, 105–124.

into networks of power and mutual aid and that these larger structures governed how people acted. Furthermore, the empire shaped these structures to the colonies' disadvantage. Provincials were exposed more openly to the ravages of greed because they were governed by men sent from a distance by the king. At the center of colonial political controversy was the problem of regulating interest under these adverse circumstances.

Some of this came out when the Massachusetts House disclosed its innermost thoughts about royal governors under the pressure of Burnet's campaign for a permanent salary. Ordinarily the House restricted itself to arguments based on its rights and privileges rather than on an assessment of its governors' motives. But faced with a determined Burnet and royal instructions, the House opened up. They told the Privy Council in 1728 that the province felt helpless and naked before a governor whose personal interests provided no incentive to advance the public good. "It is and has been very well known," the assembly noted, "in this as well as other nations and ages, that Governors at a great distance from the Prince or Seat of Government have great opportunities and sometimes too prevailing inclinations, to oppress the people." The king was not to blame for the malfeasance of his officers because "it is almost impossible for the Prince, who is the most carefull Father of his subjects, to have such matters set in a true light." What was the remedy? "We humbly crave leave therefore to suggest that it is very much for yor. Majesty's interest and very necessary to the tranquility and flourishing of this your Province, that the Governor should be induced by his own interest, as well as duty to yor. Majesty, to consult the interest and welfare of the people." The way to induce the governor's interests was through an annual salary. Otherwise "the Governor's particular interest," the House pointed out, "would be very little affected (while thus settled) by serving or disserving the peoples interest."[109]

The problem was that without the annual salary, the interests of the people of Massachusetts did not connect with those selfish impulses in the governor which the assembly knew ultimately regulated his behavior. He was caught up in another structure linking him to the crown and to England and not to Massachusetts. The annual salary was an attempt to align the interests of the governor with those of the people

109. Address of the House to the king, Nov. 22, 1728, *Cal. St. Papers*, XXXVI, 311.

he governed. Without such a connection, how could the people have confidence in him? The 1721 assembly could say with conviction that to relinquish the power of the salary would be "one of the most fatal concessions they could possibly come into."[110]

This view of how interests formed in the empire led the assembly to favor a relationship between executive and legislature different from the prescription of fashionable eighteenth-century political theory, and at odds with later American views. It was not a position in keeping with our conventional view of republicanism. The assembly asked for greater interdependence, rather than a separation of powers. Paradoxically, the advocates of separation were the British, who favored a stated salary. One of Governor Burnet's first acts upon his arrival in 1728 was to read the Massachusetts assembly a lesson on the separation of powers. The Parliament of Great Britain was the pattern for the colonial assemblies, he argued, and they must be governed by the same principles. In England, "THE *three distinct Branches of the Legislature, preserved in a due Ballance, form the Excellency of the* British *Constitution: If any one of these Branches should become less able to support it's own Dignity and Freedom, the Whole must inevitably suffer by the Alteration.*" To follow the parallel, the governor must represent the king and "*have no Inclinations, no Temptations, no Byass, that may divert him from obeying his Royal Master's Commands.*" The precarious support of an annual grant meant "the Governour must either be deprived of the undoubted Right of an Englishman, which is to act according to his Judgment, or the Government must remain without Support." It was evident that the colony's method of supporting the governors arose from "a Design to make them dependent on the People," as much "dependent on the People as if he was to be elected by them."[111] An annual salary subverted the principle of separation of powers.

In their replies, the assembly reminded the governor of all the powers he exercised that reversed the flow and made the General Court dependent on him, but on a more fundamental level the House objected to the very premises of the governor's position. He assumed that

110. *Journals of the House*, III, 99. See also *ibid.*, VIII, 302–318.
111. *Journals of the House*, VIII, 246, 274–275, 370. See also Palfrey, *History of New England*, IV, 178, 225. The arguments for a permanent salary were further elaborated in *A Letter From One in the Country, To his Friend in Boston . . .* (Boston, 1729), and *Question: Are we Obliged in this Government of the Massachusetts, by Charter, to Settle a Salary upon the Governor?* (Boston, 1729).

the components of the legislature should be independent and that ideally they exercised their respective judgments as distinct agencies, free of one another. The House disagreed. "We humbly apprehend," the House countered, "that no part of the Legislature should be so independent: We have ever conceived that it was the peculiar distinction and glory of the *British* Constitution, that every part of it had a mutual relation to and dependence on each other according to the different Powers or Priviledges respectively belonging to each: Thus it is in the Members of the Natural Body, and thus we understand it to be in the *British* Polity, and that herein it excells and differs from unlimited Monarchy."[112]

Apparently Burnet surprised the House with his talk of separation and independence. The slightly tentative "we understand it to be in the *British* Polity" suggests they were somewhat apprehensive of being out of fashion, but they were not therefore inclined to yield. A pamphlet published a little later in the controversy enlarged on the point:

> The Governor says in his Message, that it is his Majesty's Pleasure that his Governors shall be maintained honourably and independently, I am sure his Majesty is so gracious, that he never desired to be independent of his Parliament; and therefore I cannot think that he ever desired that any of his Governors should be independent of the People, they are sent to rule over. The mutual Dependence of our King and Parliament is the only support, and great Happiness of our Constitution; and the Minute that either of them can honourably subsist without any dependance upon the other, our Constitution is at an end, and the useless Member will soon be laid aside.[113]

This author and the House subscribed to an organic analogy. The members of the political community should mutually interrelate like the "Members of the Natural Body," in contrast to Burnet's interaction of separate wills.

There was a certain irony in the way the sides lined up in the province. Organic conceptions of society disturbed liberal forces in En-

112. *Journals of the House*, VIII, 279–280.
113. *Extract from the Political State of Great Britain, for the Month of December, 1730* [Boston, 1731], 14–15. See also *A Letter To the Freeholders and other Inhabitants of this Province, qualified to vote for Representatives in the ensuing Election* (Boston, 1742).

gland. In the hands of extreme monarchists, such notions had been the basis for absolutist conceptions of kingship. As the head of society, familiar with and organically connected to all its parts, the king, monarchists said, rightfully claimed supreme ruling powers comparable to a father's over a family. Locke for one rejected the idea of a common will or interest because of the uses to which Sir Robert Filmer had put the conception.[114] The Real Whigs of the eighteenth century, continuing in the same vein, deplored the interrelationship of the ministry and the House of Commons. Country party reforms arose from the desire to separate powers and to give the Commons an entirely independent voice.

Walpole, the detested enemy of the country party, was the one to speak for interdependence and organic connection as a means of moderating conflict. " 'Tis necessary," Walpole's *London Journal* said of the legislative and executive, "in order to the due exercise of government, that these powers which are distinct, and have a negative on each other, should also have a mutual dependency and mutual expectations."[115] The Massachusetts popular party found itself in the anomalous position of sharing the perspective of the ministry in England, while their opponents, the royal governors, who received their appointments from the ministry, spoke for a separation of powers in the spirit of Walpole's enemies. Governor Bernard stressed separation of powers when he spoke to the assembly (as loyalists did later on), while the Representatives lauded the virtues of mutual dependence.[116]

In practical terms, the position of the Massachusetts House is understandable in view of its political advantages in the assembly. Had the Real Whigs in England controlled the civil list as the Massachusetts assembly regulated the governor's salary, the English country party

114. Pole, *Political Representation in England and the Origins of the American Republic*, 21. Locke substituted majority rule for common interest as the means of resolving conflict. John Locke, *Two Treatises of Government*, ed. Peter Laslett (Cambridge, 1964), 350–351.
115. Quoted in Isaac Kramnick, *Bolingbroke and His Circle: The Politics of Nostalgia in the Age of Walpole* (Cambridge, Mass., 1968), 124–125. See also *ibid.*, 123; and J.G.A. Pocock, "Machiavelli, Harrington, and English Political Ideologies in the Eighteenth Century," *WMQ*, 3d Ser., XXII (1965), 549–583. Walpole opposed a statutory limit on the number of peers which the crown could create because it would make the House of Lords independent. Holdsworth, *A History of English Law*, X, 66.
116. Edmund S. Morgan and Helen M. Morgan, *The Stamp Act Crisis: Prologue to Revolution*, rev. ed. (New York, 1963), 29; Patterson, *Political Parties in Revolutionary Massachusetts*, 118; William H. Nelson, *The American Tory* (Oxford, 1962), 173.

would probably have taken a different position.[117] And by the same token, had the royal governors commanded sufficient patronage in the colonies to make dependents of the Representatives, the popular party would soon have seen the virtue of independence.

Equally important, the desire for mutual dependence reflected the House's conception of politicians as bound together in networks of interest, with each official serving those powers that advanced his interests. An appointment to office, a salary, or a bribe connected him to one network or another. The problem was not how to make him independent, but how to align his interests with the people's. Unless the governor was tied to the province by the salary, he would serve his own interests, and perhaps the crown's, but not the colony's.

In an effort to explain Massachusetts' sensitivity about its privileges, Jeremiah Dummer told his English audience, "It is generally receiv'd Opinion, that the People in the Plantations have an Interest distinct from that of the Crown; when it is supposed at the same time, that the Interest of the Governours, they being the King's representatives, is one with the Crown."[118] Thomas Hutchinson reported the same view. People in the colonies, he wrote in his history, "consider the prerogative as an interest, without them, seperate and distinct from the interior interest of the colony."[119] The salary was a small effort to close that gap by making governors dependent on the people.

The inveterate mistrust had little to do with the governors' personal failings, or dislike for the man in office. The colonists mistrusted imperial officials as a class. From the seventeenth century on, a stereotype was fixed on governors which the most virtuous and competent governors could not shake off. It was resolutely believed that imperial bureaucrats by their very nature were likely to yield to avaricious impulses. For one thing, the governors as a class were seen as lacking the large personal estates that were believed to lift men above the tempta-

117. J. R. Western, *Monarchy and Revolution: The English State in the 1880s* (Totowa, N.J., 1972), 30.
118. Dummer, *Defence of the New-England Charters*, 65–66.
119. *History of the Colony*, II, 175. It was always hoped that interests of rulers and ruled could be brought together. In good government, an early Massachusetts tract declared, there was "no difference in the Views and Interests of the Governours and Governed." *The Original Rights of Mankind Freely to Subdue and Improve the Earth* (Boston, 1722), ii. Thomas Pownall recognized that successful imperial administration depended on discovering the true interest of colonies and mother country which would blend particular interests on both sides of the Atlantic. Pownall, *Administration of the British Colonies*, 4–11.

tions of greed. The royal instructions told governors to avoid the appointment of "necessitous" men to the Council, and everyone accepted the assumption underlying that advice.[120] Poor men and men of broken fortunes were too easily tempted to use their offices for personal gain. In contradiction to that principle, governors as a group were consistently characterized as men who had fallen on hard times in England and come to the colonies to recover their fortunes.

More serious still was a lack of personal attachment to the country. Ideally, the interests of men in power so mingled with those of the people that the suffering of one brought suffering to the other. The prosperity of rulers and people advanced together. As John Wise said in behalf of lay ruling elders in church government, it was an office that drew together interests and sympathies "by the Laws of nature; that what you love, they love; what you hate, they hate."[121] That was the hope for every ruler from the king down, but it could not be realized with rulers whose property lay in a distant place and was scarcely affected by bad government. One of the first pleas of Massachusetts to the crown in their petition of 1664 was for a continuance of government "by men chosen from among themselves."[122]

The sufferings under Andros were attributed to the fact that the dominion employed outsiders to govern the province. "Of all this unhappiness," the chief gentlemen of the Council testified afterwards, "we must reckon the first step and in-let to be, that *the Governour did* so quickly neglect the great number of the Council, and *chiefly adhere unto and Govern by the advice* only of a few others, the principal *of them Strangers to the Countrey, without Estates or Interest therein to oblige them, persons of known and declared Prejudices against us, and that had plainly laid their chiefest Designs and Hopes to make unreasonable profit of this poor People."* New England was "*squeez'd* by a Crew of abject Persons

---

120. To explain colonial mistrust of officials, Dummer pointed out that "Sheriffs in the Plantations are comparatively but little Officers, and therefore not to be trusted as here [England], where they are Men of ample Fortunes." Dummer, *Defence of the New-England Charters,* 20. For instructions against "necessitous men," see Lincoln, ed., *Correspondence of William Shirley,* I, 145; Everett Kimball, *The Public Life of Joseph Dudley: A Study of the Colonial Policy of the Stuarts in New England, 1660–1715* (New York, 1911), 80.

121. John Wise, *The Churches Quarrel Espoused . . . ,* 2d ed. (Boston, 1715), 13.

122. Quoted in Greene, ed., *Great Britain and the American Colonies,* 63. In 1675 Virginia requested that their governors be resident and that the deputy governor be "such as has an estate and interest in the country." Quoted in *ibid.,* 89. See also Richard L. Morton, *Colonial Virginia* (Chapel Hill, N.C., 1960), I, chap. 12.

fetched, from *New York*" who had nothing to lose and everything to gain by oppression.[123]

A few years later, Jeremiah Dummer, the colony's agent, said bluntly that governors were too often failures in England who came to America to repair their fortunes. "It can hardly be expected but these Corruptions must happen, when one considers that few Gentlemen will cross the Seas for a Government, whose Circumstances are not a little streight at Home, and that they know by how slight and uncertain Tenure they hold their Commissions; from whence they wisely conclude, that no Time is to be lost."[124] In a frank comment to Governor Shirley in 1754, Benjamin Franklin laid down as premises on which all plans for imperial reform must be based the fact that "Governors often come to the Colonies merely to make Fortunes, with which they intend to return to Britain, are not always Men of the best Abilities and Integrity, have no Estates here, nor any natural Connections with us that should make them heartily concern'd for our Welfare."[125] In 1758 one British observer complained: "Most of the places in the gift of the Crown" in America "have been filled with broken members of Par——t, of bad if any, principles, pimps, valet de chambres, electioneering scoundrels, and even livery servants. In one word, America has been for many years made the hospital of Great Britain for her decayed courtiers and abandoned worn-out dependants."[126]

That was gross and unfair exaggeration. Governors were not ordinarily depraved characters, and as often as not the Privy Council appointed local men. The crown apparently recognized the truth of Charles Davenant's comment in 1698 that the colonies were better governed by "those who have an interest and property in the country, and who work for themselves than by governors sent from hence, whose most common aim is to grow rich by fleecing the inhabitants." Davenant throught that a native governor's colonial property was "without doubt the best caution and pledge for their good behaviour, both to the King and to his subjects in those remote parts."[127] Britain accepted that principle, and from 1691 to the Revolution, Massachusetts was under the governance of local men more than half of the

123. Whitmore, ed., *Andros Tracts*, I, 138, 13.
124. Dummer, *Defence of the New-England Charters*, 71.
125. Lincoln, ed., *Correspondence of William Shirley*, II, 103–104.
126. *Belcher Papers*, Part I, 3n.
127. Quoted in Greene, ed., *Great Britain and the American Colonies*, 148.

time. That includes the interim periods between governors when the lieutenant governor or Council held the reins, but even in terms of appointed governors, four of ten were natives.[128]

Moreover, the evidence of actual profiteering by governors is scarcely strong enough to support the great weight of suspicion they bore. The only formal charge of graft brought against a governor was the accusation against Dudley of illicit trade with the French in 1707. The alacrity of the House and Council to send out the alarm shows no hesitation in bringing charges, and yet no other cases were brought forward. Looking back, the Massachusetts governors appear generally to have been men of integrity, if of uneven ability.

The sensitivity to corruption must be understood in other terms than the actual maladministration of the royal governors. The conception of people tied together by interest was simply too powerful on both sides of the Atlantic to permit the apprehensions to die. Writing to an English audience in 1768, explaining American resistance to taxation, Benjamin Franklin stated as simple fact that colonial governors were

> not like Princes whose posterity have an inheritance in the government of a nation, and therefore an interest in its prosperity; they are generally strangers to the Provinces they are sent to govern, have no estate, natural connexion, or relation there, to give them an affection for the country. . . . they come only to make money as fast as they can; are sometimes men of vicious characters and broken fortunes . . . as they intend staying in the country no longer than their government continues, and purpose to leave no family behind them, they are apt to be regardless of the good will of the people.[129]

The New York Assembly in 1749 explained their insistence on control of public funds in almost the same words. Governors were

128. Whitmore, *The Massachusetts Civil List*, 43–44. For the efforts of native-born governors to make political capital of their birth, see Palfrey, *History of New England*, IV, 308n; *Journals of the House*, XI, 11; XIX, 64–76. Henry Ashurst said the colony had foolishly taken a beating from Dudley thinking that "*because his Family and Interest is there,*" it was "*unreasonable to Believe, that he would do any thing that should hurt the Country.*" *Deplorable State* (Mass. Hist. Soc., *Colls.*, 5th Ser., VI), 104. Douglass, *Summary, Historical and Political*, I, 418.

129. Albert Henry Smyth, ed., *The Writings of Benjamin Franklin* (Boston, 1850–1856), V, 83.

generally entire strangers to the People they are sent to govern; they seldom have any Estates . . . where they are appointed Governors, and consequently their Interest is entirely distinct . . . they seldom regard the Welfare of the People, otherwise than as they can make it subservient to their own particular interest; and as they know the Time of the Continuance in their Governments to be uncertain, all Methods are used, and all Engines set to work to raise Estates to themselves and therefore should the public Monies be left to their Disposition, what can be expected but the grossest mis-application?[130]

The prevailing belief about the failings of colonial governors deepened the ordinary doubts about rulers and made it impossible for the assembly to yield to any of its governors. Even in the absence of actual depredation, the Massachusetts House conducted itself as if it were governed by faithless strangers.

Such convictions augured poorly for the peace of colonial administration. They meant that no governor could win the trust of the assembly. The colonists chose to assume that the natural restraints on selfishness which ideally operated in good governments would not operate in theirs. The interests of a royal official would not blend with the people's; his prosperity and his family's would not suffer from oppressive taxes or avaricious judges. Private interest moved him to pillage as efficiently as possible and depart with the spoils. No matter that few governors actually behaved scandalously. The stereotypes kept alive the threat of rapine and plunder.

Through it all monarchy as a form of government was never explicitly questioned. But implicitly the structure itself was at issue. For danger could never be eliminated under the imperial constitution. So long as the power to appoint lay in England, alien officials would cross the Atlantic year after year to disquiet the lives of the colonists. At the root of the colonists' discontent was the king's right to appoint rulers. No one proposed independence; for their defense, the colonists relied on their charter rights and privileges. But dissatisfaction with the structure of empire remained as an indissoluble kernel of discontent until the Revolution brought it to life, and there grew from it both Independence and republican government.

130. Quoted in John F. Burns, *Controversies between Royal Governors and Their Assemblies in the Northern American Colonies* (Boston, 1923), 21.

PART II

The Course of Events, 1763–1776

CHAPTER 4

The Government of Empire

The political culture of provincial Massachusetts mainly formed around three words: "king," "people," and "interest." The ideas associated with those words provided what the government needed most: a moral justification for submission and a moral purpose for ruling. Culture ordered the consciences of people so that they were constrained to comply by conviction as much as by force. The culture also did what cultures must, by defining roles for people, including the good ruler, the good subject, and the loyal opposition. Room was left for criticism, along with compliance; and, in fact, one of the most sharply defined roles was that of popular leader, whose job it was to remain ever vigilant and to be uncompromising in the defense of popular rights.

It was a resilient political culture that sustained both opposition and submission. The popular party relentlessly attacked the governors, and yet the defenders of popular rights could negotiate and compromise. The politicians, after a half-century of struggle, actually resolved most of the divisive constitutional issues and reached compromises that integrated Massachusetts into the imperial system.

But the culture always retained the possibility of revolt, not buried deep within it, but near enough to the surface to trouble rulers. Imperial officials talked a lot about recalcitrance and resistance and even independence. They worried that the colonists secretly wished to free themselves of British rule, or at least to take the power of government into their own hands. After 1760 these fears were realized as Massachusetts, along with all of the colonies, took a sudden turn toward revolution. Within fifteen years after Governor Bernard's report on provincial loyalty and calm, Massachusetts fired on the king's troops at Concord. In those fifteen years, the equilibrium that had been achieved through decades of compromise and constitutional negotiation was broken, and the disruptive forces, tenuously held in check by legalistic assurances of charter rights and privileges, took over. In the stress of conflict over parliamentary taxation and regulation, monarchical government without a supporting social order proved itself incapable of disciplining the people. Events magnified the latent suspicion of royal officials, and the fear of corruption finally stretched American loyalties to the breaking point. A year after the skirmishes at Concord and Lexington, the colonies indicted the king for the failure to protect them and formed republican governments.

One of the puzzles of our history is what moved the imperial administration to pursue policies that broke up a thriving and basically harmonious empire. The specific measures that ignited controversy, the Sugar Act of 1764 and the Stamp Act of 1765, were not part of a concerted program to reform the empire. George Grenville, the chancellor of the Exchequer, and the men who surrounded and succeeded him in the ministry never laid out an integrated plan for a new American policy. They were practical politicians, trying to balance the budget and pay for the army which the king wished to keep in America after the Seven Years' War. Their immediate goals were simple and practical. What is surprising is their tenacity in doing things that provoked angry resistance. They would not have risked losing the colonies merely to support troops on an American establishment. The British must have had stronger reasons than that. Successive ministries adjusted the revenue measures to placate the Americans, reducing the molasses tariff and repealing the Stamp Act, and yet always came back with new measures offensive to the colonists. The question is, What was their purpose in pursuing policies that drove the Americans to the point of desperation?

We frequently look to the economy as a source of deep conflict, but in the eighteenth century, trade had the opposite effect. Commerce joined the interests of farmers, merchants, and manufacturers on both sides of the Atlantic, as many eighteenth-century political economists eventually perceived. Because so many benefited from it, trade strength-ened the internal bonds of empire. In this respect, the course of the imperial economy paralleled the course of imperial politics. Both overcame initial conflicts to achieve workable cooperation and even integration.

In the coming of the Revolution, the economy did play a role, but an indirect one. The economy was significant more for the reaction of politicians than for the relatively slight conflicts within the economy itself. The economy disturbed imperial politicians because one of their primary missions was to regulate trade. The main reason for sending royal officials into the colonies in the late seventeenth century was to enforce the Navigation Acts. The crown aimed to enhance British trade and thus its own revenues. Royal governors and customs officers were charged to protect the king's interests. Trouble began when the of-ficials realized they were failing.

Although the king grew rich from the American trade, colonial of-ficials only partly succeeded in their effort to enforce the crown's com-mercial policies. Trade was a wayward child. It grew by its own plan, took paths of its own choosing, broke rules. The willfulness of trade and traders, the routine disregard of restrictions, and the apparent in-subordination of colonial legislatures frustrated imperial officials. The lack of control left the powerful feeling powerless and impatient to re-gain control.

Out of this frustration were born countless schemes for reasserting authority and ending colonial insubordination. Central to virtually all was the conviction that royal officials must be independent. They must be true to the crown and not subject to the people they governed. Of-ficials sympathetic to local colonial interests would never properly en-force the Navigation Acts or carry out royal instructions. And officials would inevitably yield to local pressures if the colonial assemblies paid their salaries. The rigorous execution of royal policy required indepen-dent officials on permanent salaries. Every reformer included that simple fundamental in his scheme.

The issue took a central place because the ministry understood the position and nature of the governors exactly as the popular party did. Crown bureaucrats made no effort to defend the character of their ap-pointees against the accusations of the colonists. Whitehall believed as firmly as Elisha Cooke that a governor would pursue his own interests regardless of king or country. Like the colonists, the hard-bitten realists in Whitehall knew that governors, like all placemen, were entangled in networks of interest and would serve whichever power advanced their interests best. It was precisely because colonists and ministry thought alike on the subject that conflict occurred. To free the governors from the grasp of the people, the crown felt it must control salaries as well as appointments. Without royal officials firmly in the crown's interest, the empire could never be governed.

Colonial officials in America and England had long awaited an opportunity for change when, by sheer coincidence, the king in 1763 decided to keep his American army at near-wartime strength. Without thinking twice, Parliament enacted a colonial tax to pay expenses. The colonial reformers, seizing the opportunity, rode the coattails of the army revenue bills. The Sugar and Stamp Acts said nothing of colonial reform, but the Townshend duties explicitly provided for colonial salaries from customs revenues.

The furious reaction to both the Stamp Act and the Townshend duties caused the ministry to back away. Both revenue bills were repealed (save the tea duty, of course), and by 1770 Parliament had given up its effort to raise an American revenue for the army. The Revolutionary crisis might have ended then and there and the colonies have returned to their happy earlier state, but reformers in the ministry, having come so close, would not give up. The Townshend duties whetted their appetites for greater control and, particularly, their desire for that one basic reform, independent salaries for key officials. It was the payment of salaries to Massachusetts governors and judges that reignited the controversy in 1772 and led directly to revolution.

Innumerable other disputes, anxieties, and misunderstandings entered the course of events after 1760, but this urge governed the imperial administrators to the end. Underlying all was the century-long effort to master an empire which seemed perpetually out of control. In opposition to this effort, the popular party put every possible limit on the very officials sent to establish that control, not to evade the regulations so much as to prevent plundering. Their motives drove the two sides into head-on conflict: the imperial officials' fear of insubordination, and the provincials' apprehensions of greed and exploitation. These two opposing forces constituted the essence of the conflict that ended at last in Revolution and Independence.

i. Economic Order

Although basically well integrated, the eighteenth-century imperial economy did have its stresses and strains, and New England troubled imperial theorists more than any other region.[1] There were a number of trouble spots. Late seventeenth-century political economists worried that New England's economy resembled England's too closely and would soon compete in manufactures.[2] Later, in the eighteenth century, English sugar planters blamed New England traders for a drop in sugar prices and tried to stop trade with the French West Indies. Throughout the century, English merchants trading to America objected to Massachusetts' paper money, which was virtually useless to them. Each of the conflicts held the potential for straining the imperial system. Had the laws passed to restrain Massachusetts been enforced, the province would have severely suffered, and the economy would have become a direct cause of complaint.

But the laws were not enforced. By one device or another, usually

1. For a discussion of Massachusetts' hopes for a favored place in the empire after 1689, see Philip S. Haffenden, *New England in the English Nation, 1689–1713* (Oxford, 1974). For general studies of the Massachusetts economy, one begins with the venerable William B. Weeden, *Economic and Social History of New England, 1620–1789* (Boston, 1890). Other useful works include Percy Wells Bidwell and John I. Falconer, *History of Agriculture in the Northern United States, 1620–1860* (Washington, D.C., 1925); Douglas R. McManis, *Colonial New England: A Historical Geography* (New York, 1975); Max George Schumacher, *The Northern Farmer and His Markets during the Late Colonial Period* (New York, 1975); and Haffenden, *New England*, 149–159. Recent populations estimates project between 44,646 and 45,018 Massachusetts inhabitants in 1690. Robert Paul Thomas and Terry L. Anderson, "White Population, Labor Force, and Extensive Growth of the New England Economy in the Seventeenth Century," *Journal of Economic History*, XXXIII (1973), 655. The population figure given in U.S. Bureau of the Census, *Historical Statistics of the United States, Colonial Times to 1970* (Washington, D.C., 1975), Ser. Z, 1–19, which runs higher than the Thomas and Anderson estimates, shows 49,504 inhabitants in 1690. On economic growth, see Terry L. Anderson, "Economic Growth in Colonial New England: 'Statistical Renaissance,'" *Jour. Econ. Hist.*, XXXIX (1979), 243–258; Phyllis Deane and W. A. Cole, *British Economic Growth, 1688–1959: Trends and Structure* (New York, 1962), table 22. For a more generous estimate of 18th-century growth rates, see Russell R. Menard, "Comment on Paper by Ball and Walton," *Jour. Econ. Hist.*, XXXVI (1976), 118–125.

2. June 16, 1702, Massachusetts Archives, VI, 291, Archives Dept., State House, Boston. Sir Josiah Child, *A New Discourse of Trade . . .* (London, 1693), 160–163.

with the complicity of English commercial interests, the restraints on Massachusetts trade were circumvented. The mutual advantages of unfettered trade were too great to permit hindrances to form. England and America prospered together in the eighteenth century, and the tide of commercial growth washed away every obstacle put in its path.

The regulations to preserve mast trees were a case in point. England had long deplored its dependence on the Baltic states for an item so vital to national defense as masts and looked to America for a supply within the empire. To encourage production and to give New England a staple that would not compete with English manufactures, the Naval Stores Act of 1705 granted a bounty of £1 per ton, with a 10 percent increase in wartime, in addition to the market price. In the eighteenth century, prices for thirty-six-inch-diameter sticks, one hundred feet long, ranged up to £218 plus the bounty. The average value in the years between 1691 and 1776 for masts of all sizes was £100.[3]

Unfortunately, while masting provided a living for a number of operators, laborers, and provisioners, it was not suitable for every woodsman. Only the biggest operators could put up the capital to bring out big trees, twenty-four to thirty-six inches in diameter and as many yards long. It took as many as forty or fifty oxen to snake a big stick out of the woods to the river. There were high costs and high risks; some logs proved defective after all the trouble of getting them out. In addition, a mast merchant needed connections with English contractors who made the purchase and obtained the royal license to cut the trees marked with the king's broad arrow. Thomas Hutchinson estimated that a mast was worth ten times the value of the planks, deals, and staves that little operators sawed from the same tree, but the expense and risk made masting less profitable than straight lumbering for ordinary lumbermen.[4]

Consequently the masting regulations ran afoul of New England interests. The sawmill men wanted to log New England forest lands for one purpose, the mastmen for another. Beginning with a provision in the charter of 1691 and concluding with the White Pines Act of 1729,

3. The act is reprinted in Jack P. Greene, ed., *Great Britain and the American Colonies, 1606–1763* (New York, 1970), 133, 134.
4. Robert G. Albion, *Forests and Sea Power: The Timber Problem of the Royal Navy, 1652–1862* (Cambridge, Mass., 1926), 260–261; Thomas Hutchinson, *The History of the Colony and Province of Massachusetts-Bay*, ed. Lawrence Shaw Mayo (Cambridge, Mass., 1936), II, 190.

Parliament enacted five pieces of legislation to reserve trees of mast size (twenty-four inches in diameter and larger) and to create nurseries in which smaller trees could grow to the required girth. But the very plentitude of the legislation attests to its weakness. There was no language adequate to the task. There was always another loophole through which the sawmill men could threaten the long rafts of big trees. When the law granted control of mast trees on private land to the owners, the colonial assembly laid out a string of paper townships for the operators and thus transferred trees from the king's hands to private hands. When private ownership exclusions were restricted to lands granted before 1691, thereby invalidating the privileges of the paper townships, Elisha Cooke, leader of the popular party in Massachusetts, claimed all of Maine was private property since the beginning. Ferdinando Gorges had received it by patent from the king, and Massachusetts had purchased it from Gorges. And so it went for four decades. Every device of royal policy was countered by the colonists.[5]

In the larger perspective, however, royal forest policy succeeded. It was the surveyors general and the Board of Trade who were frustrated, not imperial interests. Lax enforcement was no hindrance to the ultimate object. In 1737, with the departure of the surveyor of woods David Dunbar to repair his political connections in England, royal forest policy lost its last zealot. There were few complaints and no further parliamentary regulations. The enforcing officers hung on limply, making no serious efforts, and yet the masts streamed across the Atlantic, as many as forty-five hundred in eighty years.[6]

After 1743, for twenty-three years, Benning Wentworth combined the governorship of New Hampshire, the office of surveyor general, and an active involvement in the timber business. In his term as surveyor general, he prosecuted no more than a dozen offenders, none of them successfully. He limited his activities to semiannual letters to the

5. William Macdonald, ed., *Select Charters and Other Documents Illustrative of American History, 1606–1775* (New York, 1914), 212; Joseph J. Malone, *Pine Trees and Politics: The Naval Stores and Forest Policy in Colonial New England, 1691–1775* (Seattle, Wash., 1964), 70–71, 75–76, 88, 98, 189; Albion, *Forests and Sea Power*, 248–256; John Gorham Palfrey, *History of New England* (Boston, 1858–1890), IV, 401, 411–412.

6. Malone, *Pine Trees and Politics*, 55, 122–123, 127–129. The later royal governors entered periodic complaints of waste in the woods, and called for more legislation, but only perfunctorily. *Journals of the House of Representatives of Massachusetts* (Boston, 1919–), XVII, 157, 180; Malone, *Pine Trees and Politics*, 129–130.

Board of Trade outlining plans. And yet in this period of relaxation, Wentworth's own crews contributed largely to the flow of masts that fitted out the navy's ships during the Seven Years' War. In the give-and-take of everyday business, Wentworth found a way to reconcile the conflicting purpose of mill men and mast men, and the Royal Navy was none the worse for it.[7]

Benning's nephew John, who succeeded to the office of surveyor general in 1767, continued his uncle's relaxed policies. John saw at once the impracticability of the regulations and brought his own en-forcement policies more into conformity with the realities of forest commerce. Lumbermen were warned away from certain preserves where infractions were strictly enforced, and given a free hand in areas where unrestricted logging made more sense. John Wentworth's recom-mendations to Lord Germain, which formed the basis of later Cana-dian legislation, deftly avoided the awkwardness of earlier white pines acts.[8] Wentworth was content to let the natural harmonies of the impe-rial economy assert themselves. The purposes of trade and empire were fulfilled despite disregard of the mast legislation. The only suf-ferers were the colonial officials who came to believe with the early surveyors of the woods that the Americans were ungovernable.

The failures of trade regulation in the West Indies repeated the ex-perience with mast laws. Mercantile regulations were no more effective there. The Caribbean offered the largest and best market for New En-gland fish, meat, grain, and lumber. The British islands absorbed large quantities of New England products in return for sugar, molasses, and bills of exchange on London.[9] But nearly half the trade went to the French islands, and the English sugar planters objected. They suffered doubly and triply from the competition. Besides lowering sugar prices in Europe, the enlarged market raised the cost of provisions and re-duced the value of molasses and rum. When French competition and a sluggish English economy brought down the price of sugar in the 1720s, the British planters pressed for legislation.[10]

7. Malone, *Pine Trees and Politics*, 132. For the Wentworth mast policy, see Jere R. Daniell, *Experiment in Republicanism: New Hampshire Politics and the American Revolution, 1741–1794* (Cambridge, Mass., 1970), 10–14.

8. Malone, *Pine Trees and Politics*, 133, 138, 140.

9. James F. Shepherd and Gary M. Walton, *Shipping, Maritime Trade, and the Economic Development of Colonial North America* (Cambridge, 1972), 135, 128, 165, 211–226.

10. Thomas C. Barrow, *Trade and Empire: The British Customs Service in Colonial America, 1660–1775* (Cambridge, Mass., 1967), 134–135; Richard B. Sheridan, "The Molasses

The Molasses Act of 1733 imposed duties that were meant to prohibit the French trade: five shillings per hundredweight on foreign sugars, nine pence per gallon on rum, and six pence per gallon on molasses.[11] Had it been enforced, the act would have devastated the New England economy. New England prosperity was delicately attuned to its largest market. When sugar prices rose in Britain after 1745, New England immediately felt the benefit.[12] The loss of nearly half of the West Indies market would have brought intolerable consequences. Besides the lost sales to the French, prices for New England provisions would have plummeted, and the cost of British molasses and rum in the islands would have shot up.

The necessity of access to French markets doomed every effort to prohibit the trade. The Molasses Act was no more successful than the White Pines Act. Only feeble attempts at enforcement were made anyway: a new surveyor and searcher was appointed in the Salem-Marblehead district, and a searcher and landwaiter added in Rhode Island. Meanwhile, pressure on Parliament let up after the British sugar planters were permitted direct shipments to the continent in 1739 and 1742. The duty and costs of reshipment which were previously required of sugar as an enumerated commodity were thus eliminated, and the British planters reaped the benefits. The Molasses Act became a dead letter, and by 1739 trade with the French islands was back to normal. War with the French after 1754 curtailed trade somewhat because of prohibitions on trade with the enemy, but commerce quickly revived after the end of hostilities.[13] Trade cut its own channels, washing away all artificial barriers, much to the chagrin of customs officials. They were left with a perpetual feeling of impotent frustration.

The currency shortage, the third source of economic conflict, was the most troubling issue, and nowhere more than in New England.[14]

Act and the Market Strategy of the British Sugar Planters," *Jour. Econ. Hist.*, XVII (1957), 62–83; Marc Egnal, "The Economic Development of the Thirteen Continental Colonies, 1720 to 1775," *William and Mary Quarterly*, 3d Ser., XXXII (1975), 206–207.

11. Barrow, *Trade and Empire*, 308.

12. Egnal, "Economic Development," *WMQ*, 3d Ser., XXXII, 206–208.

13. Barrow, *Trade and Empire*, 137, 157.

14. Still useful for information on currency issues and legislation are Joseph B. Felt, *Historical Account of Massachusetts Currency* (Boston, 1839); and Andrew McFarland Davis, *Currency and Banking in the Province of the Massachusetts Bay* (American Economic Association, *Publications*, 3d Ser., I–II [Boston, 1900–1901]). Other relevant works are Curtis P. Nettels, *The Money Supply of the American Colonies before 1720*, University of

Accommodations were reached, after extended controversy, but not before the assembly had ample opportunity to show its flagrant disregard for royal instructions. The problem ran deep. The unfavorable balance of trade made it difficult for Massachusetts to find the goods to exchange for English manufactures. Silver money of every kind flowed back across the Atlantic to pay for the British goods sold in Boston shops. The resulting shortage strained individuals all along the lines of trade. Barter and short-term credit were unsatisfactory substitutes. The lack of money distorted prices and worked innumerable injustices. Indebted farmers, rich in commodities and land, were driven to the wall because money for repayment was not to be had. Enterprising men had to forgo opportunities for lack of capital. Ordinary people had trouble raising the cash for taxes and were forced to sell their goods below their value.[15]

Massachusetts had set to work early on the problem. In 1652 the colonial government assumed the powers of sovereignty and began minting coins, variously identified as willow-tree, oak-tree, and pine-tree shillings. The crown closed the mint under the Dominion of New England, however, and refused to reopen it. In 1691 the province issued currency under another guise when it attacked the problem indirectly through deficit financing of King William's War. To meet the extraordinary expenses of an expedition against Canada, the General

---

Wisconsin Studies in the Social Sciences and History, No. 20 (Madison, Wis., 1934); Leslie V. Brock, *The Currency of the American Colonies, 1700–1764: A Study in Colonial Finance and Imperial Relations* (New York, 1975); E. James Ferguson, "Currency Finance: An Interpretation of Colonial Monetary Practices," *WMQ*, 3d Ser., X (1953), 153–180; Herman Belz, "Paper Money in Colonial Massachusetts," Essex Institute, *Historical Collections*, CI (1965), 149–163; John J. McCusker, *Money and Exchange in Europe and America, 1600–1775: A Handbook* (Chapel Hill, N.C., 1978), 125–137; Joseph Albert Ernst, *Money and Politics in America, 1755–1775: A Study in the Currency Act of 1764 and the Political Economy of Revolution* (Chapel Hill, N.C., 1973); Roger W. Weiss, "The Colonial Monetary Standard of Massachusetts," *Economic History Review*, 2d Ser., XXVII (1974), 577–592.

15. The assembly argued for currency issues as a means of making tax payments without oppression. *Journals of the House*, VII, 322, 354; VIII, 143; Mass. Arch., VII, 110–111. Another approach was to permit commodity payments. During the credit shortage in 1720 and for several years afterward, 23 items were acceptable. Davis, *Currency and Banking*, I, 108; *Journals of the House*, II, 247, 333; Samuel Sewall, *Diary of Samuel Sewall, 1674–1729* (Massachusetts Historical Society, *Collections*, 5th Ser., V–VII [Boston, 1878–1882]), II, 366, cited hereafter as Sewall, *Diary*.

Court issued bills of credit to the sum of forty thousand pounds, which were acceptable for payment of taxes, and the bills, after a momentary hesitation by the populace, gained general circulation. The bills were drawn in the next year and destroyed or held for use in further emissions.[16]

When the Peace of Utrecht halted hostilities in 1714, the Massachusetts economy faced a financial crisis. The return to a peacetime budget would mean a sharp contraction of the money supply. For the next three decades the assembly and the governor fought over an appropriate solution. The assembly made banks in 1715, 1716, 1721, and 1728. The first of these lent province bills directly to the inhabitants, securing the loans with land worth double the value of the loan. Later banks allotted the bills to the counties (1716) and the towns (1721 and 1728), who in turn lent to their inhabitants. So popular were the bills that at the same time as banks were lending notes, emissions to meet the normal expenses of government continued as before. The skirmishes with the French and Indians in 1720s resulted in average emissions of £34,900 annually between 1721 and 1730. By 1730 some £270,000 was in circulation. Governor Shirley complained in 1741 that £427,932 was overdue and that virtually every issue since 1702 had not been called in on schedule.[17]

Until 1716, royal governors sympathized with currency issues and banks. The governors needed the funds to finance the military expeditions whose success was so important to their standing with the imperial bureaucracy, and they knew the province could meet expenses in

16. For John Hull and the Massachusetts mint, see Samuel Eliot Morison, *Builders of the Bay Colony*, rev. ed. (Boston, [1964]), 150–153. Bernard Bailyn discusses the attempts to hold on to specie in *The New England Merchants in the Seventeenth Century* (Cambridge, Mass., 1955), 182–189. The Charter, or Old Colony bills, as the issues from 1691 to 1701 were called, could be paid for taxes or exchanged for whatever stock happened to be in the treasury. To overcome public reluctance, the government placed a 5% premium on the value of the bills when submitted as tax payments. Davis, *Currency and Banking*, I, 8–16.

17. Davis, *Currency and Banking*, I, 55–57, 60–62, 63, 79–80, 82–89, 155–156, 443; *Journals of the House*, VIII, 157; XVII, 158. The exact amount of circulation in a given year is now impossible to ascertain because of the discrepancies between scheduled and actual recalls and between official records and informal estimates. For differing estimates of the currency in circulation in 1740 and 1741, see Belz, "Paper Money," Essex Inst., *Hist. Colls.*, CI (1969), 159; and Malcolm Freiberg, "Thomas Hutchinson and the Province Currency," *New England Quarterly*, XXX (1957), 193.

no other way. Governor Shute, who arrived in 1716, was at first sympathetic to a public bank. His support faded quickly, however, when he saw how rapidly the bills lost their value. The crown always took the side of stable currency values, just as it favored stable weights and measures. Inflated currency worked an injustice on creditors, on widows and orphans living on interest from estates, on the clergy on fixed salaries, and above all on British merchants trading to America who had no use for Massachusetts bills.[18]

In an attempt to turn the province around, a 1720 royal instruction required the governors to include a suspension clause in all bills to emit currency. The clause suspended the bill until it was approved in England. The assembly easily got around that hindrance by taking advantage of a provision that permitted immediate emissions in case of emergency. There was always a convenient emergency. Driven to more drastic measures, the Privy Council ten years later forbade the creation of any more banks to lend bills and required that all of the outstanding bills be called in on schedule. In 1741, when the last of the currency issues were to be called in, the province's money supply would be reduced by 90 percent.[19]

18. Gov. Dudley acknowledged the need for bills but called for measures to secure their value. Davis, *Currency and Banking*, I, 54. For Shute's disillusionment with banks, see *ibid.*, 59–61. Nevertheless, Shute approved the public bank in 1721. For complaints about the currency emphasizing the hurt to British merchants, see *Journals of the House*, XI, 25, 275; XVII, 152; Board of Trade to Gov. Dudley, Feb. 4, 1706, in Noel Sainsbury *et al.*, eds., *Calendar of State Papers, Colonial Series, America and West Indies* (London, 1860–), XXIII, 43–44, cited hereafter as *Cal. St. Papers*; Lt. Gov. Dummer to Newcastle, 1729, *Cal. St. Papers*, XXXVI, 572. The British merchants would have hurt more if the bills had been made legal tender, which action would have compelled the merchants to accept the bills for debts contracted in Massachusetts. In 1712 many Boston merchants, including Jonathan Belcher, advocated this change. As it was, the bills were partially legal tender. The 1712 Act for the Relief of and to Prevent the Oppression of Debtors forbade a court execution against a debtor if he had tendered bills of credit. The debt was not wiped out, but payment was stayed. Through numerous reenactments, the act remained in effect until 1741. The House insisted the bills would not have lost their value had they been made legal tender. Sewall, *Diary*, II, 369; Davis, *Currency and Banking*, I, 99–100, 155; *Journals of the House*, VIII, 334; E. Ames and A. C. Goodell, eds., *The Acts and Resolves, Public and Private, of the Province of the Massachusetts Bay* . . . (Boston, 1869–1922), I, 700–701.

19. Davis, *Currency and Banking*, I, 63–64, 81, 114, 125–127; *Journals of the House*, VII, 329; VIII, 154; XII, 9; XVII, 152–153. The House estimated in 1739 that to meet the 1741 deadline, £100,000 a year would have to be called in. *Journals of the House*, XVII, 102, 178.

The assembly believed that the province faced economic ruin. The legislature fought the governor by every means possible, but because his signature was required to issue further bills, it was helpless. As the fatal day approached, a private land bank to issue currency was proposed, lending notes against the borrowers' land. It won supporters in every county and in nearly every town. Over nine hundred individuals signed up as subscribers and offered their land as security for the notes. In 1740 land bank notes went into circulation and were quickly broadcast across the colony.[20]

Jonathan Belcher did all in his power to crush the bank, with little effect until the news arrived in April 1741 that Parliament had extended the Bubble Act of 1720 to New England. Under its provisions, joint-stock companies were forbidden to transact business without statutory authorization. Since the land bank had never received legislative authorization (the governor would never sign such a bill), it was illegal.[21] The colony was aghast. A number of the directors seriously considered disregarding the parliamentary action and continuing the operation. In a half-dozen towns the people threatened to take up arms. The council had to issue warrants against "a design and combination with a number of evil-minded persons to come to the town of Boston in a tumultuous manner."[22]

The threat of an uprising faded, however, and the bank began the slow process of disassembling itself. William Shirley, who came to office in the midst of the crisis, alleviated the threat of an immediate economic collapse by drawing out the process of redeeming the notes. Many remained in circulation for some years. By luck, war also intervened to save the colony from collapse. In 1741 the governor was asked to raise troops for Lord Vernon's operations against the Spanish in the West Indies. The royal instructions permitted the issuance of

20. Davis, *Currency and Banking*, I, 77, 116–117, 130–132, 157; II, 130–167; Palfrey, *History of New England*, IV, 547, 549; *Journals of the House*, XVII, 151, 154, 180, 197, 210–211. The House tried to bribe the governor in 1732 with a bill to repair fortifications with bills to be withdrawn after 1741. Had Belcher been required by England to mount a war effort, he could not have held out. The House was equally determined not to contract the currency. A 1739 motion to draw in the bills failed unanimously. *Journals of the House*, XI, 107–108, 140–141; XVII, 616, 190, 235, 243–244. See also George A. Billias, *The Massachusetts Land Bankers of 1740*, University of Maine Studies, 2d Ser., No. 74 (Orono, Maine, 1959).

21. Davis, *Currency and Banking*, I, 147–151; II, 152, 160–162.

22. *Ibid.*, II, 153–154, 158–159.

bills in cases of emergency. The outbreak of hostilities and, particularly, the campaign against Louisburg in 1745 justified the governor in authorizing more bills than ever before, nineteen issues in one four-year period. Far from being drained of a currency, Massachusetts was soon awash in paper money. By 1749 more than two million pounds was in circulation, and its exchange value in sterling had dropped to less than one-tenth of its face value. Even the former advocates of bills of credit saw the need for restraint.[23]

Inflation prepared the way for a turnabout. When Britain offered to compensate the province £183,649 of sterling money for its part in the conquest of Louisburg, William Shirley and Thomas Hutchinson proposed to redeem all of the colony's paper currency and put the Massachusetts economy on a specie basis once again. Although there were cries of anguish, and fear that the merchants would once again monopolize the silver for their own purposes, the bill passed. The provincial agents purchased 217 chests of milled and pillared Spanish dollars and smaller coins and 9 boxes of small copper English coins. From March 1750 to June 1751, the provincials trooped in with their paper money and marched out with silver and copper.[24] From that time to the Revolution, Massachusetts enjoyed the benefits of a stable specie currency.

The exchange of paper for specie on the whole satisfied both crown and assembly. Like the conflicts over masting regulations and trade with the French sugar islands, the currency question was finally resolved. By mid-century, economic conflicts with the imperial government receded, just as controversies over the charter came to an end a decade earlier. The needs of commerce asserted themselves, inhibiting regulations were overcome, and so the way was prepared for an era of relative political calm.[25]

23. *Ibid.*, I, 169–170. By 1749 there were four kinds of Massachusetts money: old tenor, middle tenor, new tenor, and last tenor. Old tenor, issued between 1702 and 1738, set the terms for valuing the other three. The reason for the various tenors in addition to old tenor was the royal instruction restricting currency issues to £30,000 a year. Govs. Belcher and Shirley tried to fulfill the letter of the law by issuing currency whose face value was £30,000, but whose defined value relative to old tenor was three or four to one. To make the issues more appealing, the assembly promised redemption in silver after a few years or, in one case, within nine months. The promises were not kept, and no one believed they would be. *Ibid.*, I, 25–26, 161, 159, 165–166.
24. The dramatic story is vividly retold *ibid.*, 231–247. See also Freiberg, "Thomas Hutchinson and the Province Currency," *NEQ*, XXX (1957), 190–208.
25. A clause permitting wartime emissions vitiated Parliament's 1751 act forbidding issues of new bills in New England. For the improving standard of living during the

But royal officials could not look back on their achievements with complacency. The currency question was settled only after a thirty-year battle during which the colonists stubbornly disregarded royal instructions. The assembly doubtless would have continued to issue currency had the governor been willing to sign the bills. And while currency was no longer a problem after 1750, mast regulations and West Indies trade restrictions continued to be disregarded. Though the imperial economy prospered, officials believed the colony was headed toward independence. For many the only satisfaction was to devise elaborate schemes to bring the colonists to heel.

ii. Customs and Mores

So it was that despite their ineffectiveness, eighteenth-century British commercial regulations cast a shadow over the colonies. Because a large portion of the commodities brought into New England ports had to be entered illegally, much trading was surreptitious, carried on in the twilight of legitimacy. There was a standing agreement with customs officials to enter only a fraction of French molasses, probably less than a tenth of the whole, and then to collect only a partial duty. In more questionable cases, the captain or owner simply bribed the tidesman or searcher. If a conscientious collector cracked down in one port, cargoes went to more relaxed districts for entry. When enforcement could not be evaded, the merchants took revenge in a damage suit in a local court. The illegalities of trade soured the relations of officials

---

third quarter of the 18th century, and for the increases in British investment, see Egnal, "The Economic Development of the Thirteen Continental Colonies," *WMQ*, 3d Ser., XXXII, 208, 214–215. On the role of British war payments, see Julian Gwyn, "British Government Spending and the North American Colonies, 1740–1775," in Peter Marshall and Glyn Williams, eds., *The British Atlantic Empire before the Revolution* (London, 1980), 74–84.

26. Barrow, *Trade and Empire*, 141–142. Smuggling went on everywhere in the empire. In the 1760s Britons smuggled 7,000,000 pounds of tea into the island. Merrill Jensen, *The Founding of a Nation: A History of the American Revolution, 1763–1776* (New York, 1968), 434. In 1732 it was calculated that merchants defrauded the customs of one-third of the duties on tobacco imported into the realm. Dorothy Marshall, *Eighteenth Century England* (London, 1962), 148–150. See also Basil Williams, *The Whig Supremacy, 1714–1760*, rev. ed. (Oxford, 1962), 181.

and populace, heightening the image of arrogance on one side and disdain for authority on the other. In the messages that flowed across the Atlantic from the New England naval districts, the customs officials perpetually reproached the colonists, pleaded for stricter enforcement, and vented the bitterness and rage of their frustrating, powerless position.[26]

Officials reacted differently to their dispiriting situation. One reaction was to diagnose ills and prescribe reforms, the other to acquiesce in the infringements on the law and to blend socially with the merchants. The first group of officials became what Thomas Barrow has called "schematists," the second "creoles."

A great number of zealous but frustrated collectors and surveyors, the schematists, vented their anger at their desks in lengthy catalogs of colonial evasions and proposals for reform. From the beginning of the century to the end of the French wars in 1763, schemes for restructuring, repairing, and fortifying imperial governance piled up in the offices of the Board of Trade, the Customs Commissioners, and the Privy Council. The recommendations ranged from the obvious to the ingenious, from patchwork to drastic reconstruction: send more officials, send troops, fix fees for officials, put all navigation cases in Admiralty, grant governors a permanent salary, establish an episcopal bishop, impose a stamp tax, replace charter and proprietary with royal governments, appoint a lord lieutenant for the continent. The aim of them all was to tighten the bands and end the egregious disregard for imperial authority. Reference was made to the sacrifice of various English interests such as the loss of customs revenue, the destruction of mast trees, and the foreign invasion of England's rightful monopoly of colonial trade, but the fundamental anxiety was the loss of control. Colonial governments had "shewn too great an inclination to be independent of their mother Kingdom" and hence readily jeopardized her interests. All prudent states sought "to secure by all possible means the intire absolute and immediate dependency of their Colonies."[27] That was the primary object.

The proposals of Archibald Cummings, William Shirley, William Bollan, Robert Auchmuty, and a host of others from outside New England lay unattended in London files for decades.[28] The programs

27. Board of Trade, 1721, *Cal. St. Papers*, XXXII, 445, 446. Thomas Barrow discusses the schematists' reports in *Trade and Empire*, 81–105.

28. Barrow, *Trade and Empire*, 82, 101–102, 153–157, 302n; and his "Archibald Cum-

were not without merit; in time the ministry adopted many of the ideas emanating from the colonial officials. The sluggishness of the ministry reflects, rather, the absence of any political incentive to tighten the customs administration. No major interest stood to benefit. When manufacturing or commercial interests desired legislation, they usually got it. Hat manufacturers, iron producers, West Indian planters—all saw Parliament act in their behalf in the eighteenth century, but these interests were restricted and usually temporary. The rigid and consistent enforcement of the regulations as a whole stood to benefit no one, except the imperial bureaucracy itself, who gained from increased seizures and confiscations, higher fees, more offices, and greater authority.[29]

Faced with the failures of imperial regulations, the schematist official saw his own future in persuading the ministry of his zeal for the king's service and his grasp of the colonial situation. But theirs was not the only course of action. Another group of officials bent with the wind. These more pliable men, properly called creoles, saw only trouble and pain in strict conformity to the law. The customs officer in Lord Bellomont's time was "much hated by the Marchants here, but 'tis (for ought I can find) for being carefull and Exact in the Execution of his office." "A Collectors is the most ungratefull Office in these plantations that can be; if he is Just to his trust in looking into their Trade they hate him mortally."[30] On occasion that hate could turn to violence. Two crew members, who turned evidence for the crown in a 1723 smuggling case involving eighteen skins of Spanish leather and twelve jars of Spanish oil, felt the fury of Boston's commercial men. At the end of the hearing, some merchants and masters of ships "with a great number of other persons in a violent and mobbish manner assaulted the said evidences, kicked and pushed them downstairs and beat one of them so unmercifully dragging him thro' the streets that it is not yet known what may be the consequences."[31] With only ten regular customs officers in all of New England (after 1733), and no police force at his command, a collector or surveyor lived every day with the fact of

---

mings' Plan for a Colonial Revenue, 1722," *NEQ*, XXXVI (1963), 383–393; *Boston Evening-Post*, July 4, 1737. Various schemes are conveniently reprinted in Greene, ed., *Great Britain and the American Colonies*, 171–214.

29. Barrow, *Trade and Empire*, 88–90.

30. Quoted *ibid.*, 97.

31. *Ibid.*, 88–90.

his powerlessness.[32] If he was not often in danger of physical assault, he was perpetually threatened with damage suits in local courts whenever he chose to press charges in vice-admiralty.

Governor George Clinton in 1752 wrote that customs officers were "Sensible that the only way for them to prosper, or to be rewarded, is by Neglect of their Duty, and that they must Suffer by a performance of it."[33] Judging from the results, most Massachusetts officials chose to prosper. Instead of turning to the crown for satisfaction as the schematists did, the creole official joined the society of local merchants and took pleasure in it. Added to the modest salary of one hundred pounds, fees and the collector's share of seizures brought his official income, after payments to clerks and the deputy, to eight hundred to one thousand pounds annually. On top was the informal income of lemons and wine and not infrequent payments of gratitude. Flexible officials had long, peaceful, and uneventful careers. John Jekyll, the nephew of Sir Joseph Jekyll, received his appointment as collector at Boston in 1707. When he died in 1733, his son John took his place and served until 1740, thirty-three years for father and son. The Commissioners of Customs sent Hilbert Newton to Nova Scotia in 1724 as collector. One son subsequently received an appointment as surveyor and searcher; another succeeded his father as collector. For fifty years one family controlled the Nova Scotia customs. Jonathan Pue was Boston surveyor and searcher from 1727 to 1751; John Stackmaple served as New London collector for twenty-three years.[34]

None of the collectors made news. At most they added a little glitter to fashionable drawing rooms, as did Sir Charles Frankland for a time after 1740. They did not figure in the debates in the General Court as did John Bridger, the obstreperous surveyor of woods, or David Dunbar in the same post. The creole official was honored, rewarded, and invisible. The *Boston Weekly News-Letter* said it all in the elder John Jekyll's obituary. "By his courteous Behaviour to the Merchant," the *News-Letter* noted appreciatively, "he became the Darling of all fair Traders . . . with much Humanity [he] took pleasure in directing Masters of Vessels how they ought to avoid the Breach of the Acts of Trade."[35] The difficulty of their office and the natural processes of as-

32. *Ibid.*, 136.
33. Quoted *ibid.*, 152.
34. *Ibid.*, 81, 96–97, 129–130, 139–140, 169, 305n.
35. Quoted *ibid.*, 169.

similation turned the officials into appendages of the merchant group. "We are here removed at a great distance from Our Superiors," one report observed, "and Continuing long in the same place degenerate into Creoles, and at length forget Mother Country and her Interests."[36]

The creole officials occupied their compromised position without any evident loss of self-respect. Among the colonials, their connivance in evasion of the Navigations Acts did not make them objects of disgust or pity. Indeed, the Customs Commissioners themselves implicitly countenanced the compromises by leaving a Jekyll or a Stackmaple in office year after year, decade after decade. Royal governors themselves defended the benefits of illicit trade.[37] From 1756 to 1760, if Molasses Act duties are excepted, only sixteen pounds a year on the average was collected on mainland colonial goods.[38] The very hopelessness of strict enforcement diluted the evil of systematic dereliction of duty. The prevalence of smuggling in every imperial port accustomed everyone to the disjunction of law and performance.

Implicit in the creole's strategy of compliance was the perception of another good. The merchants of America and the merchants of England acted in the conviction that the larger interest of the empire, the growth of its trade and manufacturing, was better served by disregarding unreasonable trade restrictions. Interference in the currents of trade was an artificial and damaging manipulation of the natural commercial order. In disregarding the Molasses Act and frequently breaching other Navigation Acts, no great harm was done. When the Revenue Act of 1764 attempted to stop the French island trade, New England was righteously indignant. Within weeks a fully formed rationale for an open trade was in print. The merchants believed in smuggling and could defend their position. The arguments, first published in 1763 when circumstances demanded a public statement, doubtless circulated in less sophisticated forms before 1763 and weakened the resolve of the customs officials who dined with merchants, married sons to daughters, and met them daily on the wharves and in the marketplace.[39] In a letter to George Washington in 1769, George Mason summed up the American belief that the empire's gain and the mer-

---

36. Quoted *ibid.*, 142.
37. Jensen, *Founding of the Nation*, 46.
38. Barrow, *Trade and Empire*, 75.
39. *Massachusetts Gazette. And Boston News-Letter*, Nov. 24, 1763; Charles M. Andrews, "'State of the Trade,' 1763," Colonial Society of Massachusetts, *Publications*, XXIX (Boston, 1916–1917), 379–390. For the intellectual origins of the merchants' views,

chant's profit sailed in the same ship. "Our supplying our Mother Country with gross Materials, and taking her Manufactures in Return," Mason wrote, "is the true Chain of Connection between Us; these are the Bonds, which, if not broken by Oppression, must long hold Us together, by maintaining a Constant Reciprocation of Interest."[40]

That perspective was not shared by George Grenville, who became first lord of the Treasury and chancellor of the Exchequer in 1763. Grenville took his ideas from the backlog of schematist reforms floating about the colonial office and partially put into practice during the French and Indian War. The complete bureaucrat and master of finance, Grenville understood the elaboration of enforcement procedures, the appointment of new officials, the precise calculation of the return of duties. The Revenue Act of 1764, besides lowering certain duties to levels calculated to be profitable, contained detailed procedures to prevent the passing of French molasses through the British islands and other forms of evasion. Among the requirements were certificates from the British owners or growers of sugar, detailed descriptions of every package on board, and bonds to guarantee that cargoes reached their announced destinations and not forbidden ports, with confiscation awaiting captains who failed in any particular. That was precisely the kind of program the schematists appreciated. The course of the complacent creoles was discredited and that of the schematists validated. Customs officials who had lived in obscurity began to make news.

The series of riots, pamphlets, and speeches against the customs officers after 1760 tended to obscure the fact that a coalescence of interests rather than conflict characterized the imperial economy right up to the eve of Independence. The great commercial interests were not at war. It was the frustrated bureaucracy which sounded the dissonant notes and which now with renewed support from the ministry attempted to fill the role long projected for it. Unable to grasp properly the significance of the powerful commercial networks binding colony to mother country, a Grenville could only partially appreciate the stability and coherence of the transatlantic empire which had come into being by 1760.

---

see Joyce Appleby, "The Social Origins of American Revolutionary Ideology," *Journal of American History,* LXIV (1977–1978), 935–958.
40. Quoted in Thad W. Tate, "The Coming of the Revolution in Virginia: Britain's Challenge to Virginia's Ruling Class, 1763–1776," *WMQ,* 3d Ser., XIX (1962), 335.

iii. The Governor and Imperial Policy

In their essentially personal decisions about the conduct of their offices and the direction of their lives, the creole officials contributed largely to the integration of the British and American economies that came about in the eighteenth century in the face of contravening laws. Although implicit acknowledgment of the creoles' wisdom was widespread, the contradiction between official expectations for the empire and the commercial actualities troubled imperial relations from the mid-seventeenth century on. A disconcerting feeling prevailed that imperial business was unfinished, that the colonies were slipping away, and that merchant interest and imperial interest conflicted. Either the pleas of the schematists for more authority or a revision of official expectations in the creole direction was necessary for a resolution.

The perplexities of colonial rule had long been recognized. The Lords of Trade grasped the problem soon after they had gone a few rounds with New England in the 1660s and 1670s. They saw one basic solution: Massachusetts must have a royal governor, "all agreeing that it must be a Governor wholly to be supported and maintained by his Majesty."[41] They got a royal governor in 1691, but not the other requisite—an independent salary. Every English observer of Massachusetts government urged the ministry to insist on one.[42] The Board of Trade complained to the king in 1703 after a decade of fruitless attempts to get a permanent salary that the Massachusetts assembly had "kept your Majesty's Governors there in a continual dependence upon them for voluntary presents."[43] Bellomont wanted still greater dependence for royal officials: he preferred that no "men of the country" be appointed and that all officials be Englishmen.[44] The Board of Trade did not go that far as a matter of policy, but it saw no hope for effective administration without a royal governor made independent through a

41. Quoted in Palfrey, *History of New England*, III, 314.
42. *Ibid.*, 343; J. R. Western, *Monarchy and Revolution: The English State in the 1680s* (Totowa, N.J., 1972), 92; Haffenden, *New England in the English Nation*, 114; Members of the Church of England to the Board of Trade, Feb. 4, 1706, *Cal. St. Papers*, XXIII, 36; Greene, ed., *Great Britain and the American Colonies*, 146; Patricia U. Bonomi, *A Factious People: Politics and Society in Colonial New York* (New York, 1971), 153.
43. Quoted in Palfrey, *History of New England*, IV, 255. See also Court Records, Sept. 5, 1705, Mass. Arch., VIII, 147.

fixed salary. In fact the board was inclined to rest nearly the whole of administrative reform on the creation of such an officer.

After 1680, England dismantled proprietary and charter government at every opportunity, thus replacing proprietor-appointed and elected officials with royal governors.[45] A 1701 bill in the House of Lords sought to resume all colonial charters because of the failure to obey royal commands. But the centerpiece of crown policy was the demand for permanent salaries for royal appointees to give them the desired independence. The imperial administration eventually got results in eighteen royal colonies, even though in a number the funds came from revenues that otherwise would have gone to the crown. Royal instructions after 1703 also forbade gifts to the governors, lest dependence be reestablished surreptitiously through an assembly's ostensible generosity. In the holdouts—New York, New Hampshire, New Jersey, and Massachusetts—the struggle went on to the end of the colonial period. The imperial government unanimously concurred in Burnet's judgment that his majesty's authority would be dangerously dissipated if England gave up the salary. The compromise of Belcher's administration did not mark a change in royal policy. The demand was merely postponed to await a riper moment and a better strategy.[46]

The structure of imperial government made it impossible for the administration ever to relent. The royal governor was virtually the only link to the colonies, and he had to be wholly devoted to the execution of his duties. How else could royal policy be effected? No laws of Parliament applied to the colonies unless specifically indicated, and except for the Navigation Acts, Parliament showed a notable reluctance to exercise its authority outside the realm.[47] Virtually the only line from London to the colonies was the set of instructions issued to the governor with his commission and subsequently supplemented as needed,

44. Quoted in Palfrey, *History of New England*, IV, 177.
45. Board of Trade to the Crown, Sept. 8, 1721, *Cal. St. Papers*, XXXII, 445 – 447.
46. Palfrey, *History of New England*, IV, 200; Jack P. Greene, *The Quest for Power: The Lower Houses of Assembly in the Southern Royal Colonies, 1689 – 1776* (Chapel Hill, N.C., 1963), 129; Leonard Woods Labaree, *Royal Government in America: A Study of the British Colonial System before 1783* (New Haven, Conn., 1930), 323, 325 – 327, 335 – 337; Gov. Burnet to the Board of Trade, Sept. 30, 1728, in *Cal. St. Papers*, XXXVI, 213.
47. Labaree, *Royal Government*, 4 – 5; Palfrey, *History of New England*, V, 536; *Journals of the House*, XI, 171; Newcastle to Burnet, June 26, 1729, *Cal. St. Papers*, XXXVI, 412 – 413.

and instructions were a tenuous connection at best.[48] The governor was, of course, bound to comply at the risk of jeopardizing his appointment, but the assembly's only compulsion was its respect for the royal will and pleasure. Governors scolded the House for ingratitude and disloyalty and vaguely threatened royal retribution, but exercised no sanctions.[49] While acknowledging their obligation to regard the royal instructions, the House easily evaded them when it chose. Most commonly they contended that charter and instructions conflicted and that the charter took precedence.[50] Or more simply, the House complained that an instruction opposed the people's best interests, and when adequately informed, the king would withdraw the offending command.[51] By the end of the colonial period, a number of colonial politicians explicitly denied that instructions bound the assemblies, and thereby weakened still further royal power in the provinces.[52]

The disregard shown for unpopular royal instructions left the imperial administration nearly helpless when action was required. Except for the restraints of the veto, governance depended on the good will of the people. A few frustrated royal officials came to believe that royal instructions should be the law of the land in the colonies and thus en-

48. Between 1700 and 1783, a set of instructions on the average contained 93.5 paragraphs. Labaree, *Royal Government*, 16–17. For the use of instructions in British governance, see David L. Keir, *The Constitutional History of Modern Britain, 1485–1951*, 5th ed. (London, 1953), 122; Sir William Blackstone, *Commentaries on the Laws of England*, 12th ed. (London, 1793–1795), I, 108.

49. *Journals of the House*, III, 17, 39, 107; VIII, 144, 155, 306, 308, 363, 368; XI, 34, 81, 215, 278, 279; Labaree, *Royal Government*, 32, 434–435; *Belcher Papers*, (Massachusetts Historical Society, *Collections*, 6th Ser., VI–VII [Boston, 1893–1894]), Part I, 287, cited hereafter as *Belcher Papers*; Burnet to Board of Trade, Aug., 1728, *Cal. St. Papers*, XXXVI, 226; Board of Trade to Shute, Aug. 23, 1721, *Cal. St. Papers*, XXXII, 393.

50. *Journals of the House*, III, 107; VII, 322–328; VIII, 279; XI, 64–65, 67–68, 111–112, 115–116, 119, 185; Palfrey, *History of New England*, IV, 404, 518–519.

51. *Journals of the House*, III, 17; VIII, 146–147; XI, 65, 185–189; XVII, 149, 179; Labaree, *Royal Government*, 32–35.

52. *Journals of the House*, XI, 187; XXV, 53, 128; Greene, *Quest for Power*, 435, 439; Labaree, *Royal Government*, 28, 192; M. Eugene Sirmans, *Colonial South Carolina: A Political History, 1663–1763* (Chapel Hill, N.C., 1966), 183; John F. Burns, *Controversies between Royal Governors and Their Assemblies in the Northern American Colonies* (Boston, 1923), 23; William Douglass, *A Summary, Historical and Political, of the First Planting, Progressive Improvements, and Present State of the British Settlements in North-America* (Boston, 1747–1752), I, 472; Jack P. Greene, "The Role of the Lower Houses of Assembly in Eighteenth-Century Politics," in Jack P. Greene, ed., *The Reinterpretation of the American Revolution, 1763–1789* (New York, 1968), 98.

forceable in the courts.[53] Riders were attached to bills before Parliament in 1744 and 1749 automatically invalidating colonial acts which contradicted instructions, bringing the instructions one step closer to law, but antiprerogative forces rallied against the measures. Royal proclamations between 1539 and 1547 enjoyed the same standing as statutes until Parliament detected the danger and repealed the law so investing them. Subsequently, royal proclamations had been enforced in the hated Star Chamber. Instructions with a degree of statutory authority partook too much of Stuart autocracy for Parliament to accept the 1744 and 1749 bills.[54]

Those defeats left responsibility for imperial policy entirely in the hands of the royal governors. Either their determination and skill, and their wholehearted compliance with their instructions, carried royal policy, or the policy failed. Unfortunately, governors were known to be weak reeds. The ministry in England had no higher regard for the character of the men who held the office than did the colonists. The ministry entertained repeated complaints about official avarice without ever attempting to defend the character of appointees. Spokesmen for the colonies showed no more compunction about denigrating governors in testimony before the Privy Council than they would in a Boston tavern. Dummer's *Defence of the New England Charters*, written for the Board of Trade and Parliament, explained without embarrassment why the colony clung to its charter: to prevent greedy governors from draining them dry. The attorney for the Virginia House of Burgesses in the pistole fee controversy was Robert Henley, who went on to become attorney general in the Devonshire-Pitt administration and lord keeper of the great seal. In his statement before the Privy Council in 1754, Henley observed, as had the Massachusetts House in 1728, that governors always abused their authority. The pistole fee served "merely to gratify the avarice of one Man." "If your Lordships do not restrain officers within due bounds," Henley said, "they will abuse

53. Grenville expressed this opinion to Franklin in 1759. Bernhard Knollenberg, *Origin of the American Revolution: 1759–1766* (New York, 1960), 51.

54. *Ibid.*, 49; Labaree, *Royal Government*, 33–35; Greene, "Role of the Lower Houses," in Greene, ed., *Reinterpretation of the American Revolution*, 102; G. R. Elton, *England under the Tudors* (London, 1955), 170; J. P. Kenyon, ed., *The Stuart Constitution, 1603–1688: Documents and Commentary* (Cambridge, 1966), 119–120. Roger Manwaring exemplified the high prerogative view of royal commands in a 1627 sermon printed in Kenyon, ed., *Stuart Constitution*, 15.

their Authority; they always have; your Lordships know, that Governors of all others always did, and always will, endeavour to oppress the Subject."[55] Royal officials likewise complained to the Board of Trade of corruption in each other. Edward Randolph warned against the appointment of gentlemen who came to America to make their fortunes, and indignantly reported Bermuda governors' seizing ships as wrecks when they had barely touched the rocks. Customs officials indicted governors for corruption, and governors replied in kind.[56] The level-headed Malachy Postlethwayt, whose two-volume work, *Britain's Commercial Interest Explained and Improved* (1757), advocated greater colonial dependence on the crown, also cataloged for the benefit of his readers in the government the numerous "acts of oppression" perpetrated by the governors because "suited to their private interests."[57] Perhaps moved by the reputed scandals of the Dominion of New England or perhaps by the unfavorable report on Governor Berkeley delivered by royal commissioners after Bacon's Rebellion, the Parliament in 1700 enacted an "Act to Punish Governors of Plantations in this Kingdom, for Crimes by them committed in the Plantations." The statute provided punishment for governors found guilty at King's Bench or before commissions of oppressing their subjects or breaking the law.[58]

The alleged venality of the governors resulted, as Postlethwayt noted, in both "detrimental encroachments upon the crown, and acts of oppression upon the subject." Covetousness cut both ways. The ministry, of course, was more concerned about encroachments on the prerogative. From the British perspective, unless properly oriented, the governor's private interest inevitably weakened his resolve in the interminable controversies with the assembly. Even if they did not yield to

---

55. Quoted in Jack P. Greene, ed., "The Case of the Pistole Fee: The Report of a Hearing on the Pistole Fee Dispute Before the Privy Council, June 18, 1754," *Virginia Magazine of History and Biography*, LX (1958), 412, 413.

56. Michael Garibaldi Hall, *Edward Randolph and the American Colonies, 1676–1703* (Chapel Hill, N.C., 1960), 89–90; Randolph to the Board of Trade, Nov. 15, 1700, *Cal. St. Papers*, 936; Jordon D. Fiore, "The Temple-Bernard Affair: A Royal Custom House Scandal in Essex County," Essex Inst., *Hist. Colls.*, XC (1954), 58–83.

57. Quoted in Greene, ed., *Great Britain and the American Colonies*, 294, 296–297.

58. Sir. William S. Holdsworth, *A History of English Law*, VI (Boston, 1927), 402; XI (1938), 100; Thomas Pownall recommended half-pay pensions for retired governors to reduce the temptation to make their fortunes by dishonorable means while in office. Thomas Pownall, *The Administration of the British Colonies*, 5th ed. (London, 1774), I, 84–85.

crass greed, governors shaded their judgment, temporized under pressure, or compromised in private to protect their own interests. Indeed, the Board of Trade characteristically blamed the governors for colonial troubles and the failures of imperial policy. Royal governors "frequently abused their authority," it was charged in 1721, and dissipated royal landholdings in America without reserving quitrents to the king.[59] In a report on Governor Belcher's failure to control the New Jersey Assembly during his administration there, a dissatisfied Board of Trade observed, "That his dependence upon the Assembly [for salary] has been the motive of his conduct may be hard to say, but very easy to believe."[60] A number of Board of Trade proposals, including the riders of 1744 and 1749, were aimed at the governors. Had the governors done their duty conscientiously, their vetoes would have automatically eliminated assembly actions contrary to instructions, and the riders would have been superfluous.[61]

The governors' acknowledged weakness and venality made the crown's demands for a permanent salary all the more insistent. The board told Massachusetts agents at the height of the salary controversy that the crown's aims were simple. The ministry sought only "that the Governor might be made by any means independent of the people, and not lie under the temptations of retailing the prerogative of the crown or the interest of Great Britain to the said Assembly for his daily bread."[62]

Perhaps the British government's greatest administrative error in the provincial period was to believe that a single appointee with proper determination could implement royal policy in the colonies. The obvious lack of patronage, the weak statutory backing for policy which made the governor dependent on the cooperation of the assemblies, and the overwhelming advantage of the popular party in the legislature never erased the conviction that sufficient resolve and skill could overcome the deficiencies of real power. William Douglass expressed a typical attitude when he wrote to Cadwallader Colden in 1727, "We

59. Quoted in Greene, ed., *Great Britain and the American Colonies*, 179–180.
60. Quoted in Labaree, *Royal Government*, 345.
61. Douglass, *A Summary, Historical and Political*, I, 472.
62. Quoted in Palfrey, *History of New England*, IV, 534. Even less could be expected of the elected governors of the two charter colonies, Connecticut and Rhode Island. See the discussion of Governor Bernard's plan for reform in Edmund S. Morgan and Helen M. Morgan, *The Stamp Act Crisis: Prologue to Revolution*, rev. ed. (New York, 1963), 27.

are here a great people, and from the indulgence, indolence, or weakness of former governors, have got a habit of doing every man what is right in his own eyes with a leveling principle."[63] As late as 1752, after so many decades of experience, the Board of Trade warned governors about departures from their instructions as if stricter heed would by itself make the difference. Lord Hillsborough told Governor Bernard in 1768 in the midst of trouble in Boston, "It is You, to whom the Crown has delegated its Authority, and You alone are responsible for the due Exercise of it."[64]

The shortsightedness of the English government and the stubbornness of the colonials caught the royal governors in a merciless vise. After the Boston Massacre, when Captain Preston's lynching appeared likely, Governor Thomas Hutchinson lay "awake whole nights in America, fearing I should be called to account in England for neglect of duty to the King."[65] And, indeed, criticisms of his leniency in the tea affair ultimately did lead to his recall. Despite his uncompromising integrity and loyalty to the crown under the most severe pressure, Hutchinson lost the confidence of Bernard, Pownall, Hillsborough, Lord North, and the Parliament. Seemingly, it was believed that greater resolve, firmer resistance to colonial intimidation and bribes, or some impossible force of character could have reversed the Revolutionary tide.[66]

The dilemma in which the imperial administrators found themselves drove them to make these excessive demands. In the absence of alternatives, conventional political understanding compelled them to depend on governors for the implementation of policy, while the same conventions predicted that private interests would dissolve all higher loyalties. The ministry had no choice but to expect impossible accomplishments from officials whom they knew to be sorely tempted to retail power for personal gain. What could the administration do but admonish the governors, punish them for their weakness, and attempt to

63. Douglass to Colden, Nov. 20, 1727, Mass. Hist. Soc., *Colls.*, 4th Ser., II (Boston, 1854), 175.
64. Quoted in John J. Waters, Jr., *The Otis Family in Provincial and Revolutionary Massachusetts* (Chapel Hill, N.C., 1968), 169. Knollenberg, *Origin of the American Revolution*, 50.
65. Quoted in Bernard Bailyn, *The Ordeal of Thomas Hutchinson* (Cambridge, Mass., 1974), 28n.
66. *Ibid.*, 5, 8, 347–348.

reduce the temptations? Among the list of proposed reforms for the recalcitrant middle and northern colonies was always an independent salary. Interests would out, and only the assurance of a salary secured against popular caprice would enable officials, as James II had observed, to avoid the "necessity of base compliance with others to the King's prejudice, by which to get one shilling to himself he must lose ten to the king."[67]

iv. A Colonial Civil List

After 1754 the Seven Years' War brought into sharp focus the varied discontents among imperial administrators and finally precipitated action where before there were only querulous complaints, threats, and delay. The notorious inability of the colonies to cooperate in their own defense and the stinginess of the assemblies hindered the war effort on every hand. After a conference with colonial governors in 1755, General Edward Braddock concluded that voluntary appropriations were a hopeless cause. Pitt succeeded in mobilizing the colonists only by promising reimbursement from the British Treasury for a large part of the costs of war. By the same token, the failures of the governors to enforce the Acts of Trade, a tolerable shortcoming in peacetime, became an egregious dereliction in war, when illicit trade with the French sugar islands aided the enemy. In 1756 the Board of Trade ordered an embargo on all colonial vessels unless bound for another British port, and in 1757 Parliament forbade the export of most provisions to any places but Britain, Ireland, and other British colonies.[68] Neither order had any effect, and the feeling that something had to be done intensified. Lord Loudoun, soon after he took over command of British

---

67. Quoted in Western, *Monarchy and Revolution*, 88. Thomas C. Barrow has seen more clearly than anyone else the critical importance of the civil list in the agenda of imperial reform after 1763. "The Old Colonial System from an English Point of View," in Alison Gilbert Olson and Richard Maxwell Brown, *Anglo-American Political Relations, 1675–1775* (New Brunswick, N.J., 1970), 125–139. My analysis is heavily indebted to his.

68. Jensen, *Founding of a Nation*, 44, 59; John Shy, *Toward Lexington: The Role of the British Army in the Coming of the American Revolution* (Princeton, N.J., 1965), 45; George Louis Beer, *British Colonial Policy, 1754–1765* (New York, 1907), 52–71.

forces in America, wrote home, "The truth is governors here are ciphers; their predecessors sold the whole of the king's prerogative, to get their salaries; and till you find a fund, independent of the province, to pay the governors, and new model the government, you can do nothing with the provinces."[69]

The dramatization of colonial lethargy and smuggling during the Seven Years' War did not by itself bring the century-long grievances of imperial administrators before Parliament. The complaints of the Board of Trade still lacked the power to penetrate parliamentary indifference. Were it not for tangential matters, Parliament would not have dealt any more firmly with the colonies after 1763 than it had in the decades of salutary neglect. The determining elements in the favorable vote for the colonial revenue acts in the 1760s were English, not American. American questions absorbed the ministries of Bute, Grenville, and Townshend more than their predecessors, but not Parliament as a whole.

Parliament laid taxes on the colonies to pay for the army, not to reform colonial administration or to pay salaries. The fateful decision to keep troops in the colonies after the Seven Years' War originated primarily in the desire of George III to cut back on the wartime strength of the army as little as possible. The king needed the patronage which the additional regiments afforded and was loath to destroy the networks of favor and dependency lacing every regiment. Knowing Parliament's anxiety over the national debt, which doubled during the war, and the Commons' determination to hold the line on taxes, the ministry proposed to distribute the army burden among other dependencies of the crown. Ireland already had a legal obligation to support twelve thousand men. On the recommendation of Halifax, lord lieutenant of Ireland, the ministry planned to raise the number to eighteen thousand or twenty thousand and to require the colonies to pay for ten thousand more. The cost estimates were based on eighty-five regiments, virtually full wartime strength.[70]

Debate in the House focused entirely on the Irish increase. The economy-minded opposition behind Newcastle forced the ministry to

---

69. Quoted in Robert Zemsky, *Merchants, Farmers, and River Gods: An Essay on Eighteenth-Century American Politics* (Boston, 1971), 99.

70. Shy, *Toward Lexington*, 69–77. See also Thomas C. Barrow, "Background to the Grenville Program, 1757–1763," *WMQ*, 3d Ser., XXII (1965), 93–104.

pull back to the original twelve thousand on the Irish establishment, but was unable to reduce the number of American troops. When the formidable Pitt spoke in the House in favor of a large army to avert unemployment and to keep the nation in readiness for the renewal of hostilities which he expected momentarily, the Newcastle opposition gave way, and the revised bill sailed through. The possible consequences of an American army troubled the House so little as to earn their complete disregard. To speed passage, the ministry promised to tax the colonies to pay for the twenty regiments to be stationed there. The precedent of an Irish army paid from Irish revenues apparently foreclosed any doubts about the suitability of the idea.[71]

A simple desire to save the British taxpayer seems to have motivated the House to pass each of the three major revenue bills which followed: the Sugar Act of 1764, the Stamp Act of 1765, and the Townshend duties of 1767. Each bill came before the House as an expedient for paying for the army without adding to the burdens on Britain. Bute, Grenville, and Townshend, however, welcomed Parliament's support for reasons not mentioned in debate. They knew of the perplexities of colonial rule, had read the reports of the self-styled colonial experts, and conscientiously worked at improving imperial administration. They accepted the assignment of twenty regiments to America as a means of regulating the Indian trade and pacifying the frontier. Like many of their predecessors, they believed the presence of British forces would also make the colonial assemblies more compliant with royal instructions and the customs officers less subject to intimidation.[72]

The assignment of troops to America, however, was a fortuitous gift of George III, not an essential element of the ministers' own plans for reform. The Board of Trade had not campaigned for a permanent detachment of troops in the colonies. After 1763 the ministry as a whole lost interest in the American army and ultimately, in 1768, ordered withdrawal from many of the Indian posts. The confusion in Whitehall over the best means of deploying the troops betrayed a lack of clear purpose. Townshend favored a reduction of the total, and Dartmouth in the North ministry said the colonists themselves should specify the

---

71. Shy, *Toward Lexington*, 77–80; P.D.G. Thomas, *British Politics and the Stamp Act Crisis: The First Phase of the American Revolution, 1763–1767* (Oxford, 1975), 38.
72. Barrow, *Trade and Empire*, 184. Thomas, *British Politics*, documents the view that Parliament understood the tax bills as payments to the army.

size of the American forces. Hillsborough ordered further withdrawals in 1771.[73]

Higher among the reformers' own priorities was a permanent civil list for the colonies, a list of colonial officials to be paid from designated revenues. The list would aid imperial administration everywhere, not just in the four northern royal colonies which kept their governors dependent on annual salary grants. In the other colonies there were officials other than the governor who depended on the assemblies: lieutenant governors, the king's attorneys, and justices of the superior courts. The dependence of these officials weakened royal administration nearly as much as the governors' beggary in New York, New Jersey, Massachusetts, and New Hampshire. Britain supported these other officials only in Nova Scotia, East and West Florida, and Georgia. The salaries of all those on the projected civil list for the colonies probably came to less than £50,000 annually, a trivial amount compared to the £359,000 which the army was expected to cost. The ministry believed the expense of these few salaries could in time be paid from one of the revenue bills, and the benefits would be enormous.[74]

The Board of Trade under Halifax (1748–1761) believed strongly in the necessity of an independent revenue for colonial officials. The instructions to Sir Danvers Osborne drafted by Charles Townshend in 1753 as Osborne was about to assume the governorship of New York stressed the point more than ever:

> And whereas nothing can more effectually tend to reestablish good order and government within our said province and promote its future peace and prosperity than the having a permanent revenue settled by law upon a solid foundation for defraying the necessary charges of government, for want of which great inconvenience and prejudice have hitherto arisen to our service and to the affairs of our said province . . .

Osborne was to recommend "in the strongest manner" that provisions be made "for the salary allowed by us to our captain general and governor in chief of our said province, and likewise for competent salaries

73. Shy, *Toward Lexington*, 258–266, 324–325; Thomas, *British Politics*, 34, 344–345; Barrow, *Trade and Empire*, 244.
74. Thomas, *British Politics*, 38, 54. Beer estimated that the charge for the military and the civil establishment in America would be £380,000. *Colonial Policy*, 268.

to all judges, justices, and other necessary officers and ministers of government" and for all other charges "as may be fixed and ascertained."[75]

The board must have understood the futility of such language. Townshend, then a junior minister at the board, like many who preceded him, believed that only a permanent crown revenue raised by act of Parliament would achieve the purpose.[76] By the end of the war, the repeated failures of the colonial assemblies, the force of opinion at the Board of Trade, and the continual recommendations of colonial observers at last awakened the ministry. After studying the report of William Knox, one of the distressed observers of colonial affairs, Lord Bute acknowledged that Canada was not the only area in North America requiring attention in 1763. "We ought to set about reforming our old colonies," Bute was reputed to have said, "before we settled new ones."[77] Governor Shirley in 1755 commented that Britain need not fear the incipient spirit of independence in America following a conquest of Canada, "provided the Governors and principall Civil Officers are Independent of the Assemblies for their Subsistence."[78]

After he replaced Bute in 1763, Grenville apparently had extensive plans for colonial reform, beyond the increase of revenues from the French island trade, but he refused to fund a colonial civil list in 1764 when the Sugar Act was passed.[79] He and Halifax heatedly discussed the point over dinner without reaching agreement. The fears of Jasper Mauduit, Massachusetts agent in 1764, that the ministry intended to pay colonial salaries from the new revenue measures turned out to be premature. The fact that Grenville estimated the revenues from the Sugar Act at little more than a fifth of the expenses of the American army must have affected the decision.[80]

75. Quoted in Greene, ed., *Great Britain and the American Colonies*, 284. On Townshend's authorship of the instructions, see Sir Lewis Namier and John Brooke, *Charles Townshend* (London, 1964), 37.

76. Barrow, *Trade and Empire*, 175; Knollenberg, *Origin of the American Revolution*, 35; James A. Henretta, "*Salutary Neglect*": *Colonial Administration under the Duke of Newcastle* (Princeton, N.J., 1972), 339–340.

77. Quoted in Thomas, *British Politics*, 34.

78. Quoted in Beer, *British Colonial Policy*, 266n.

79. Thomas, *British Politics*, 35–36; Barrow, *Trade and Empire*, 181–182, 184–185; cf. Jack M. Sosin, *Whitehall and the Wilderness: The Middle West in British Colonial Policy, 1760–1775* (Lincoln, Nebr., 1961), 79n.

80. Thomas, *British Politics*, 35–36; Barrow, *Trade and Empire*, 179–180, 182; Sosin, *Whitehall*, 79n. Richard Jackson, another colonial agent, also expected a civil list and

The Stamp Act held no greater promise of producing sufficient revenues for salaries and the army. In December 1764, Grenville told his colleagues at the Treasury that the stamp duties would possibly yield £100,000, bringing total American revenue to £150,000 against army costs of £350,000. The major point of the Stamp Act, judging from the debates, was more to establish the principle of internal taxation than to alleviate British taxpayers or reform colonial government.[81]

In 1767 Townshend, by then chancellor of the Exchequer, reversed the reform strategy. American taxation had proven entirely inadequate to meet army expenses. British taxpayers still carried nearly the full burden of the swollen peacetime army which the king had desired. Townshend apparently gave up on exacting a contribution from the colonies for their defense and turned his thoughts to the civil list. He initially presented the plan for duties on American imports as still another approach to financing the army. When it became evident, however, that he projected a measly revenue of only forty thousand pounds, Townshend explained that his purpose was rather to fund a colonial civil list for which such an amount was sufficient. After a brief delay, Parliament enacted the duties, possibly without fully realizing that they promised no relief to British taxpayers. Townshend's measures simply transferred salary payments from American treasuries, sustained by assembly taxes, to the British Treasury and Parliamentary taxes. The Commons primarily desired to establish the principle of parliamentary taxation, and Townshend assured them that the duties met colonial objections. His own greatest satisfaction, however, lay in the fulfillment of his long-held desire to set imperial officials free of the American assemblies.[82]

However befuddled the House of Commons may have been about the purpose of the Revenue Act of 1767, officials of the Board of Trade rejoiced in the enactment. The preamble stated clearly that the revenue "should be raised . . . for making certain and adequate provisions for defraying the charge of the administration of justice, and the support of civil government in such provinces where it shall be found neces-

---

queried Grenville about it in 1765. John L. Bullion, *A Great and Necessary Measure: George Grenville and the Genesis of the Stamp Act, 1763–1765* (Columbia, Mo., 1982), 147.
81. Thomas, *British Politics*, 86–87; Morgan and Morgan, *Stamp Act Crisis*, 87.
82. Barrow, *Trade and Empire*, 217, 226; Thomas, *British Politics*, 338, 346–348, 352, 354–357; Namier and Brooke, *Charles Townshend*, 140, 172–175, 179.

sary," as well as "further defraying the expenses of defending, protecting, and securing the said dominions."[83] Governor Bernard enthusiastically declared that "a civil list is a measure most immediately wanting to the regulation of the American governments" and appended a detailed account of the Massachusetts assembly's abuse of its financial powers.[84] Edward Sedgwick, undersecretary for American affairs under Halifax, applauded Townshend in 1767

> for having provided for the expense of the whole civil administration in the colonies, and made the several officers concerned in it independent of the people. This step ought to have been taken, for the want of it has been sufficiently felt, many years ago. Without it, it was absurd ever to think of preventing smuggling or collecting any revenue whether old or new. But now we may hope to see the laws observed and many evils corrected which have hitherto been incorrigible.[85]

Townshend did not foresee wholesale or immediate assumption of the colonial civil lists. The preamble spoke of "the support of civil government in such provinces where it shall be found necessary." In 1764 Governor Bernard had recommended that the taxing power remain with the colonial assemblies so long as they provided salaries according to the specifications of Parliament. That principle governed the ministry from 1767 on. In 1768 Hillsborough, the secretary of state for the new American department, proposed repeal of the Townshend Revenue Act for colonies with permanent civil lists.[86] The North ministry adopted the same policy and insisted that as soon as the colonies promised "a revenue for the support of the Civil Government and of such military force as they themselves shall desire to have among them," the duties would be lifted.[87] The same idea underlay Lord North's belated plan for reconciliation in February 1775. In the meantime, however, the ministry began selectively paying salaries in those colonies where the British most desired greater control: the attorney general of New York and chief justice of Massachusetts in 1768, the

83. Quoted in Barrow, *Trade and Empire*, 217.
84. Quoted in Thomas, *British Politics*, 361.
85. Quoted in *ibid.*, 36.
86. Bailyn, *Ordeal of Thomas Hutchinson*, 87; Morgan and Morgan, *Stamp Act Crisis*, 27–28; Thomas, *British Politics*, 352n; Jensen, *Founding of a Nation*, 323.
87. Lord Dartmouth quoted in Barrow, *Trade and Empire*, 244.

governors of New York and Massachusetts in 1770, and chief justices of New York and New Jersey in 1772. In 1772 the Treasury scheduled payment of the salaries of Massachusetts' attorney general, solicitor general, and five lower judges.[88]

v. Protest

Massachusetts watched apprehensively as the ministry bolted together the taxation machinery in 1763. Rumors spread of a plan to pay official salaries almost as soon as Grenville made known his intentions of raising a colonial revenue. The ministry did not have to declare its purposes; the threat of a British-paid officialdom had hovered over the colonies ever since Jeremiah Dummer, Massachusetts' agent, wrote that the salary question would be laid before Parliament in 1729. Governor Bernard had spread the word, before taking up his duties as governor, that the proposal that governors' salaries "should be settled by Parliament so as to make them independent of the people" was "much talked of and cannot be done too soon."[89] The tax bills of 1764 and 1765 each brought in its train news of an impending civil list for the colonies. The *Boston-Gazette* in September 1765 predicted that success in imposing the Stamp Act would be followed by a colonial civil list, and a year later accused Governor Bernard of promoting crown salaries. When Townshend actually put together a revenue measure to support colonial officials, Americans heard about it at once.[90] Franklin wrote home on April 11, 1767, two months before final passage, that a project was "on Foot, to render all the governors and magistrates in America independent of the annual support they receive of their several Assemblies."[91]

Townshend did not announce who would benefit from the revenue, but Massachusetts suspected at once that Chief Justice Thomas Hutchinson would be among the first. The premonition was accurate.

88. Jensen, *Founding of a Nation*, 581; Thomas, *British Politics*, 361–362.
89. Quoted in Barrow, *Trade and Empire*, 175.
90. Palfrey, *History of New England*, IV, 525; Thomas, *British Politics*, 36, 352; *Boston-Gazette, and Country Journal*, Sept. 30, Oct. 7, 1765.
91. Leonard W. Labaree *et al.*, eds., *The Papers of Benjamin Franklin* (New Haven, Conn., 1959–), IV, 109.

Through the fall of 1767 Hutchinson received assurances that his salary would be forthcoming as soon as revenue from the duties had accumulated. Lord North said informally in December that the chief justice ranked first among American officials, immediately after the customs commissioners.[92] The popular party did not require official confirmation of their suspicions to begin the attack. The *Boston-Gazette* ran a five-part series in August 1767 against Townshend's avowed intention to render crown officers independent of the people.[93] In January and February 1768, the House of Representatives issued a series of documents against the Townshend duties: a petition to the king, a series of letters to ministry officials, and a circulatory letter to the speakers of other houses of representatives on the American continent. A recurrent paragraph begged leave to submit "whether the people can continue free, while the Crown in addition to its uncontroverted right of appointing a Governor, may appoint him such stipends as it shall judge fit, at the expence of the people and without their consent."[94] The same question was raised regarding justices:

> Whether, while the Judges of the land, at so great a distance from the throne, the fountain of justice, may be altogether independent on the people for their support, it may not probably happen, that in some future time, the principles of equity may be subverted even on the Bench of Justice, and the people deprived of their happiness and security.[95]

Labeled a pensioner, Hutchinson failed of election to the Council in May 1768 and was refused his salary as chief justice without having received a penny of his promised two-hundred-pound supplementary stipend from Britain.[96]

Hutchinson was more successful after his appointment as governor in 1770. He and Andrew Oliver, the lieutenant governor, were surreptitiously paid from the duty on tea. Again, Boston radicals suspected the truth before the facts were out. In the spring of 1771, Hutchinson's delay in approving salary appropriations provoked the House to ask whether he was getting support from an unprecedented source. Hutch-

92. Bailyn, *Ordeal of Thomas Hutchinson*, 121n, 147.
93. *Bost.-Gaz.*, Aug. 17, 1767.
94. *Journals of the House*, XLIV, 226, 228, 230–231, 236, 238.
95. *Ibid.*, 226.
96. Bailyn, *Ordeal of Thomas Hutchinson*, 121, 147.

inson replied evasively that the Parliament had decided that he was to have a more certain form of support and said no more. Believing the worst, Samuel Adams and Thomas Young condemned the salary in the fall of 1771 before the news was official. They restrained their wrath, however, until June 1772, when the truth of the rumors was confirmed. Two months later the province learned that four justices of the superior court, besides the chief justice, also were to be paid. The news set the province aflame. In July the House voted eighty-five to nineteen to oppose the salary for the governor. In November, a little more than a month after news of judicial salaries was received, the Boston town meeting voted to correspond with town meetings throughout the province in an effort to mobilize public opinion.[97]

Boston took a chance in making a direct appeal to the backcountry, since they had no poll of opinion on the salary. The response in late 1772 and early 1773 was all the more heartwarming for coming as something of a surprise. More than 144 of 260 towns and districts replied, and the Committee of Correspondence jubilantly expressed its "unspeakable satisfaction . . . that their [the towns'] sentiments so nearly accord with ours."[98] "A uniformity of sentiment, tho' express'd in a variety of languages runs thro' Them all."[99]

The town committees had no trouble in recognizing the danger in crown salaries. The Boston committee listed twelve grievances in summary of all the violations of rights since 1763. Beverly acknowledged the list was "Rightly and Justly drawn up . . . particularly in the Sixth article wher mention is made that our Governor is rendred intirely Dependant on the Crown for his Support which is an infringment on our Charter Rights an innovation and has a direct Tendancy to the Destruction of our Happy Constitution."[100] "All civil officers are or ought to be Servants of the people," Braintree wrote, "and dependent upon

97. *Ibid.*, 165n, 166, 169, 199, 203; Richard D. Brown, *Revolutionary Politics in Massachusetts: The Boston Committee of Correspondence and the Towns, 1772–1774* (Cambridge, Mass., 1970), 49–52; Harry A. Cushing, *History of the Transition from Provincial to Commonwealth Government in Massachusetts*, Columbia University Studies in History, Economics and Public Law, VII, No. 1 (New York, 1896), 37–39.
98. Quoted in Brown, *Revolutionary Politics*, 140.
99. Boston Committee of Correspondence to Lexington, Jan. 18, 1773, Letters and Proceedings received by the Boston Committee of Correspondence (photostats), Mass. Hist. Soc., Boston.
100. Beverly to the Boston Committee of Correspondence, Dec. 21, 1772, *ibid.*

them for their official Support; and every instance to the contrary from the Governor downwards tends to crush and destroy civil liberty."[101]

The virtual unanimity on the point cannot be attributed solely to editorials in the *Boston-Gazette* or declarations in the House, for the salary question had not been at the center of attention for some years. The quick reaction suggests, rather, a common understanding of political forces acquired through the years of struggle with the prerogative. Although withholding or curtailing the salary had never been used to any effect, the grant of money was believed to create dependence. That fact everyone understood. The transfer of payment from assembly to the British Treasury represented in every provincial mind a significant loss of power. The officials moved from the people's network of interests to the crown's, and the people's influence over them diminished accordingly. Even friends of government like Israel Williams, one of the Connecticut Valley river gods, disliked the creation of a civil list.[102] One-sided assembly votes like eighty-five to nineteen, and ninety-two to seventeen, and the defection of the Council from the governor's cause were partly the consequence of agreement on the point.

The towns' views closely resembled those of the assemblies of the 1720s and 1730s. Rather than a mechanical balancing of forces, the towns wished for bonds of interest and affection to align the governor's desires with their own. Brimfield held it a "great Greivance" that the governor should be paid "in a Way so appearantly tending to alienate His Affections from His People; and clearly tending to destroy Their mutual Confidence, upon which The welbeing of the Province so much depends."[103] "Confidence" was the word they chose to describe the desired interdependence and common interest. "The Governour of this Province has been made independant of the Generall Assembly of this Province for his support," Ashby said; "thereby the Connection between him and his people is weakned and their Confidence in him as their Governor is much lessned."[104] Deprived of this measure of control over the passions and will of the executive, provincials lost confidence in his regard for their well-being. Franklin observed that the im-

---

101. Braintree to Boston Committee of Correspondence, Mar. 2, 1773, *ibid.*
102. Brown, *Revolutionary Politics*, 50.
103. Brimfield to the Boston Committee of Correspondence, Jan. 14, 1773, Letters and Proceedings.
104. Ashby to Boston Committee of Correspondence, May 13, 1773, *ibid.*

perial government, having forbidden governors "to take any salaries from their provinces . . . the people may no longer hope [for] any kindness."[105]

Hutchinson earnestly answered the protests with the classic argument Burnet had introduced forty years earlier. In communications to the assembly and in the *Censor*, the newspaper which he and Andrew Oliver founded in November 1771 to return the fire of the *Gazette* and radical pamphleteers, they repeatedly reviewed the crucial importance of independence in the three branches of government. Each should check the other through the constitutional powers vested in them such as the veto, but none should be dependent on the other. Dependence warped the judgment and made one branch of government the tool of another, thus destroying the desired equilibrium. So patently obvious was the truth of the principle that even English friends of the colonists like Thomas Pownall accepted the necessity of a royal salary, but Hutchinson's repeated statements were entirely futile. The provincials' refusal to accept so clear and simple an idea convinced him that his enemies had lost their reason.[106]

The Boston Committee of Correspondence acknowledged the validity of Hutchinson's point at least so far as to state that in a mixed government "a due proportion or balance of power should be established among the several branches of legislative," but claimed that the charter permanently fixed the proper balance, including assembly control of the governor's salary. "Every thing which renders any one branch of the Legislative more independent of the other two than it was originally designed" destroyed the equilibrium.[107] Balance meant simply keeping things as they were.

The sticking point was dependence. Hutchinson accepted the necessity of checks, but no form of dependence. The more complete the independence of each branch, the better, even if changes had to be made. The provincials required dependence or interdependence. "An independent ruler, [is] a monster in a free state," John Adams said.[108] The

105. Albert H. Smyth, ed., *The Writings of Benjamin Franklin* (Boston, 1850–1856), VI, 134.

106. Bailyn, *Ordeal of Thomas Hutchinson*, 199–204.

107. *The Votes and Proceedings of the Freeholders and other Inhabitants of the Town of Boston, In Town Meeting assembled . . .* , in Merrill Jensen, ed., *Tracts of the American Revolution, 1763–1776* (Indianapolis, Ind., 1967), 245.

108. In *Bost.-Gaz.*, July 6, 1772.

Boston committee claimed, "It has always been held, that the dependence of the Governor of this Province upon the General Assembly for his support, was necessary for the preservation of this *equilibrium*." Through a royal salary, "the ancient connection between him and this people is weakened, the confidence in the Governor lessened and the equilibrium destroyed."[109] The key point was how to maintain confidence in the governor, not how to free him to act independently.

The payment of judicial salaries angered the colony just as much. "Nothing has alarmed us more," Lunenburg wrote the Boston committee in January 1773, "than the information we have lately received that the Judges of our superior court have their stipends otherwise than by the free grants of the people."[110] In this instance, there was some difference over the question of independence. Brimfield stated that, in principle, judges "ought rather to be independent of the King and People." But unfortunately, American judges held their positions at the pleasure of the crown rather than on good behavior. Governors had the power to dismiss a judge who refused to fall in with the executive's schemes. The best the colonists could do, therefore, was to make judges "equally dependant" on king and people. The assembly's payment of their salaries "tended to keep a Ballance of Affection in them to the Prince and Subjects."[111]

The majority of town opinion overlooked this subtlety and simply repudiated any measure "rendring them independent of the People and dependent on the Crown for their support."[112] "What security can we have of Liberty, Life and Property, when our Governor is wholly dependent on the crown, and the Judges who are by him commissioned, and enjoy their offices during pleasure, receive their support from those who may be disposed to injure oppress and destroy us?" Lunenburg resolved "that our judges, who, we are credibly informed, now [receive] their salaries from the Crown, may again be paid by this

109. *Votes and Proceedings of the Freeholders*, in Jensen, ed., *Tracts of the American Revolution*, 245.
110. Lunenburg to the Boston Committee of Correspondence, Jan. 18, 1773, Letters and Proceedings.
111. Brimfield to Boston Committee of Correspondence, Jan. 14, 1773, *ibid*. See also the newspaper war between John Adams and William Brattle, discussed in Brown, *Revolutionary Politics*, 99–100.
112. Sheffield to the Boston Committee of Correspondence, Jan. 12, 1773, Letters and Proceedings.

people, whose Judges they are, in whose interest and for whose service, they ought to employ their time and abilities."[113] The pressure of public opinion persuaded four of the justices to renounce their salaries. In February 1774, Chief Justice Peter Oliver, the only one to refuse, suffered impeachment in the Massachusetts House.[114]

The salary issue was enmeshed in a complex debate over parliamentary power and was but one aspect of the confrontation of British and American political power after 1763. But the salary had a singularly important role in the coming of the Revolution. By 1770 Parliament had given up its efforts to raise a revenue to support an American army. The 1764 duty on French molasses was reduced from three-pence a gallon to an acceptable one penny. The Stamp Act was repealed. All of the Townshend duties save that on tea were likewise gone. After 1770 British and American relations enjoyed two years of peace. With the constitutional issues apparently resolved, the popular party as before lapsed into quietude.

Then the century-old need of strengthened imperial government reasserted itself. In 1772 the announcement of royal payment of official salaries ignited resistance once again. Not only the Boston radicals, but farmer politicians in remote Massachusetts villages recognized the danger. The province was on the alert when the unfortunate accident of the Tea Act provoked Boston to violence once more, starting the train of events that led to Independence.

113. Lunenburg to the Boston Committee of Correspondence, Jan. 18, 1773, *ibid.*
114. Bailyn, *Ordeal of Thomas Hutchinson*, 265. Only the suspension of the legislature in 1774 prevented trial before the Council.

CHAPTER 5

Enslavement

The payment of salaries in 1772 alarmed people all over the colony because of what salaries signified. They were thinking about the ties of interest formed by the salary and the loss of the governor's affection and sympathy when Britain, instead of the province, paid him. In the same way, it was the significance given events by political culture that made the other imperial reform measures so disturbing. The jurisdiction of vice-admiralty courts, a standing army, customs collection, episcopacy, and many other matters also set off alarms in the colonists' minds.

Parliamentary taxation, the issue raised by the Stamp Act of 1765, was the most troubling of all. The colonists felt that a parliamentary tax destroyed their best defense against avarice and oppression. Although Parliament failed to see the implications of the stamp tax, to the colonists it was a nightmarish culmination of the worst in provincial politics. Parliament passed the act almost without a second thought, as incidental to the support of an American army. It seemed like a mild tax for a good purpose and well within the Parliament's rights. To its surprise, Americans were outraged. The colonies exploded in a burst of riots, petitions, and boycotts. It was not that the tax was strange and new. To the contrary, the problem was that it reawakened the colonists' oldest and deepest fears.

The Stamp Act released the very forces that Massachusetts politicians had fought to hold in check for nearly a century. From 1691 on, the popular party had used every possible means to contain the avarice of imperial officials, who were suspected of taking colonial posts for the purpose of making a fortune. Most of the constitutional maneuvering in the assembly aimed to prevent the governor from diverting public money to his own use. The audit of accounts confronted the question most directly, but control of the salary, limitations on military expenditures, and defense of the assembly's privileges all sought to keep imperial placemen in rein and to preserve the legislature as a bulwark against official rapacity.

Parliamentary taxation bypassed the province's established line of defense and negated all the safeguards built up over the years. The Stamp Act drew money from the people without the permission of a colonial assembly and put it at the disposal of the British ministry and their appointees. The representatives of the provincial population who knew and shared the interests of the people lost control. The ministry could drain the colonies and put the revenues to whatever corrupt purpose they chose. The decision to use the taxes to pay for British regulars in America and to make governors and judges independent of the colonial legislatures realized all the old fears. The horror of a rapacious band of alien officials ravaging the province, the danger foreseen for seventy-five years, seemed about to be enacted.

But the stamp tax was more than a horrible culmination; it was the beginning of a new kind of politics. The most obvious effect was to bring the whole population into the controversy. That would probably have happened merely because of the enormity of parliamentary taxes, but the Stamp Act also changed the structure of political forces in such a way as to involve the populace more systematically. The crisis spread from the assemblies, where opposition had long been located, to the streets. Most political disputes earlier had been fought in the legislative chambers, spilling over occasionally into newspapers and pamphlets. From the Stamp Act on, the Revolutionary crisis took place in city lanes and at country crossroads. A broad cross-section of the population from all over the province actively participated. The legislative debates of the popular party were transformed into a far-reaching popular movement, in which the latent anger of the people, expressed before only in infrequent riots and the occasional acquittal of critical newspaper editors, was acted out day after day.

This change after 1765 had consequences for political culture. In the first place, the extent of popular acceptance of the politicians' beliefs was measured for the first time. It became evident after 1765 that the political culture of the assembly was the political culture of the people. The leaders spoke in Boston, and ordinary farmers in country towns understood. In conventions, riots, and letters, farmers and artisans all over Massachusetts showed that provincial political culture belonged to them. More particularly, the addresses and petitions from the country towns showed that people understood political sociology alike. It was universally believed, as the popular leaders in the assembly had always thought, that officials were tied into networks of interest and would act as their interests dictated. Though seemingly a small point, it made a great difference in the understanding of events. It led people to believe that a salary or appointment could pull rulers away from the interest of the people and turn them from friends into enemies. It also pointed the province toward republican government as the obvious defense against oppression.

In the second place, the pressure of events after 1765 clarified and elaborated the meaning of traditional political culture. In writing to arouse the people, the whigs spoke much more openly than popular leaders had ever felt free to do. Regard for political stability inhibited politicians in less frenzied times. Popular leaders like the Cookes had concentrated on legal issues and avoided elaboration of their darker apprehensions. The whigs felt less compunction and explained much more fully the meaning of popular principles. The whigs clarified particularly the connections between abstract rights and social organization. The enslavement towards which imperial policy carried the colonies, the whigs made clear, encompassed lands and houses, human relations in every village, and even personality. Taxation, they believed, threatened to destroy their society. The provincials were convinced that the ministry conspired to drain the province of its wealth, perhaps strip them of their freeholds, and erect an oppressive social order in which officials and their lackeys would be the lords of all. In these last feverish expressions of popular protest, we glimpse the compelling necessity for abandoning monarchy and fleeing to republican government for refuge.

i. The Invasion of Parliamentary Power

Parliamentary taxation shocked the Massachusetts Bay political system far more severely than the appointment of a royal governor under the second charter of 1691. Parliamentary taxes were a stunning invasion of power. Successfully to accommodate this new force would have required far more complicated and contentious negotiations than those that ensued after 1691. And yet, the severity of the shock notwithstanding, some of the province's most experienced statesmen believed that Massachusetts would react to the intrusion of parliamentary power in 1765 as the colony had reacted to the intrusion of royal power in 1691. Compromises would be worked out step by step to safeguard both provincial rights and imperial interests, and eventually an equilibrium would be reestablished. Thomas Hutchinson's strategy in this sense resembled Increase Mather's in 1691. Both opposed Whitehall's proposed reform; both yielded a point when they judged no vital interests were at stake; both believed Massachusetts would benefit most from cooperation with imperial government. The Mathers' sponsorship of the second charter eventually won over public opinion against the objections of a vociferous popular party, and by 1736 Massachusetts was firmly laced into the imperial commercial and political network. Thomas Hutchinson believed another accommodation could be achieved after 1765. Through give-and-take on both sides, the imperial connection would remain intact despite the protests of the popular party.

Unfortunately for the reasonable men who chose the moderate path, history did not repeat itself in 1765.[1] Accommodating statesmen like Hutchinson needed time to work out a compromise, and time was not

1. The best narratives of the Stamp Act period are Edmund S. Morgan and Helen M. Morgan, *The Stamp Act Crisis: Prologue to Revolution*, rev. ed. (New York, 1963); and Merrill Jensen, *The Founding of a Nation: A History of the American Revolution, 1763–1776* (New York, 1968), 36–182. For Massachusetts, see Leslie Joseph Thomas, "Partisan Politics in Massachusetts during Governor Bernard's Administration, 1760–1770" (Ph.D. diss., University of Wisconsin, 1960); and Stephen E. Patterson, *Political Parties in Revolutionary Massachusetts* (Madison, Wis., 1973). The popular party in time took control of the once conservative Council. Francis G. Walett, "The Massachusetts Council, 1766–1774: The Transformation of a Conservative Institution," *William and Mary Quarterly*, 3d Ser., VI (1949), 605–627.

granted them. It took more than forty years after the issuance of the second charter to lay to rest the question of the permanent salary and the other constitutional issues which the charter raised. Time of such magnitude was not permitted Hutchinson and the Olivers. Inevitably parliamentary taxation called the popular party back to life and in no mood for extended negotiations. The threat of parliamentary taxes rallied huge majorities to the popular cause. James Otis, Oxenbridge Thacher, and, later, Samuel Adams once again enjoyed the unfailing support which Cooke had at his disposal in the 1720s. Under these leaders, politics after 1765 moved at a dizzying pace. The popular party did not seem to follow the accepted rules of political conduct, leaving no time and no inclination for compromise. Hutchinson could conclude only that the population had lost its reason and placed its destiny in the hands of madmen.[2]

What Hutchinson could not perceive was that the Parliament's own action had turned politics upside down. The Stamp Act called into being a new mode of operation, evoked a new language, and accelerated enormously the pace of political change. The reason for the acceleration of events was Parliament's adoption of a new method of rule. Except for commercial regulation, which the colonies accepted or evaded, the major instrument of imperial governance before 1765 was royal instructions to the governors. Whenever one of the London agencies of government wished to establish a policy, it cast its wishes as a command of the king to his servant, the governor, for transmission to the people. The request for a permanent salary, the recruitment of troops, and the limitation on currency emissions, for example, took this form. Until enactment by the legislature, however, royal instructions carried no sanctions. They could not be enforced in the courts, and punishment could not be meted out for noncompliance. The only sanction applied to the governor. His persistent refusal to obey brought dismissal. The governor warned the assembly that neglect of the royal command would bring down the king's wrath, but

2. On the English side, Lord Dartmouth, colonial secretary, took the position that time would heal Anglo-American wounds. Like all experienced English statesmen, he knew the wisdom of avoiding constitutional issues, preferring pragmatic solutions. Dartmouth was disturbed when Hutchinson reopened the debate in 1773 with his lengthy reply to the House. Bernard Bailyn, *The Ordeal of Thomas Hutchinson* (Cambridge, Mass., 1974), 122.

these threats were empty. Only the governor himself was in any immediate danger.[3]

Before 1765 the structure of imperial rule made the legislature the scene of major political confrontation. To resist royal policy, the popular party had only to rally a majority in one house of the assembly. So long as the legislature held firm, imperial power could be contained. Only when instructions became law could they be enforced. Since Massachusetts was pretty much of one mind on questions of its rights within the empire, the task of popular party leaders was relatively simple. They needed only to state their position as a clear defense of acknowledged colonial rights, and the country representatives fell into line. The required legislation of the instructions met a stout wall of resistance. The one caution to be observed was to avoid the appearance of disloyalty. Displays of independence or hints of rebelliousness might indeed stir up Parliament or the crown and bring a curtailment of colonial privileges. Fortunately, the language of right legitimated in the Glorious Revolution gave Cooke and his associates plenty of leeway. They could draw upon the most commonplace of English political ideas and arouse the backcountry deputies without trespassing the limits of English tolerance. So long as their arguments rested on the charter and the common law, the popular party sounded, at worst, troublesome rather than rebellious or disloyal.

Parliamentary taxation overturned the structure of colonial resistance. A parliamentary measure, unlike a royal instruction, arrived in the colonies with the force of law. Since Parliament was a legislature, its measures did not require enactment to be enforced in the courts. Colonial officials could compel the obedience of all subjects through normal judicial procedures. In a stroke, the colonial assembly became obsolete as a line of defense against imperial power. Official avarice could run its course regardless of the people's objections. The assembly could serve as a rallying point for libertarian sentiments, but not as a check on power. The schematists' ambition to circumvent excessive democracy was fully realized.

The only recourse of the popular forces in 1765 was to the citizenry at large. If the legislature could no longer stop oppressive measures, each individual could. The imperial government might punish a few

3. Gov. Shirley in 1748 admitted that royal instructions bound the governor, not the House. *Journals of the House of Representatives of Massachusetts* (Boston, 1919–), XXV, 128.

recalcitrants; it could not discipline an entire population—without resort to arms. Politics therefore moved into the streets, first to attack the instruments of parliamentary policy, the stamp men, but more generally to arouse the entire populace to civil disobedience.

Popular party leaders after 1765 played a dual role. Earlier they strove to win the confidence of the deputies; and Otis, Thacher, Adams, and Warren, like the Cookes, continued to write petitions and addresses and to direct the House vote by their speeches on the floor. But at the same time, the whigs also turned to the public at large, through newspapers, pamphlets, and town meetings. They adopted the methods of the English opposition and mobilized a party press to inform and animate the people. For the first time in the history of the Bay colony, popular party leaders became public figures. Unlike the Cookes, the leaders of the Revolutionary generation left a body of writings— tracts, newspaper essays, letters, and political treatises. The much broader public to which the whigs appealed required communication through public media.[4]

Furthermore, the mode of political activity changed from words to action. Politics in the streets involved pageants, the harassment of officials, and nonimportation and nonconsumption agreements. Although circumspect about public order, the popular party could not foresee the ultimate consequences of action politics. When politics were carried to the public, the new devices proceeded to extremes beyond the intentions of either side. Only force could control resistance in the population at large. Eventually the recourse was to arms. Moderates looked on helplessly as events carried the province pell-mell toward armed conflict and independence, with no time for the arts of compromise and negotiation to have their way.[5]

ii. The Provincial Reaction

The British at first persuaded themselves that a small cadre of radicals formed the only determined resistance to imperial rule. The tories

4. John C. Miller, *Sam Adams: Pioneer in Propaganda* (Boston, 1936), 95–96. For general studies, see Philip Davidson, *Propaganda and the American Revolution, 1763–1783* (Chapel Hill, N.C., 1941); and Arthur M. Schlesinger, *Prelude to Independence: The Newspaper War on Britain, 1764–1776* (New York, 1958).
5. Pauline Maier, *From Resistance to Revolution: Colonial Radicals and the Development of*

credited the whigs' propaganda skills for the intense popular reaction. Looking back late in 1774, the tory Daniel Leonard marveled at the ingenuity of the popular leaders. "They were intimately acquainted with the feelings of man," Leonard commented, "and knew all the avenues of the human heart." The whigs religiously noted the anniversaries of popular resistance activities as, before, the colonists had remembered the king's birthdays. "The fourteenth of August was celebrated annually as a festival in commemoration of a mob's destroying a building, owned by the late Lieutenant Governor, which was supposed to have been erected for a stamp-office." The anniversary of the Boston Massacre was another holiday, when "annual orations were delivered in the old south meeting house." These occasions permitted the popular party to keep up a steady drumbeat of propaganda. "The people were told weekly that the ministry had formed a plan to enslave them. . . . This perpetual incantation kept the people in continual alarm."[6] The government party was outraged when Samuel Adams wanted a gallery installed in the House of Representatives. The whigs, it seemed, wished to seat the assembly in a building "equal to the most finished playhouse."[7]

But contrary to conservative opinion, skill in dramatization cannot by itself account for the popular reaction. Whig success in mobilizing the population could not have been accomplished by manipulation alone. At the very least the political leaders and their audiences had to have shared a common political language and a few basic attitudes. It seems more likely that the source of whig strength was a common political culture. Probably that was true of the earlier popular parties. John Leverett and Thomas Danforth commanded popular majorities in the seventeenth century. The opposition to compromise on the first charter gave evidence of wide backing. In the early eighteenth century, the consistent support of the Cookes in the assembly measured the commitment of country towns to popular party principles. The crowd's

---

American Opposition to Britain, 1765–1776 (New York, 1972), treats in detail the nature of violent resistance.

6. J. Adams and [Leonard], *Novanglus, And Massachusettensis; Or Political Essays, Published in the Years 1774 and 1775* . . . (Boston, 1819), 149–150.

7. Quoted in Miller, *Sam Adams*, 110. On the anthropological and psychological significance of these performances, see Peter Shaw, *American Patriots and the Rituals of Revolution* (Cambridge, Mass., 1981). Although Philip Davidson's term "propaganda" casts doubt on the radicals' sincerity, he offers a useful description of their activity in *Propaganda and the American Revolution*.

reactions to impressment and the jury support of newspaper opposition to government suggested even more vigorous suspicion of rulers among the people at large than among their elected representatives. But the uprisings in Boston in 1765 and the later conventions and riots in the country revealed as never before the strength of support for popular party principles. Since whig influence depended almost entirely on words and symbols, the popular party's success measured the reach and force of provincial political culture.

The resort to the public in 1765 made visible, especially in Boston, a host of clubs, circles, crowds, networks, and juntos ready for action and quick to run into the streets when the alarm sounded. The city had long been interlaced with fire companies, tavern clubs, dining clubs, Masonic lodges, militia companies, and Scottish and Irish societies, meeting for conviviality and political discussion. Seemingly spontaneously, without direction from elected officials, these groups took it upon themselves to resist Parliament.[8]

At first the backcountry lagged behind Boston, but not far. The town meeting and the informal networks of kin and neighborhood served as well as caucus and club to carry news and form opinion. In Worcester, the American Political Society of sixty-three members functioned like the Boston caucuses. The towns knew enough about the Stamp Act by the fall of 1765 for more than forty of them to join in adopting the instructions which John Adams framed for Braintree's representative to the General Court, urging firm opposition to the tax.[9] When the town of Boston called for a convention of towns in September 1768 to state the opinion of the province on the arrival of two regiments of British troops, more than a hundred sent delegates, despite the questionable legality of the convention. From 1765 on without exception, the backcountry representatives to the assembly backed the popular party leaders by large majorities. In December 1772 the Boston Committee of Correspondence asked the towns to state their opinions on the payment of the salaries of superior court justices. Replies from 144 towns and districts out of some 260 survive,.enough to show that in towns of

8. G. B. Warden, *Boston, 1689–1776* (Boston, 1970), 156; Miller, *Sam Adams*, 37–38; Carl Bridenbaugh, *Cities in Revolt: Urban Life in America, 1743–1776* (New York, 1955), 292–295, 363–364.
9. The editor of the *Massachusetts Gazette; and the Boston Weekly News-Letter* asked John Adams for a copy of the Braintree instructions and printed them. Other towns copied. Page Smith, *John Adams* (Garden City, N.Y., 1962), I, 81.

all sizes, wealth, and commercial development, scattered from the coast to the Berkshires in the west, committees pondered the Boston statement of rights and grievances, formulated their replies, and presented them to the town meetings for approval. The delighted Boston Committee expressed its "unspeakable satisfaction . . . that their [the towns'] sentiments so nearly accord with ours."[10]

The manifestos, the processions, the newspaper essays, the banquets, speeches, and effigies revealed hundreds of people taking a part in politics. The Stamp Act crisis was the opportunity of a lifetime to play a role on a broad stage. Events did not pull these people reluctantly from shops and countinghouses. The painters, braziers, and distillers of the Loyal Nine moved deftly and enthusiastically into the organization of the August 14 riot. Ebenezer MacIntosh gave every appearance of enjoying his position at the head of Boston processions, decked out in a caricature costume of a military officer.[11] Samuel Adams was an obscure tax collector until the Stamp Act offered a field for his remarkable talents. So in scores of towns in 1772, at least one man knew how to state the principles of American rights and stepped forward with pen in hand. The Boston Committee of Correspondence delightedly observed, "We seem to have a Solon or Lycurgus in every second or third town and district."[12] The small conspiratorial gang of tory mythology was in reality a large corps of willing accomplices in every corner of Boston and in town after town throughout the province.

The political traditions of many generations, the celebrated controversies of recent years, tavern talk of politicians and traders who went to Boston, sermons, and litigation in the local courts had spread and

10. Quoted in Richard D. Brown, *Revolutionary Politics in Massachusetts: The Boston Committee of Correspondence and the Towns, 1772–1774* (Cambridge, Mass., 1970), 140. For description and analysis of uprisings in Boston and the country, see Dirk Hoerder, *Crowd Action in Revolutionary Massachusetts, 1765–1780* (New York, 1977).

11. George P. Anderson, "Ebenezer Mackintosh, Stamp Act Rioter and Patriot," Colonial Society of Massachusetts, *Publications*, XXVI (Boston, 1927), 15–64, and "A Note on Ebenezer Mackintosh," *ibid.*, 348–361; Warden, *Boston*, 164, 170; Morgan and Morgan, *Stamp Act Crisis*, 163, 173.

12. Boston Committee of Correspondence to New Salem, Apr. 6, 1773, Letters and Proceedings received by the Boston Committee of Correspondence (photostats), Massachusetts Historical Society, Boston. For the involvement of English middle classes in politics in the 1760s, see John Brewer, *Party Ideology and Popular Politics at the Accession of George III* (New York, 1976).

kept alive the rudiments of political culture.[13] In its reply to West-borough, the Boston committee commented in 1773, "The knowledge of the true spirit of our Constitution, which was spread even to the remotest parts of the Province, must astonish those who represent us as ignorant, as savages."[14] A fluid continuum of discourse flowed from the press into the taverns and from the Boston Committee of Corre-spondence to the rural town meetings.

Significantly, city and country had more in common than a raw dis-like of the British ministry. They understood the mechanisms of politi-cal society alike. The returns from the towns expressed the same ap-prehension of interest networks and dependencies that underlay the assembly's opposition to the permanent salary. It was commonly ac-cepted that officials were attached by interest to one power or another, that they conformed to the wishes of whatever power advanced the of-ficials' own interest, and that if not attached to the people, rulers would exploit and oppress the population they governed. That idea loomed large enough that country people freely used violence to prevent a separation of their own from their ruler's interests.

The people had frequent occasion to express their commitment to these ideas after 1772. Town replies to the Boston committee on the payment of salaries to judges condemned the separation of the gover-nor's from the people's interest. The salaries and the question of inter-est made it impossible for Bostonians to accept the Tea Act of 1773 as an innocent mistake made in an attempt to bail out the East India Company. It was easy to surmise that the ministry paid the salaries from the tea duty, and cheap tea was a device to persuade the colonists to acquiesce in making judges dependent on the home government alone. Even more alarming was the passage of the Massachusetts Gov-ernment Act. The popular reaction to all these measures revealed the concern about officials tied by interest to the crown alone with no de-pendence on the people.

Of them all, the Massachusetts Government Act was most reprehen-sible. Passed in Parliament May 20, 1774, in answer to the Boston Tea Party of December 1773, the act decreed that, beginning August 1, 1774, the members of the Council would receive their appointments

13. Gary B. Nash, "The Transformation of Urban Politics, 1700–1765," *Journal of American History*, LX (1973–1974), 605–632.
14. Boston Committee of Correspondence to Westborough, Jan. 19, 1773, Minute Book, V, 361 (photostats), Mass. Hist. Soc., Boston.

from the king without nomination of the Massachusetts House, that the attorney general, the inferior judges, sheriffs, and justices of the peace would be appointed and removed by the governor without the advice and consent of the Council, and that sheriffs would select juries rather than their being elected or summoned by local constables.

The whig leaders in Boston were aghast. The act in effect abrogated the charter of 1691 by legislative fiat. More important, the entire apparatus of government fell under the control of the governor, who was in turn the puppet of the British ministry. All were entangled in the webs of patronage. Every constitutional safeguard which had protected Massachusetts through eighty-three years of royal government was eradicated. The province's property and liberty lay at the mercy of ministers and placemen. "Gentlemen," a June 8 circular from the Boston Committee of Correspondence declared, "the evils which we have long foreseen are now come upon this town and province, the long meditated stroke is now given to the civil liberty of this country."[15]

No explanation from Boston was required to stir people in the country towns. In August of 1774 the Massachusetts countryside rose in wrath. For more than a decade thereafter the western counties exceeded the east in their demands for independence and democracy. Not waiting for the House of Representatives to assemble or for the Boston Committee of Correspondence to prompt them, the people in county after county came together in conventions and crowds to wreak their will on their enemies.[16]

The conventions based their opposition on the same principles that had motivated the popular party for over a century. The overriding concern was the dependence of appointed officials. Under the Massachusetts Government Act, the web of patronage and dependence reached from governor to sheriff to justices of the peace, tying all their interests to the ministry, and severing all connections by salary or appointment to the people. Every judge, every juror, it was believed, became the lackey of the ministry. Because officials were in no way beholden to the people, judges, customs officers, and tax collectors could combine to strip the colony of its property.

Virtually every region of Massachusetts resolved to resist the Mas-

15. Circular broadside, June 8, 1774, Mass. Hist. Soc., Boston.
16. Brown, *Revolutionary Politics*, 212, 231, 233; Patterson, *Political Parties in Revolutionary Massachusetts*, 91–124; Robert J. Taylor, *Western Massachusetts in the Revolution* (Providence, R.I., 1954), 52–69.

sachusetts Government Act. In practice resistance meant refusal to acknowledge the authority of any appointed official. The principle on
which the counties acted had been clearly enunciated in the previous
year and a half as the payment of the governor and superior court
judges had become public knowledge. In March 1774 the town of Worcester laid down the grounds for noncompliance:

> The Governor and Judges of the Superior Court, rendered inde-
> pendent of the people of the province, for whose good only they
> were appointed, for which service they ought to depend on those
> they serve for pay: and, we are constrained to say, that to have
> these who are to determine and judge on our lives [and] property
> paid by a foreign state, immediately destroys that natural depen-
> dence which ought to subsist between a people and their officers,
> and [is,] of course, destructive of liberty. For which reason, we are
> of opinion, that we [are] not in the least bound in duty to submit
> to the ordering and determining of such officers as are not depen-
> dent on the grants of the people for their pay.

In Worcester, the very legitimacy of authority depended on the payment of salaries. The salary represented "that natural dependence
which ought to subsist between a people and their officers." Breaking
the bonds of interest released the people from their obligations to
government.[17]

Beginning in July 1774 in Berkshire and then in quick succession
through August in most other counties, conventions met to force resignations of officials and to prevent the sitting of county courts. The
crowds did not always repudiate individuals. In Worcester County the
people requested that all the justices of the peace resign their commissions from the governor, and immediately voted to continue the eleven
who complied. Personal vengeance was a minor theme. The crowds
aimed to separate every official from "the System of Despotism" and
return each to dependence on the people.[18] They worried that the gift
of an office would lure officials into the grasp of the ministry.

Thomas Young reported to Samuel Adams in early September 1774
that the western counties feared the British ministry would always be
tempted to attack Massachusetts, and "a creature of the Minister hav-

17. Quoted in William Lincoln, *History of Worcester, Massachusetts, From Its Earliest
Settlement to September, 1836 . . .* (Worcester, Mass., 1862), 77.
18. Boston Committee of Correspondence, minutes, Aug. 27, 1774, quoted in Brown,
Revolutionary Politics, 230.

ing all posts of honor and profit in his disposal will still have it in his power to draw many aside from their duty to their Country." With the lure of office, "a party is so easily made of the most powerful men in every County and even town against the common People" that it was impossible to "frustrate their machinations."[19] The only answer to a party of dependent placemen was a purge of officeholders through forced resignations. On October 21, the Provincial Congress resolved that all persons holding commissions under the Massachusetts Government Act should resign in ten days or be treated as rebels.[20]

This moment of revolutionary opposition revealed how deeply imbedded in the popular consciousness were the maxims of eighteenth-century political culture, and also where those principles led. The abstract ties of salary and appointment were in the minds of country people the very bonds of legitimacy and allegiance. On October 4, 1774, Worcester elected Joshua Bigelow to the General Court and instructed him in the course he was to follow. The town said that if the right to elect councillors were not restored, "You are to consider the people of this province as absolved, on their part from the obligation therein contained, and to all intents and purposes reduced to a state of nature." The loss of the right to nominate councillors was sufficient to dissolve government and return people to a state of nature. Worcester told Bigelow he was to work for a new government wherein this central privilege was assured. "You are to exert yourself in devising ways and means to raise from the dissolution of the old constitution, as from the ashes of the Phenix, a new form, wherein all officers shall be dependent on the suffrages of the people for their existence as such."[21] The obvious remedy for excessive dependence on the ministry was popular election, that is, republican government. Worcester did not consult with pundits or theoreticians before proposing the idea, nor did they see election of officials as a radical departure. Given their assumptions about dependency and interest, election by the people, along with popular control of salaries, was the natural reaction to the dangers facing the province.

East and west were said to disagree on what new form to raise

19. Thomas Young to Samuel Adams, Sept. 4, 1774, quoted in Brown, *Revolutionary Politics*, 232.

20. Harry A. Cushing, *History of the Transition from Provincial to Commonwealth Government in Massachusetts*, Columbia University Studies in History, Economics and Public Law, VII, No. 1 (New York, 1896), 118–119.

21. Lincoln, *History of Worcester*, 91–92.

"from the ashes of the Phenix." James Warren told Samuel Adams in September that "almost all in the western counties, are for taking up the old form of government, according to the first charter." Under the charter of 1629, the people elected the governor as well as the two houses of the legislature and thus were in effect a republic with complete control over appointments and legislation. Some in the eastern counties thought that "the connection between the king and the people is dissolved by his breaking the compact made between them." They favored the negotiation of a new compact, with "a certain limited subjection to the king, as they shall judge convenient, which he may accept or reject as he pleases."[22] But whether a return to the first charter or the construction of a new constitution, many seemed resolved by the fall of 1774 to refuse submission and to bring rulers under the control of the people.[23]

iii. The Sociology of Corruption

The appointment of mandamus councillors and the change in Massachusetts government in 1774 touched a raw nerve in the province. The reaction nearly everywhere was immediate, spontaneous, and violent. For many, cutting off officials from their connections with the people meant an end of legitimate authority, and townsmen everywhere combined to close down courts and force resignations. The reasons were obvious. Making officials entirely independent of the people and giving them, in effect, unchecked taxing power overstepped all the limitations the popular party had tried to impose on officials since the issuance of the second charter in 1691. Ministerial policies appeared to allow the very thing the popular party had fought to prevent, the release of rapacious officials to plunder the province. In basic theme and purpose, Revolutionary politics were a continuation of popular party politics of the entire provincial period.

But the whigs were more candid than the older leaders. Licensed by the times to speak freely, whigs went deeper into the consequences of

22. Joseph Warren to Samuel Adams, Sept. 12, 1774 (should be Sept. 14, 1774), quoted in Brown, *Revolutionary Politics*, 231–232. On resumption of the old charter, see Patterson, *Political Parties*, 119–120.
23. See Chapter 2 above.

unchecked political power. They explained what rulers who were independent of the people would do and, more particularly, how the policies of the ministry went beyond politics to undermine the foundations of society. Rather than merely checking the greed of a few transient officials, the provincials believed that they faced a general social degradation, a deterioration toward a state they called ruin, destruction, or, most commonly, slavery.

On the eve of the Revolution, the town of Athol, writing to the Boston Committee of Correspondence, saw danger "rushing in upon us like a flood from the artful devices of a Corrupt and Designing ministry," who aimed to "put in Execution their avoritious Schums for enriching and agrandizing themselves and their favour rights although it be at the expence of Enslaving a free and Loyal People."[24] Those words warned of an impending transformation of the social order growing out of the recent changes in government. Enslavement implied a reorganization of all the fundamental social relations of work, authority, and personal regard. The petitioners seemed to forecast, if in abbreviated and encoded form, a rapid and debilitating social degeneration.

As Athol understood the process, enslavement followed in the wake of designing ministers aggrandizing themselves and a circle of friends. The image of a combination was significant. Although corruption began with a single greedy person in power, it did not end there. The greed of one multiplied and expanded. Favorites and friends had to be fed, and their numbers incessantly increased. In an obvious attack on the British ministry, a 1775 sermon sketched the circle of dependents which the notorious Old Testament tyrant Haman the Premier gathered around him.

> *Haman* the *Premier,* and his junto of court *Favourites, flatterers,* and *dependants* in the royal city, together with *governors* of provinces, *counsellors, boards of trade, commissioners* and their *creatures, officers* and *collectors* of *REVENUE, solicitors,* assistants, *searchers* and *inspectors,* down to tide-waiters, and their *scribes,* and the good Lord knows whom, and how many of them, together with the coachmen and servants of the whole made a *formidable* number through

24. Athol to the Boston Committee of Correspondence, July 20, 1774, Letters and Proceedings. See also Amherst to Boston Committee of Correspondence, Jan. 26, 1774, *ibid.*; Berwick to Boston Committee of Correspondence, Jan. 3, 1774, *ibid.*

that great empire, all dependant upon the breath of *Haman* the court *favourite*, and with him breathing the same spirit, and expecting to share with him some part of the *spoil.*[25]

The horror of parliamentary taxes, as John Dickinson observed, was that the minister "may divide the spoils torn from us in what manner he please" and "reward the most profligate, ignorant, or needy dependents on himself or his friends, with places of greatest trust."[26]

The network of recipients was more than a system for dividing the spoils. It was a recognizable kind of society, bound by mutual obligations. The ruler was the patron of the lesser men, their protector and giver of gifts, a horrible caricature of the great patron the king. The minister's dependents, like all dependents and clients, were bound by duty, gratitude, and interest to yield and obey. The patronage network created power for the minister just as protection gave power to the king. In Haman's system all were "dependant upon the breath" of the premier. Wealth, favors, and places flowed downward through the network, and obedience flowed up. The great patron, like God, made men his creatures by bestowal of favors. The same forces of gratitude and interest, the traditional moral cohesives, bound patron to client and compelled obedience. The difference was that self-indulgence, greed, and lust for power motivated the parties to the compact, rather than regard for the public welfare and zeal for the king's service.

The tentacles of the patronage networks reached into Parliament, the royal bureaucracy, and across the seas, right alongside legitimate government. The blind compliance of ministerial dependents in the Parliament partly accounted for the egregious trespasses on the colo-

25. Oliver Noble, *Some Strictures Upon The Sacred Story Recorded In The Book of Esther, Shewing The Power and Oppression of State Ministers tending to the Ruin and Destruction of God's People . . .* (Newburyport, Mass., 1775), 17–18.

26. [John Dickinson], *Letters from a Farmer in Pennsylvania, to the Inhabitants of the British Colonies* (Philadelphia, 1768), 49. "*Wherein consisteth the ministers* powerful and *Political* preservation *of his creatures?*" a pamphlet of 1771 asked. "It consisteth, in prefering them to *places* and *pensions,* giving them *salaries* independent of the people." *A Ministerial Catechise, Suitable to be Learned by all Modern Provincial Governors, Pensioners, Placemen, etc.* (Boston, 1771), 4–5. See also Mercy Otis Warren, *The Adulateur, a Tragedy, As it is now Acted in Upper Servia* (Boston, 1773), 9; William Gordon, *Discourse Preached December 15th, 1774 . . .* (Boston, 1775), in John Wingate Thornton, ed., *The Pulpit of the American Revolution* (Boston, 1860), 204n; Samuel Webster, *The Misery and Duty of an oppress'd and Enslav'd People, Represented in a Sermon Delivered at Salisbury, July 14, 1774 . . .* (Boston, 1774), 23–24.

nists' rights: dependents in the Commons voted for ministerial measures at whatever cost to principle. So with the imperial bureaucracy.
English attorneys and solicitors, after taking their training at the turf
and gaming tables, came to the highest stations "in the Courts of Law,
without any other recommendation than a servile disposition to pros-
titute the Law and the Constitution, whenever their Masters should require it of them."[27] That fact explained the outlandish instructions issued from royal offices ostensibly in the king's name.

From Whitehall, selfishness and dependence flowed outward, pol-
luting the system of government in every provincial county and remote country town. The governor served not his people, but, as Samuel Adams said, "some other person residing in Great Britain, whose
instructions the Govr, must punctually observe upon pain of forfeiting
his place." By the same token, the governor's appointees, the justices
and militia officers, catered to his wishes with no regard to the people.
The lust for office and salaries made them sacrifice all to greed. The
whole point of taxes was to finance this vast network and to extend its
reach. Samuel Adams hated the tea duty because he believed the
money would go "for the support of standing armies and ships of war;
episcopates and their numerous ecclesiastical retinue; pensioners,
placemen, and other jobbers, for an abandoned and shameless ministry; hirelings, pimps, parasites, panders, prostitutes, and whores."[28]
Taxes enabled the ministry to purchase an army of lesser officials and
through them to impose on people in every corner of the empire. By
1775 Pittsfield radicals believed that by means of the governor's power
"a secret poison" has "spread thro' out all our Towns and great Multi-

27. Harry Alonzo Cushing, ed., *The Writings of Samuel Adams* (New York, 1904–
1908), II, 42.
28. *Ibid.*, II, 166–167, 247. See also Lexington to Boston Committee of Correspondence, Dec. 15, 1773, Letters and Proceedings. Cato much earlier had sketched in the
dynamics of enslavement:

No man, or small Number of Men, can support themselves in Power upon their
own proper Strength, without taking in the Assistance of a great many others;
and they can never have that Assistance, unless they take in their Interests too,
and unless the latter can find their own Account in giving it: for Men will laugh at
bare Arguments brought to prove that they must labour, be robbed of that Labour, and want, that others may be idle, riot, and plunder them. Those Governments therefore, which are founded upon Oppression, always find it necessary to
engage Interests enough in their Tyranny to overcome all opposition from those
who are tyrannized over, by giving separate and unequal Privileges to the Instru-

tudes have been secured for the corrupt Designs of an abandoned Administration."[29]

In the minds of popular leaders, the true conflict after 1765 lay not between Great Britain and the colonists, but between those who were part of the ministerial patronage network and those who resisted. The popular party leaders recognized the distinction immediately upon passage of the Stamp Act. They directed attacks not at Great Britain as a nation, and not at Grenville and his associates alone, but even more fiercely at the stamp men who accepted office and became his dependents. The traitors who joined the network of corruption merited condemnation equally with their British masters. "Will the Cries of your despairing, dying Brethren be Music pleasing to your Ears?" one essayist asked the stamp man in August 1765. "If so, go on! bend the Knee to your Master Horseleach, and beg a Share in the Pillage of your Country." He feared that the desire to join in the plunder would lead the colonists to yield themselves to the dispensers of spoils. "Have many already become the Tools of your Oppression? and are numbers now cringing to become the Tools of your Oppression? and are numbers now cringing to become the Tools of those Tools?"[30] The war was not with another nation or with a legitimate government, but with an insidious social order and shadow government forming both in the colonies and at home.

The trouble was that the wealth and power offered by the ministry were an irresistible lure. Inconceivable as it seemed, men like Thomas Hutchinson, one of Massachusetts' favorite sons, "bone of our bone, and flesh of our flesh, *born* and *bred* among us," would "for a wedge of gold, detach themselves from the *common* interest, and embark in *another* bottom" in hopes one day of triumphing "in the ruins of their country."[31] John Adams thought that was the point of all the taxes.

---

ments and Accomplices of their Oppression, by letting them share the Advantages of it, by putting Arms in their Hands, and by taking away all the Means of Self-Defence from those who have more Right to use them.

John Trenchard and William Gordon, *Cato's Letters; or, Essays on Liberty, Civil and Religious, and other Important Subjects*, 3d ed. (New York, 1969 [orig. publ. London, 1724]), III, 266.

29. Petition of Pittsfield, Dec. 26, 1775, in Robert J. Taylor, ed., *Massachusetts, Colony to Commonwealth: Documents on the Formation of its Constitution, 1775–1780* (Chapel Hill, N.C., 1961), 18.

30. *Boston Post-Boy and Advertiser*, Aug. 26, 1765.

31. Cushing, ed., *Writings of Samuel Adams*, II, 149.

They were not to be applied "for public purposes, national or provincial, but merely to corrupt the sons of America, and create a faction to destroy its interest and happiness."[32] The process fed on itself. Corruption, "like a cancer," John Adams said, "eats faster and faster every hour."

> The revenue creates pensioners, and the pensioners urge for more revenue. The people grow less steady, spirited and virtuous, the seekers more numerous and more corrupt, and every day increases the circles of their dependents and expectants, until virtue, integrity, public spirit, simplicity, and frugality, become the objects of ridicule and scorn, and vanity, luxury, foppery, selfishness, meanness, and downright venality swallow up the whole society.[33]

As one appointee after another yielded to enticement and let the patronage tentacles wrap around him, the purposes of government were hopelessly perverted. Inevitably the people would "grow less steady, spirited, and virtuous."

The consequences of this expanding network of dependents were as devastating for the economy as for government. Unless it were uprooted, the network of dependents would grow into a great parasitic vine, sapping the life of the provincial economy. Ministers and placemen sought power so as to gain property. "The present Ministry is Endeavouring to plunder this people, first of their constitutional Rights and Liberties," Elbridge Gerry wrote Samuel Adams in 1772, "and then (the point at which they are ultimately driving) of their Interest."[34] The whigs saw at once that the Stamp Act revenues were intended to make jobs in the colonies for court favorites, to keep "lazy fellows in ease, idleness, or luxury, in mother Britain's lap."[35] The ministry had exhausted the resources of England and Ireland. "The long and scandalous list of placemen and pensioners, and the general profligacy and prodigality of the present reign" accounted for Britain's financial straits. "America was the only remaining spot to which their oppression and extortion had not fully reached, and they considered

---

32. J. Adams and [Leonard], *Novanglus, And Massachusettensis*, 37.
33. Charles Francis Adams, ed., *The Works of John Adams*, IV (Boston, 1851), 43.
34. Elbridge Gerry to Samuel Adams, Oct. 27, 1772, Samuel Adams Papers, New York Public Library.
35. *Boston-Gazette, and Country Journal*, Aug. 12, 1765.

her as a fallow field from which a large income might be drawn."[36] The tax drain, though small at first, if not checked, would suck the life-blood from the people. Accept one small tax, and others would follow. "When once they have found the way to rob us," the Boston Committee of Correspondence warned of the tea duty in November 1773, "their avarice will never be satisfied until our own manufactures and even our land, purchased and cultivated by our hard labouring Ancestors, are taxed to support the extravagance and vices of wretches whose vileness ought to banish them from the Society of Men."[37]

Ultimately the population would be sharply divided into laborers and the idle, those who worked and the great network of indolent task-masters who lived off the workers' toil. Everything the industrious portion of society produced would be taxed to support lazy placemen and pensioners. There would be "an increase of *taxes* and *duties* on the necessaries of life, on lands, food and cloathing, whereby the people are reduced to straits and poverty, while these *Supernumeraries* live in idleness, affluence and luxury, on the labors of the honest and industrious."[38] Because their appetites were insatiable and their numbers were ever increasing, in time "a great part of the wealth of a state, must in this case, fall a prey to their insatiable avarices."[39] "We may have the honor," a preacher told his congregation in December 1774, "of burning under the heats of summer and freezing under the colds of winter

36. Noble, *Some Strictures*, 10, 17–18. See also Bernard Bailyn, ed., *Pamphlets of the American Revolution, 1750–1776* (Cambridge, Mass., 1965), I, 78–79. A caricature of Sept. 3, 1768 has Grenville say as he saddles the American Beast with taxes, "I say Saddle the Beast, she will be able to bear great burdens for plac——n and PENSIONERS." M. Dorothy George, *English Political Caricature: A Study of Opinion and Propaganda* (Oxford, 1959), I, 156.

37. Circular Letter, Nov. 23, 1773, Boston Committee of Correspondence, Minute Book, VI, 455 (photostats), Mass. Hist. Soc., Boston. The Dedham town meeting resolved not to drink tea, because it was the tea duty that furnished "so large a sum toward the maintenance and support of an almost innumerable multitude who live upon the fruits of the honest industry of the inhabitants, from the odious Commissioners of the Customs down to the dirty informers that are employed by them." Frank Smith, *A History of Dover, Massachusetts as a Precinct, Parish, District, and Town* (Dover, Mass., 1897), 86.

38. Peter Whitney, *The Transgressions of a Land punished by a Multitude of Rulers . . .* (Boston, 1774), 24.

39. Noble, *Some Strictures*, 8. See also Lexington to Boston Committee of Correspondence, Dec. 15, 1773, Letters and Proceedings; *Bost.-Gaz.*, Jan. 8, 1770; Jensen, *The Founding of a Nation*, 434.

in providing for the luxurious entertainment of lazy, proud, worthless pensioners and placemen."[40]

That was the very essence of slavery: to labor and not to enjoy the fruits of one's toil. When Athol spoke of "enslavement," it meant the word literally. The loss of political liberty implied the loss of one's labor, working not for one's own gain, but another's. "Those who are governed at the will of another, or of others, and whose property may be taken from them by taxes, or otherwise, without their own consent, and against their will, are in the miserable condition of slaves."[41] Liberty was the power "which every man has over his own Actions, and his Right to enjoy the Fruit of his Labour, Art, and Industry," and when lost, slavery ensued.[42] Taxes enacted without consent of the people, to support in luxury bands of rapacious officials, were as truly slavery as legal bondage.

Tyranny meant impoverished slavery for workers, and luxury and magnificence for rulers and their minions. "Liberty and Property" were polar opposites to "Slavery, Wooden Shoes, and Beggary."[43] As dependency grew ever larger, "minions, and court parasites, those blood-suckers of the constitution," would gluttonously devour the wealth of the people, and in the declining nation, "poverty and misery [would] come upon its industrious inhabitants, like the breaking in of mighty waters."[44] The enslavement of the Massachusetts countryside

40. Gordon, *Discourse*, in Thornton, ed., *Pulpit of the American Revolution*, 203.
41. Stephen Hopkins, *The Rights of the Colonies Examined* (Providence, R.I., 1764), in Merrill Jensen, ed., *Tracts of the American Revolution, 1763–1776* (Indianapolis, Ind., 1967), 43.
42. Trenchard and Gordon, *Cato's Letters*, II, 245. The Continental Congress made the connection in an address "To the oppressed Inhabitants of Canada," May 29, 1775: "By the introduction of your present form of government, or rather present form of tyranny, you and your wives and your children are made slaves. You have nothing that you can call your own, and all the fruits of your labour and industry may be taken from you, whenever an avaritious governor and a rapacious council may incline to demand them." Worthington Chauncey Ford *et al.*, eds., *Journals of the Continental Congress, 1774–1789* . . . , II (Washington, D.C., 1905), 69.
43. *Boston Weekly News-Letter*, Jan. 16, 1746. In English caricature, the wooden shoe symbolized slavery. Herbert M. Atherton, *Political Prints in the Age of Hogarth: A Study of the Ideographic Representation of Politics* (New York, 1974), 156; George, *English Political Caricature*, I, 79, 83, 100, 114.
44. Gordon, *Discourse*, in Thornton, ed., *Pulpit of the American Revolution*, 203.

as patronage and dependency spread would ultimately reduce all honest farmers to abject poverty.[45]

iv. Lordships

There were no systematic treatises on this social transformation. Elaborate explanations of the consequences of parliamentary taxation were not required. The writers of Revolutionary tracts assumed their audiences would understand. Great changes were compressed into a phrase or even a word like "enslavement." The publicists concentrated on vivid description and slashing hyperbole and yet consistently described in passage after passage the selfsame process of social degradation.

Occasionally words flashed in their writings that portended still more ominous changes, words like "tenantry" and "lordships," suggesting that in whig minds, impoverishment was not the end of enslavement. Samuel Adams was explicit about the loss of property. "If Parliament can take away Mr. Hancock's wharff and Mrs. Rowe's Wharf," he reasoned, "they can take away your Barn and my house."[46] If granted one tax, would not Britain send for more, "and rise in their demands the next time? and why not for all? And then for our real estates?"[47] That was the power inherent in taxation. Those who were "taxed at pleasure by others, cannot possibly have any property, can have nothing to be called their own," and "are indeed reduced to the most abject slavery."[48] Ultimately, these passages suggest, Americans would lack property altogether or at best be "Tenants of their real and personal Estates at the will of a Government infinitely beyond their reach and Controul."[49]

45. For a poetic picture of an impoverished village, see John Trumbull, "An Elegy on the Times," discussed in Leon Howard, *The Connecticut Wits* (Chicago, 1943), 68–89.

46. Cushing, ed., *Writings of Samuel Adams*, III, 288–289.

47. Joseph Emerson, *A Thanksgiving–Sermon Preach'd at Pepperrell, July 24th, 1776* (Boston, 1766), 13. See also *Boston Post-Boy and Advertiser*, Nov. 4, 1765, and Pelham to the Boston Committee of Correspondence, Nov. 16, 1773, Letters and Proceedings.

48. Hopkins, *Rights of the Colonies Examined*, in Jensen, ed., *Tracts of the American Revolution*, 54.

49. Quoted in George Athan Billias, *Elbridge Gerry: Founding Father and Republican Statesman* (New York, 1976), 27. See also Taylor, *Western Massachusetts in the Revolution*, 62. The *Craftsman* in 1731 said the party out of power was on the light end of the scale

In talking of property and tenantry, the whig publicists left behind distant ministries and the machinations of royal governors and brought the conflict into the everyday work lives of provincial farmers and tradesmen. At these points social circumstances and ideology converged. The meaning of the publicists' words can be understood only in light of the actual circumstances of the ordinary farmers who, along with their families, composed the bulk of the provincial population. In light of the strains in the rural economy, it can be seen that parliamentary taxes aroused long-standing rural fears, just as parliamentary taxes raised an old specter in the minds of the popular party.

The problem was that farmers lost control when they were forced to operate in the money economy where taxes were collected. Farmers were secure within their local exchange economy. They could always trade what they had, whether it was a pair of oxen to rent, some surplus pasturage, or their own labor, for whatever they needed, corn, hay, shoes, or wood. Within the elaborate exchange networks of town and neighborhood even farmers of limited means could garner a sparse but adequate living. The trouble came when they had to pay in money, for farmers could not always get money. Though they had surplus animals or corn to sell, the prices might have fallen or, even worse, money was not to be had. The province's shortage of currency, because of the unfavorable balance of trade with England, was a terrible burden for each individual farmer. When he had to pay a debt with money, he could not be assured of getting it, or he would have to pay exorbitant amounts of his grain or meat to obtain a few shillings in currency.[50]

Failure to pay could mean foreclosure, auction, and loss of one's land. That was why currency emissions were so critical to the province and why the governor could believe rumors of an uprising when Parliament closed down the land bank in 1741. When money was not

---

and continually losing weight, "so that in a certain process of time the losing party must dwindle to nothing, and that the prevailing party, by continuing in employments of profit, must become able to purchase all the lands in the Kingdom." Quoted in Isaac Kramnick, *Bolingbroke and His Circle: The Politics of Nostalgia in the Age of Walpole* (Cambridge, Mass., 1968), 122.

50. For the exchange economy within rural communities, see Richard L. Bushman, "Family Security in the Transition from Farm to City, 1750–1850," *Journal of Family History*, VI (1981), 239–243; Michael Merrill, "Cash Is Good to Eat: Self-Sufficiency and Exchange in the Rural Economy of the United States," *Radical History Review*, VII (1977), 42–71.

circulating, farmers were in trouble. Without access to currency, they were in danger of losing their land and ready to take desperate measures.

The problem was acute because most farmers were in debt; circumstances made it nearly unavoidable. The storekeeper was not the biggest worry. The book debts recorded in the storekeeper's account books could be paid in butter or corn just like the exchanges with a neighboring farmer. Major money debts more commonly arose out of land purchases, a much larger expenditure and, for most, a virtually inescapable involvement sometime in the course of life. Older sons who inherited the father's farm often had to pay the other heirs for their share or provide for the mother who received the widow's dower. Sons who lacked an adequate inheritance went in debt to get started on a farm. Fathers who wished to give their sons a good start tried to purchase extra land.[51] Indebtedness was integral to the rural life cycle as one generation attempted to assist the next to begin life, and as each new cohort of young people struggled to obtain farms for themselves. By the late provincial period, entanglement in debt worried an ever larger number of people. The number of litigants in debt cases in five rural counties between 1761 and 1765 equalled 22 percent of the total adult male population. In Berkshire County, it was 76 percent.[52] Oscar Handlin has observed that in Berkshire in the years 1774 through 1776, for some people "all problems of government revolved about the necessity for saving the land from creditors."[53]

The danger of losing land on the auction block was not new in the 1760s. It surfaced earlier as a major issue in rural life in the writings of the currency controversy that raged in Massachusetts from 1715 to 1750. Both advocates and opponents of currency emissions recognized the farmer's plight, and both saw that the social order could regress toward feudalism. The conservative Edward Wigglesworth opposed

---

51. On problems of passing land down the generations and of getting started, see Christopher M. Jedrey, *The World of John Cleaveland: Family and Community in Eighteenth-Century New England* (New York, 1979), 58–94; and more specifically on borrowing to buy farms, J. M. Bumsted, "Religion, Finance, and Democracy in Massachusetts: The Town of Norton as a Case Study," *JAH,* XVII (1970–1971), 825–826.

52. John M. Murrin, "Review Essay," *History and Theory,* XI (1972), 250–251.

53. Oscar Handlin and Mary Flug Handlin, *Commonwealth: A Study of the Role of Government in the American Economy: Massachusetts, 1774–1861,* rev. ed. (Cambridge, Mass., 1969), 18.

liberal emissions of currency because he thought that they encouraged farmers to go deeper into debt, with all that entailed. He wanted to curtail currency so "that the Estates should continue as at present in many mens hands," rather than "that a few Gentlemen should be Landlords, and all the rest of the Country become tenants."[54] A writer in favor of paper money argued differently, but saw the same result. He thought an "archy, Shy Set of Men" at one point had favored emissions and then after monopolizing the bills wanted to contract the currency. The shortage of money would bring debtors to their knees and precipitate the country's estates into the hands of the monopolizers.[55] "If such Men had their Wills, there should no common Man own a Canoe, Fishing Boat, Sloop," nor should "any Countryman own one Inch of improved Land between *Boston* and the *Blue Hills*." These financial conspirators sought "to deceive the People into Debt over Head and Ears, so *they have contrived a Scheme, to have no Money amongst Us*." Then "we must sell our Lands to pay them; then go and Work upon their Farms, or Starve, or go to Sea as their Slaves, or go to—Jail."[56] The currency advocates commonly saw in currency manipulations a design to reduce most people to tenants and laborers while a few became great lords. A 1720 pamphlet asked what did the "few *Muck-worms*, who have *monopoliz'd* vast Hoards of Bills" drive at so furiously but "to *engross* all the *Estates* in the Island; and themselves being *Lords*, the rest by consequence their *Slaves?*"[57] By the same token, the merchants' plan for a silver bank in the mid-1730s, because it implied a monopoly of currency, was thought to give them power to get lesser men in their debts and then build great estates.[58]

Taxes like the Stamp Act gave the same power to government as

54. [Edward Wigglesworth], *A Letter From One in the Country to his Friend in Boston* . . . (Boston, 1720), in Andrew McFarland Davis, ed., *Colonial Currency Reprints, 1682–1751* (Boston, 1910–1911), I, 439–441. There was no debate between advocates and opponents of currency emissions over the eventual outcome of agrarian indebtedness: farmers would lose their lands and become tenants to great landlords. The only question was whether generous currency emissions helped or not. Davis, ed., *Colonial Currency Reprints*, II, 325–326; III, 55, 446; IV, 57, 443.

55. *Ibid.*, II,17, 246; IV, 362.

56. *Massachusetts in Agony: or, Important Hints To the Inhabitants of the Province* . . . (Boston, 1750), in *ibid.*, IV, 438–439.

57. *New News from Robinson Cruso's Island* . . . (n.p., 1720), in *ibid.*, II, 132.

58. *The Melancholy State of this Province Considered, in a Letter, From a Gentleman in Boston to his Friend in the Country* ([Boston], 1736), in *ibid.*, III, 143.

creditors had over debtors. The lands of farmers who were unable to pay went on the auction block, and the fortunate few who acquired public office and enjoyed the profits could gain control. Those who imposed taxes were in the same position as the monopolists of money. The networks of parasitic officials were in line to become feudal lords, while all the rest were beggars. Parliamentary taxation thus aroused the same apprehensions as underlay the currency controversies before 1750.[59] Subsequently, those same fears played themselves out in Shays's Rebellion when farmers again lacked currency to pay their debts, in the Jacksonian controversy over the monster bank, and in the Populist demand for free silver coinage. From a rural viewpoint, the Revolutionary conflict was of a piece with the major agrarian conflicts which began in New England in the eighteenth century (and in England much earlier) and continued in the United States through the nineteenth century.

The whigs knowingly played upon these enduring tensions in rural life. Although never a major theme in whig writings, the danger of lordships' arising in America hovered in the background as the ultimate doom of an enslaved country. Daniel Leonard, the tory spokesman, who wrote under the title "Massachusettensis" in late 1774, said that, following the Boston Massacre, "lists of imaginary grievances were continually published; the people were told weekly that the ministry had formed a plan to enslave them; that the duty upon tea was only a prelude to a window tax, hearth tax, land tax, and poll tax; and these were only paving the way for reducing the country to lord-

59. On the strength and nature of the currency crisis of the 1740s, see J. M. Bumsted, "The Report of the Pembroke (Massachusetts) Town Committee on the Currency, March 24, 1740/41," *New England Quarterly*, XL (1967), 551–560; Robert Zemsky, *Merchants, Farmers, and River Gods: An Essay on Eighteenth-Century American Politics* (Boston, 1971), 114–122; and George A. Billias, *The Massachusetts Land Bankers of 1740*, University of Maine Studies, 2d Ser., No. 74 (Orono, Maine, 1959). On the threat of an uprising in 1741, Gov. Belcher to Thomas Hutchinson, May 11, 1741, *Belcher Papers*, (Mass. Hist. Soc., *Collections*, 6th Ser., VI–VII [Boston, 1893–1894]), Part II, 388. Reflecting back, John Adams said there was a greater uproar over the constriction of the currency in 1741 than over the Stamp Act. C. F. Adams, ed., *Works of John Adams*, IV, 49. See also Andrew McFarland Davis, "Threat to Burn Governor Shirley's House," Col. Soc. of Mass., *Publs.*, III (1900), 207–211. Thomas Hutchinson reported that a decade later the authors of the bill to exchange the Louisburg reimbursement of paper money were threatened, and the government had to pass an act against riots. Thomas Hutchinson, *The History of the Colony and Province of Massachusetts-Bay*, ed. Lawrence Shaw Mayo (Cambridge, Mass., 1936), II, 337.

ships."[60] By the last, Leonard meant that the whigs were saying, in the words of the easy currency advocate in 1736, that we "shall in a little Time have no middling Sort." "We shall have a few, and but a very few Lords, and all the rest Beggars."[61]

Two months later, in February 1775, John Adams replied to Leonard point by point in the *Novanglus* essays. Leonard meant to discredit the whigs by pointing out their bloated exaggerations of the ministry's intentions, but in this instance rather than deny the charge, Adams said it was all true. The ministry indeed designed to enslave the colonists, and one tax led to more, "paving the way for reducing the country to lordships." "Were the people mistaken in these suspicions?" Adams asked. "Is it not now certain that governor Bernard in 1764, had formed a design for this sort?"[62] Referring to Leonard's observation that the threat of lordships was a bait "the more easily swallowed, as there seems to be an apprehension of that kind hereditary to the people of New-England," Adams agreed that "it is true that the people of this country in general, and of this province in special, have an hereditary apprehension of and aversion to lordships, temporal and spiritual. Their ancestors fled to this wilderness to avoid them—they suffered sufficiently under them in England. And there are few of the present generation, who have not been warned of the danger of them by their fathers or grandfathers, and injoined to oppose them." Adams, who had grown in up Braintree, studied in Worcester, and ridden circuit court to various country towns in Massachusetts, sensed in the minds of New Englanders a picture of a social order based on lordships that was the end result of political tyranny and oppression.[63]

60. J. Adams and [Leonard], *Novanglus, And Massachusettensis*, 150.

61. *The Melancholy State Of This Province*, in Davis, ed., *Colonial Currency Reprints*, III, 143.

62. J. Adams and [Leonard], *Novanglus, And Massachusettensis*, 42. For the basis of Adams's accusation, see Governor [Francis] Bernard, *Select Letters on the Trade and Government of America; and the Principles of Law and Polity, Applied to the American Colonies* (London, 1774), 83.

63. J. Adams and [Leonard], *Novanglus, And Massachusettensis*, 42–43, 150. An unpublished drama written in 1732 at the time of the salary controversy foresaw a similar outcome of salary payments to the governor. A character in the play congratulated the town of Boston for not complying with the instruction for a permanent salary. "Your utter ruin would have been the Consequence, for Consider my friends, the King sais We must pay £1000 a year to the Governour, next year he may say £2000, and so on, till at last We Shall be forced to sell our Estates to Support the Price and Arrogance of a Governour, and Send our Children beyond Sea, to begg their Bread." "A Play," Boston, 1732, MS, 11–12, Mass. Hist. Soc., Boston.

It made no difference that lordships were rare in New England and had never seriously threatened small farmers. In Concord, and probably most other country towns, 80 percent of the taxpayers owned land.[64] The English author of *American Husbandry*, writing on the eve of Revolution, marveled at the prevalence of "little freeholders who live upon their own property, and make much the most considerable part of the whole province." The important thing was that the farmers understood that freeholds were not secure. They could be gobbled up. In England, *American Husbandry* went on, "the great, when grown wealthy as well as powerful, have purchased such little freeholds as joined their estates, and thereby exterminated one of the most useful sets of men." Beyond that, "taxes, tythes, rates, and repairs, with the increase expences of living, have almost driven [small farmers] from the face of the earth."[65] After two and a half centuries of increasing concentration of ownership, landlords owned three-quarters of English land; freehold farmers worked only 15 to 20 percent. The number of small freeholders was constantly diminishing, pressed to the wall primarily by high taxes and debt.[66] Touring Ireland and Scotland in 1772, Benjamin Franklin noted "Landlords, great Noblemen, and Gentlemen, extramly opulent, living in the highest Affluence and Magnificence," and alongside them "the Bulk of the people Tenants, extramly poor, living in the most sordid Wretchedness, in dirty Hovels of Mud and Straw, and cloathed only in Rags." His thoughts turned to "the Happiness of New England, where every Man is a Freeholder, has a Vote in publick affairs, lives in a tidy, warm House, has plenty of good Food and fewel, with whole cloaths from Head to Foot, the Manufacture perhaps of his own Family."[67] The contrast favored America, but the New England farmer's exceptional privileges were unsettling rather than comforting. At the forefront of liberty, he was also exposed

64. Bettye Hobbs Pruitt, ed., *The Massachusetts Tax Valuation List of 1771* (Boston, 1978), 194–200. But for the strains in managing the land, see Robert A. Gross, *The Minutemen and Their World* (New York, 1976).

65. Harry J. Carman, ed., *American Husbandry*, Columbia University Studies in the History of Agriculture (New York, 1939 [orig. publ. anon., London, 1775]), 49–50.

66. G. E. Mingay, *English Landed Society in the Eighteenth Century* (London, 1963), 19, 24; H. J. Habakkuk, "English Land Ownership, 1680–1740," *Economic History Review*, X (1940), 2–17.

67. Albert Henry Smyth, ed., *The Writings of Benjamin Franklin* (Boston, 1850–1856), V, 362.

and vulnerable, in danger of being reduced to the normal condition of agricultural life in the empire—tenantry and lordships.

Some Americans were aware of Ireland's condition, where two-thirds of the land was owned by absentee landlords and offices in the Irish establishment sustained a horde of English placemen. Jonathan Swift's 1727 description of Ireland could have served as a perfect picture of the slavery Americans were fighting to prevent.

> One-third of the rents of Ireland is spent in England, which, with the profits of employments, pensions, appeals . . . and other incidents, will amount to a full half of the income of the whole kingdom, all clear profit to England. . . . The rise of our rents, is squeezed out of the very blood, and vitals, and clothes, and dwellings of the tenants, who live worse than English beggars. . . . The miserable dress and diet . . . of the people; the general desolation in most parts of the kingdom; the old seats of the gentry and nobility all in ruins, and no new ones in their stead; the families of farmers, who pay great rents, living in filth and nastiness without . . . a house so convenient as a hog-sty to receive them.[68]

The Scotch-Irish immigrants in Pelham and Colrain, Massachusetts, recognized the British designs on America as a repetition of what they had seen at home.

> It plainly appears to us that it is the design of this present administration to serve us as they have our brethren in Ireland first to raise a revenue from us sufficient to support a standing army as well as place men and pentioners and then laugh at our Calamities and glut themselves on our spoil (many of us in this town being eye witnesses of those crewel and remorseless enemies).[69]

The life of small farmers in Ireland and England was proof enough that enslavement could actually occur, that taxes and patronage could reduce farmers to tenants and day laborers, and that the cost of supporting a standing army and networks of dependent placemen was ul-

---

68. Quoted in Giovanni Costigan, *A History of Modern Ireland, With a Sketch of Earlier Times* (New York, 1969), 103.
69. Colrain to the Boston Committee of Correspondence, Jan. 31, 1774, Letters and Proceedings. On the contrast of Ireland and Massachusetts, also see John Phillip Reid, *"In a Defiant Stance: The Conditions of Law in Massachusetts Bay, the Irish Comparison, and the Coming of the American Revolution* (University Park, Penn., 1977), 12–15.

timately degradation to tenantry under a vulgar American version of what E. P. Thompson has called "patrician banditti."[70]

The Boston committee warned the towns that, should the ministry succeed, "which God forbid, slavery would be the consequence, this good land would be divided into lordships, and instead of being masters, we would be servants to as an abandoned set of men as ever the earth produced."[71] The ultimate humiliation resulting from parliamentary taxation was laid out again for the towns in the committee's statement of rights issued in 1772: "If the breath of a British house of commons can originate an act for taking away all our money, our lands will go next or be subject to rack rents from haughty and relentless landlords who will ride at ease, while we are trodden in the dirt."[72] Property in the famous slogan of the Revolution, "Liberty and Property," seems to have meant, besides cash money, the land the colonists farmed, the houses they lived in, and their way of life as independent freeholders.[73]

v. Servility and Virtue

The opposition to taxes thus was far from an abstract principle of political right. Judging from pamphlets, newspaper essays, private correspondence, and statements approved in town meetings by common

70. E. P. Thompson, "Patrician Society, Plebeian Culture," *Journal of Social History*, VII (1974), 382–405. For John Dickinson's awareness of the Irish parallel, see *Letters from a Farmer in Pennsylvania*, 49–57. W.E.H. Lecky believed that Americans were conscious of Ireland with its "hereditary revenue, the scandalous pension list, the monstrous abuses of patronage" and were "resolved not to suffer similar abuses in America." Quoted in Bailyn, *Ordeal of Thomas Hutchinson*, 392.

71. Westborough echoed the fear: "Should they succeed in this arrogant this execrable Design, the Land holder must look upon himself to be a Tenant at Will, and may be ejected from his Freehold, whenever his british masters shall think proper." Quoted in Davidson, *Propaganda and the American Revolution*, 119.

72. *The Votes and Proceedings of the Freeholders and other Inhabitants of the Town of Boston, In Town Meeting assembled . . .* (Boston, 1772), in Jensen, ed., *Tracts of the American Revolution*, 241.

73. In the midst of war in 1778, a New Englander complained of poor men's paying more taxes than the rich, because the poor might be forced to sell their property and become "tenants of their rich neighbors," and thereby "one main part of that slavery against which the present war was profesedly undertaken" would be established in New England. *Connecticut Journal* (New Haven), May 6, 1778. See also the sermon by

farmers all over the province, the people of Massachusetts Bay believed they were opposing the creation in America of elaborate networks of dependents, whether in church, state, army, or on the land, dependencies that were the essence of social relationships in Britain. The colonists believed chains of political patrons and their ravenous clients would impoverish honest and industrious farmers and ultimately deprive them of their farms. Some sensed that the engine of oppression fueled by parliamentary taxation could turn New England back toward a feudal order, to use John Adams's word, and degrade independent farmers to the status of tenants, laborers, and paupers. They fought to maintain the independence and freedom that had always distinguished life in the New World from the oppression and dependence of the Old, when British policies seemed about to create a monarchical society in America, consistent with monarchical government.

Beyond the deterioration of the social order, many observers foresaw the degeneration of personality. Tyrants not only treated their subjects abominably but had the power to reduce them to despicable weakness. "Deprived of liberty, oppressed, and enslaved," a Plymouth clergyman warned his congregation, "men not only sink below the primitive standard of humanity . . . they become stupid, and debased in spirit, indolent and groveling, indifferent to all valuable improvement, and hardly capable of any."[74] They grew inured to their bondage, insensitive to the abuses heaped upon them, and even honored the tyrants who kept them in chains. Samuel Adams feared that the people of Massachusetts might become "so accustomed to bondage, as to forget they were ever free."[75] "The Sweeds were once a free, martial and valient people," he wrote in the Boston committee's letter to the towns. "Their minds are now so debaced, that they rejoice at being subject to the caprice and arbitrary power of a Tyrant and kiss their Chains."[76]

George Duffield, *Declaration of Peace* . . . (Philadelphia, 1783), in Frank Moore, ed., *The Patriot Preachers of the American Revolution* (New York, 1862), 358–359. For a somewhat fuller explication of the lordship theme, see Richard L. Bushman, "Massachusetts Farmers and the Revolution," in Richard M. Jellison, ed., *Society, Freedom, and Conscience: The American Revolution in Virginia, Massachusetts, and New York* (New York, 1976), 77–124.

74. Gad Hitchcock, *A Sermon Preached at Plymouth* . . . (Boston, 1775), 17.

75. Samuel Adams to Arthur Lee, July 31, 1771, in Cushing, ed., *Writings of Samuel Adams*, II, 190.

76. *Votes and Proceedings of the Freeholders*, in Jensen, ed., *Tracts of the American Revolution*, 254–255.

Whig writings proceeded on the assumption that the people had to be aroused. They showed a fatal somnolence, as if tempted to yield to power and give themselves up to the will of the despot. There were, of course, always those who lusted for the profits of office and willingly sacrificed their country for their own gain. "These vermin crawl forth in every department and condition of life." Even some of "the most profligate among the poorer sort were dazzled with the ideas of distinction" and turned informers for a price.[77] But beyond those self-interested motives, John Adams detected in 1769 timidity, indolence, and undue respect that turned too readily into "infamous tameness and submission," as if tyranny were already sucking them under.[78] The easy course, the way of weakness, was to yield to might and splendor. Against that effeminate passivity, the whig writers set their wills and issued what Westborough called "a loud Call to Every one to awake from Security and in Earnest Strive to Secure his Liberty, least he Politically perish."[79]

The repeated rehearsals of colonial rights were meant to enlighten and thus to enliven a people whose energy was being sapped by despotism. Barring popular knowledge of the constitution, the designing ministry could lay one indignity after another on the province. People would enter into a descending spiral of degradation. The secret of American liberty, the town of Westborough noted in 1773, was that "the knowledge of the true Spirit of our Constitution" had "spread even to the remotest parts of the Province." This fact "must astonish those who represented us as ignorant as savages." Otherwise, Westborough went on, the province might be "imposed upon in what manner they pleased without the least opposition or complaint."[80] Limp and lifeless, an ignorant people lacked the spirit and sense to react when trod upon.

The essayists ultimately were testing the virtue of the people, and the proof of virtue was willingness to resist. Trespasses on liberty filled a man of virtue with indignation, while the slave cowered in fear. "There cannot be a greater affliction to a man of sentiment," a minister insisted in 1771, "than the insult of such despicable creatures" as the

77. *Ministerial Catechise*, 177.
78. C. F. Adams, ed., *Works of John Adams*, III (1851), 460.
79. Westborough to the Boston Committee of Correspondence, Jan. 4, 1773, Letters and Proceedings.
80. *Ibid.*, Jan. 19, 1773.

ministry put in office. "They, who are willing to be made slaves and to lose their rights, as Issachar, without one struggle, justly deserve all the miseries and insults an imperious despot can put upon them. They richly deserve to be trampled on by the whole chain of wretches, and instruments of the minister, from the grand tool the *pensioner*, to the dirty office of *informer*."[81] No matter if the resistance were in vain. "It is noble to struggle for freedom, and should power and oppression prove superior, the attempt was laudable, and we fall like men." When the citizens of Boston rioted against the stamp men, it was celebrated "as the happy Day, on which Liberty arose from a long Slumber."[82] Resistance was "the first, and highest social Duty of this People," and therefore God and Nature warranted "the use of every rightful art, and energy of policy, stratagem And force."[83] Proper indignation was a sign of character and spirit.

Underlying the declarations of all who argued for resistance was the choice of becoming slaves in spirit (as they became serfs on the land) or of standing like men. "Now brethren," the Boston committee wrote in November 1773, "we are reduced to this dilemma, either to sit down quiet under this and every other burthen that our Enemies shall see fit to lay upon us, as good natured Slaves, or rise and resist this and every plan laid for our destruction as becomes wise freemen."[84] By choosing resistance, whether or not the province's endeavors succeeded, "posterity might know that we understood our Rights and Liberties and were neither afraid nor ashamed to assert and maintain them." Then in themselves they could "have (at least) this Consolation in our Chains that it was not through our neglect that this People were enslaved."[85] They had refused "patiently to take the Yoke upon our Necks," but stood as men and freemen.[86]

In using words like those, whig writers touched their listeners at many levels. The claims on behalf of colonial rights appealed ra-

---

81. *Ministerial Catechise*, 8. See also *Bost.-Gaz.*, Feb. 16, 1761.
82. Cushing, ed., *Writings of Samuel Adams*, II, 201.
83. Petersham to Boston Committee of Correspondence, Jan. 4, 1776, Letters and Proceedings.
84. Circular Letter, Nov. 23, 1773, Boston Committee of Correspondence, Minute Book, VI, 457.
85. Stoughton Protestors, Mar. 31, 1773, *ibid.*, III, 239.
86. Billerica to Boston Committee of Correspondence, June 6, 1774, Letters and Proceedings.

tionally to the Americans' sense of justice; it seemed only fair that American colonists should enjoy political privileges equal to every Englishman's. At a deeper level, the strength of Revolutionary writing came from the sense of danger to their lands and houses, and beyond that to their integrity and dignity as human beings. Here the whigs did not have to invent phantasms to stir their audiences, but played on apprehensions that had long disturbed provincials, fears of avaracious and conspiring royal officials, of impoverishment and foreclosure, and of personal debasement. Channeled by whig rhetoric, the most troubling anxieties of provincial political and economic life flowed into the Revolutionary conflict.

The sequence of events after 1765, particularly the Massachusetts Government Act, made these dangers real and imminent. By 1775 some form of relief had to be found. Until that year the province had avoided dark thoughts about its king, but then George III put himself into the center of controversy. It was obvious by 1774 that the king was unable to protect the colonies from depredation, but in 1775 his actions made it clear that he was chief among the people's enemies. The king and the people at last faced one another as antagonists instead of partners in government as they had long been.

CHAPTER 6

Independence

The Massachusetts Government Act brought the province to the verge of revolution by the fall of 1774. That act, added to all the others, so undermined the legitimacy of royal government that large segments of the population simply denied the authority of the king's officers. People believed that the ministry's measures so endangered liberty and property that rulers could not be obeyed. Parliamentary taxation enabled avaricious officials to bleed the province of its wealth, and salary payments from the royal treasury cut off an important link to the people. Under the Massachusetts Government Act, direct appointment of councillors, sheriffs, and justices of the peace, without the advice and consent of the people's representatives, severed the remaining ties of common interest. All the bonds between rulers and people were broken. With all the barriers down, the colonists foresaw great chains of dependent placemen extorting wealth from the province and living in idleness and luxury on their ill-gotten gains. In time rulers would take over the people's property, and in the end a debased feudal order of servile tenants and haughty landlords would threaten Massachusetts' society of independent farmers.[1] The people had to stop tyranny from taking its destructive course.

1. It did not require a revolutionary frame of mind to see the dangers in the Massachusetts Government Act. The lords who protested its passage in the House of Lords

As the province struggled against oppression, the necessity of forming a republican government became increasingly evident. The answer to both the immediate crisis and the constitutional controversies of the entire provincial period was to make rulers dependent on the people, not for salaries alone but also for appointments. No one had set out to overthrow the king, but the election of officials was now seen to be imperative, and that implied the end of monarchy. The king's presence in the government, while always honored, was seen to be the source of the province's difficulties. Royal appointments created the networks of officials who ostensibly came to execute imperial policy, but actually, it was believed, used their power for personal gain. To establish a republic with all authority in one moral center, the people—rather than in two, king and people—would prevent the networks from forming. Ultimately the best way to control rulers should be to make them dependent on the people alone.

The proper course was obvious to Samuel Adams and others by the fall of 1774, but monarchy was not so easily dispatched. In the final months of the Revolutionary crisis, the person and authority of the king, a remote presence for most of the provincial period, came to the fore. Monarchical loyalties and habits ran deep. The province, for all its discontent, was uncertain of the legitimacy of government without a king and delayed for two years before taking full authority to itself. Before Massachusetts could declare its independence and form a republic, the imposing moral authority of the monarch had to be encountered and overcome.

i. The Last Days of the King

As a practical matter, Massachusetts became a republic in September 1774. On September 1, General Thomas Gage, who had replaced Thomas Hutchinson as governor the previous June, issued writs for an

---

commented that the Massachusetts governor and Council had powers greater than the English Privy Council. They "have the means of returning such a jury in each particular cause, as may best suit with the gratification of their passions and interests, so that the lives and properties of the subject are put into their hands without control." Quoted in William Gordon, *The History of the Rise, Progress, and Establishment, of the Independence of the United States of America* . . . (London, 1788), I, 356.

election of the General Court to sit at Salem on October 5. As turmoil spread, he reversed himself on September 28 and declared it inexpedient for the assembly to convene. Elections occurred anyway, and ninety representatives assembled in Salem, waited three days for the governor to appear, and then organized themselves into a convention and determined to form a Provincial Congress. Unrepresented towns were invited to elect delegates, and the Congress met at Cambridge on October 17, 1774.[2] With the assembling of the Provincial Congress, royal government was at an end. From September 1774 on, no courts sat under royal commission. The governor was never again to call a legislature into session. The Provincial Congress ordered towns to pay taxes, not to Harrison Gray, the royal appointee, but to the Congress's own receiver general. Gage's military authority was restricted to Boston. Elsewhere town militias under popularly elected or long-standing officers drilled on the town greens and assembled supplies.[3] The Provincial Congress took upon itself virtually all the functions of government.

And yet Massachusetts was not independent. The Provincial Congress was not a legislature, and royal government still hung by a single thread: loyalty to the king, or, more accurately, loyalty to the idea of a king. The county conventions of 1774 inserted into their resolves the habitual pledges of allegiance to the monarch, and an occasional sermon appealed to "the mildness, tenderness, and affection of our sovereign."[4] But these were perfunctory or desperate. The large body of vocal citizens had lost confidence that the king would rescue Massachusetts from its plight. The province was bound to the monarch not by affection, but by a principle: the belief that a true legislature was a meeting of king and people.

The English constitution rested on the idea that only in the agree-

2. Before convening in Cambridge, the Congress met briefly in Concord.
3. For an analysis of the political issues in the Congress, see Stephen E. Patterson, *Political Parties in Revolutionary Massachusetts* (Madison, Wis., 1973), 110–117; and Merrill Jensen, *The Founding of a Nation: A History of the American Revolution, 1763–1776* (New York, 1968), 557–567. For a detailed description of the Provincial Congress at work, see L. Kinvin Wroth *et al.*, eds., *Province in Rebellion: A Documentary History of the Founding of the Commonwealth of Massachusetts, 1774–1775* (Cambridge, Mass., 1975), 31–145.
4. Peter Whitney, *The Transgressions of a Land punished by a Multitude of Rulers . . .* (Boston, 1774), 46. On the caution of the county conventions, see Patterson, *Political Parties*, 97; Richard D. Brown, *Revolutionary Politics in Massachusetts: The Boston Committee of Correspondence and the Towns, 1772–1774* (Cambridge, Mass., 1970), 215.

ment of monarch and subjects could laws be made. The people had assembled in the provincial congresses, acting through elected representatives, but the king's delegate, the governor, was missing. His absence prevented the Provincial Congress from making laws which could be enforced in the courts. For nine months they collected taxes, managed nonimportation, raised military forces, and after April 19, 1775, conducted a war without the power to legislate. The advocates of a return to the 1629 charter implicitly sought to eliminate the king from the legislature, for in seventeenth-century Massachusetts the governor was elected, not appointed, and had no veto over legislation. But these radicals lacked the strength to carry the day, and the Provincial Congress limped along through the winter and spring of 1775 without a legislature and hence without laws, and for the most part without courts. For nine months the Congress waited on the king to appear in the form of a trustworthy governor.

The three Provincial Congresses that met from October 1774 to July 1775 took their precedent from the English convention Parliament which met after James II took flight in 1688 and which asked William and Mary to assume the throne. An assemblage of representatives of the people could, as the Provincial Congress declared, "collect the wisdom of the province . . . to concert some adequate remedy for preventing impending ruin, and providing for the public safety."[5] A convention, or congress, collected the wisdom of the people, but it could not enact laws. It could do only as the Stamp Act Congress and the Continental Congress had done, pass resolves expressing the will of the people. Taxes, military orders, and price stabilization took the form of congressional resolves or orders, with the force of public opinion behind them, but not the force of law. Trespassers upon the orders of the Congress could be harassed and humiliated, but they could not be arrested, tried, and punished by established legal procedures in a court of law.[6]

It was tenuous government at best. The county conventions repeatedly congratulated themselves on the good order in society in the

5. William Lincoln, ed., *The Journals of Each Provincial Congress of Massachusetts in 1774 and 1775* (Boston, 1838), 17.
6. On congresses and conventions, see Gordon S. Wood, *The Creation of the American Republic, 1776–1787* (Chapel Hill, N.C., 1969), 306–328; Oscar Handlin and Mary F. Handlin, eds., *The Popular Sources of Political Authority: Documents on the Massachusetts Constitution of 1780* (Cambridge, Mass., 1966), 4–5.

absence of formal government, with only patriotism and public virtue restraining the people.[7] Writing much later, Mercy Otis Warren remembered these months as a time when Massachusettts was "reduced nearly to a state of nature" "without any legal government, without law, and without any regular administration of justice, but what arose from the internal sense of moral obligation." She marveled that "the principles of rectitude and common justice should have been so generally influential."[8] The proclamation of the Provincial Congress in January 1776 noted proudly that "mankind has seen a Phenomenon without Example in the political World, a large and populous Colony, Subsisting, in great Decency and order, for more than a year, under such a Suspension of Government."[9]

At the time, the Congress itself was less sanguine. In November 1774 Joseph Warren foresaw the difficulties, and wrote Josiah Quincy, Jr., that "it will require a very masterly policy to keep this province, for any considerable time longer, in its present state."[10] In March, when some towns failed to pay taxes, the Provincial Congress could only plead for cooperation. By April 1, 1775, the Congress was ready to reinstate the king's representative, the governor, and once again become a legislature despite its suspicions and the governor's hostility. With the traditional time for annual elections approaching, the Provincial Congress advised the towns to respect a writ for elections from the governor and choose representatives with the sole proviso that, when organized as a house, they transact no business with the infamous mandamus councillors.[11] Presumably the governor would take his place once more, and laws could be passed.

The skirmishes with British troops at Lexington and Concord on April 19 foreclosed any possibility of cooperation with Governor Gage, and the Congress revoked its suggestion in May. At the same time, the need for the authority of a legislature increased dramatically. The as-

7. Harry A. Cushing, *History of the Transition from Provincial to Commonwealth Government in Massachusetts*, Columbia University Studies in History, Economics and Public Law, VII, No. 1 (New York, 1896), 90–92.

8. Mercy Warren, *History of the Rise, Progress and Termination of the American Revolution* (Boston, 1805), I, 226–227.

9. Handlin and Handlin, eds., *Popular Sources*, 66.

10. Quoted in Richard Frothingham, *Life and Times of Joseph Warren* (Boston, 1865), 395.

11. Lincoln, ed., *Journals of Each Provincial Congress*, 116.

sembling of town militia units in Cambridge following the April 19 battle placed unbearable strains on public order. In May, Joseph Warren in desperation wrote Samuel Adams at the Continental Congress of "the necessity of establishing civil government here." "I assure you *inter nos,* that, unless some authority sufficient to restrain the irregularities of this army is established, we shall very soon find ourselves involved in greater difficulties than you can well imagine. The least hint from the most unprincipled fellow, who has perhaps been reproved for some criminal behavior, is quite sufficient to expose the fairest character to insult and abuse among many."[12] Respect, deference, even property lay exposed to the caprice of unprincipled fellows. The delegation laid Massachusetts' case before the Continental Congress, and in June the Congress authorized the Provincial Congress to organize as a government.

The Continental Congress recommended a plan for effecting government much like one proposed by Samuel Adams the previous fall. Under the provisions of the 1691 charter, in the absence of the governor and lieutenant governor, the Council assumed executive functions. The provision enabled government to continue in case of the untoward death or illness of the governor. Adams proposed to use the clause for another purpose. He suggested that the councillors elected in May 1774, before the Massachusetts Government Act called for the appointment of mandamus councillors, be invited back to function as a Council, with the Provincial Congress as House, thus constituting two houses of the legislature. Knowing that the governor and lieutenant governor would never countenance such a body, those two officials could be declared absent and the Council take over the executive's role, including approval of laws.[13]

The failure of the councillors to cooperate defeated Adams's plan in the fall of 1774, but in June 1775 the Continental Congress recommended a variation of his proposal. The Provincial Congress was to issue writs for an election of representatives (illegal, but justified under the circumstances), and this body was to elect a Council which was to sit without confirmation from the governor. When the governor refused to appear, his chair was to be declared vacant, and the Council was to take over as executive (a legal step under the charter). No Brit-

12. Frothingham, *Life and Times of Joseph Warren,* 495.
13. Cushing, *History of the Transition,* 165–166.

ish court would sustain these actions, but they maintained the forms of legitimate government to satisfy the colonists' own desire for constitutional propriety.[14]

On July 19, 1775, the new House of Representatives met, elected a Council, declared the governor's seat vacant, and henceforth assumed the powers of civil government, including the right to legislate. To prop up government as best it could, the new Council and House on August 23 retroactively transformed the enactments of the Provincial Congress into near law and required that they be recognized in court. Whereas the colony had been for many months deprived of "its usual powers of government," the act began, "which has necessarily occasioned the publick business thereof to be conducted by congresses," the standing of its actions was indeterminate in the courts. "The legality of such resolves, doings and transactions may hereafter be called in question, and may occasion much litigation, unless confirmed and established in some known constitutional manner." Therefore, the House and Council enacted that the "resolves, doings and transactions of the several provincial congresses of this colony," from October 4, 1774, to July 20, 1775, "are confirmed and established as lawful and valid to all intents, constructions and purposes whatsoever, as fully and effectually as if the same resolves, doings and transactions had been done by any general court or assembly of this colony."[15] Belatedly the Provincial Congresses were vested with a semblance of the legislative authority they had lacked after the demise of royal government.

And yet, having gone so far, Massachusetts had still not snapped the thread binding it to the king. However twisted and abridged, the royal charter still directed provincial government. The legitimacy of the new House and Council rested on the fiction that they waited for the king to appoint a governor who would rule them by the charter. The government organized in 1775 recognized that it was a temporary expedient, awaiting the restoration of normal royal rule. The king of this fiction, devoted to his people's rights and well-being, would at last recognize the lies of his ministers, repudiate the infamous Massachusetts Government Act, send them a faithful governor, and restore the privileges of the people.

Few if any in Massachusetts in 1775 believed the fiction. Royal

14. *Ibid.*, 169–172.
15. In Handlin and Handlin, *Popular Sources*, 57–58.

troops had attacked the colonists again in June in Charlestown at the battle of Bunker Hill. General Washington had taken command of the Continental armies in Cambridge and laid Boston under siege. Redemption and reconciliation seemed out of the question. And yet ingrained loyalties and the ancient principles of king and people required that the fiction of an absent royalty be maintained a few months longer until the king should present himself undeniably as traitor and enemy to his people. Only then could Independence be declared a moral reality, as it had long been a political and military fact, and a permanent government put in place.

ii. The End of Monarchy

Massachusetts clung to these last vestiges of royal government while fighting a war with the king's troops. But the king gave no sign of sympathy for American suffering. The destruction of the tea in Boston harbor enraged George III. He meant every word of his message to Parliament on March 7, 1774, which referred to the "outrageous proceedings at Boston," and called for powers to stop disorders. He gladly signed the Massachusetts Government Act and, when it met resistance, urged Gage to use force against the provincial militia. The pretense that the monarch would rescue his people from their oppressors and restore charter government was the flimsiest of the fictions underlying Massachusetts civil government in the summer of 1775. In point of fact, the king was as responsible for the colony's sorrows in 1775 as were the ministry and Parliament.

The last vestige of loyalty survived a year and a half of outright warfare because of the ancient wall protecting the good name of the king.[16] His fortress was the fundamental axiom of monarchical culture that the king could do no wrong, with its corollary that all evil was the fault of his ministers. Since the monarchical state was founded on the principle of the king's benevolence, criticism had to be deflected to ministers and advisers. They took the blame for ill-conceived or op-

16. William Liddle has found that Americans as a whole kept up their confidence in the king until late in 1775. "'A Patriot King, or None': Lord Bolingbroke and the American Renunciation of George III," *Journal of American History*, LXV (1978–1979), 951–970.

pressive measures. They were thought to prevent the king from hearing of his people's sufferings and to control his ear and judgment. Words from the king's mouth were construed as put there by evil advisers.[17] Even in 1776, Abigail Adams spoke of "Ministerial troops" in Boston, avoiding direct implication of the king.[18] Such circumlocutions sustained the various fictions about royal benevolence through 1775 and early 1776.

The king's own actions stretched this regard for the proprieties to the limit in the summer and fall of 1775.[19] George III fully believed in the right of Parliament to tax the colonies. If anything, he was in advance of his advisers in advocating force to suppress resistance. He selected from American reports those facts that justified repression, and showed impatience with any attempts to plead the colonial cause. In April 1775 he at first refused to hear a petition from the City of London begging for a change in the ministry's American policy and, when persuaded at last to listen, received the petition coldly. After the news of Concord and Lexington reached England, the king opened negotiations with Russia and the German states for mercenaries. With the Bedford faction he brought around the Privy Council in August 1775 to favor a proclamation declaring the colonies in open rebellion. It announced that all subjects were "bound by law to be aiding and assisting in the suppression of such rebellion."[20] Ten days before the proclamation was issued, Richard Penn arrived with a petition from the Continental Congress, once again affirming colonial loyalty and praying for royal intervention in their favor. The king refused a hearing until a

17. In the early 1770s, this traditional construction of royal acts was denied occasionally in the colonies and more commonly in England. Pauline Maier, *From Resistance to Revolution: Colonial Radicals and the Development of American Opposition to Britain, 1765–1776* (New York, 1972), 208–209.

18. Abigail Adams to John Adams, Mar. 16, 1776 in L. H. Butterfield *et al.*, eds., *Adams Family Correspondence* (Cambridge, Mass., 1963), I, 357. The attribution of the troops to the ministry was common. Liddle, "'Patriot King, or None,'" *JAH*, LXV (1978–1979), 965.

19. In the account that follows I rely on Jerrilyn Greene Marston, "King and Congress: The Transfer of Political Legitimacy from the King to the Continental Congress, 1774–1776" (Ph.D. diss., Boston University, 1974), 109–185. See also Richard Frothingham, *The Rise of the Republic of the United States* (Boston, 1881), 403–455.

20. Peter Force, ed., *American Archives: Consisting of a Collection of Authentick Records . . . Forming a Documentary History of the Origin and Progress of the North American Colonies; of the Causes and Accomplishment of the American Revolution . . .* (Washington, D.C., 1837–1853), 4th Ser., II, 240–241.

week after the proclamation of rebellion, and then refused to receive the petition on the throne.

Through the fall of 1775, George III single-mindedly pursued his policy of suppression. On October 26, 1775, at the opening of Parliament, he reported that the Americans "now openly avow their revolt, hostility and rebellion." "It is now become the part of wisdom . . . to put a speedy end to these disorders by the most decisive exertions."[21] On December 22, 1775, he signed into law the American Prohibition Act, forbidding all commerce with the American colonies. The act contained directions for distributing prizes taken during the rebellion. His proclamation declared all ships trading with the colonies forfeit to the king "as if the same were the ships and effects of open enemies."[22] The protestations of loyalty from America were dismissed as "vague expressions" meant "only to amuse."[23] In word and deed the king put the colonies outside of his protection and turned on them as his enemies.

News of the king's words filtered across the Atlantic in the fall and winter of 1775–1776. In early November the colonists heard of the August 23 proclamation. "We find by a Vessell from Cork," John Pitts wrote to Samuel Adams, "a Proclamation from that stupid ———— Wretch of K——g declaring us all Rebels."[24] James Warren wrote his friend John Adams with Mercy Warren sitting at the table. Mercy insisted on the inclusion of a paragraph of hers telling Adams the Congress "should no longer piddle at the threshold. It is time to leap into the theatre, to unlock the bars, and open every gate that impedes the rise and growth of the American republic."

> At leisure then May G——ge his reign review,
> And bid to empire and to crown adieu.[25]

Writing to George Wythe in January 1776, John Adams himself drew the conclusion that "by an act of Parliament, we are put out of the

---

21. *The Parliamentary History of England, from the Earliest Period to the Year 1803* (London, 1806–1820), XVIII, 695–696.
22. Force, ed., *American Archives*, 4th Ser., IV, 377. See also Jensen, *Founding of a Nation*, 649–650.
23. *Parliamentary History*, XVIII, 695–696.
24. Pitts to Adams, Nov. 12, 1775, quoted in Marston, "King and Congress," 176.
25. James Warren to Adams, Nov. 15, 1775, in [Worthington Chauncey Ford], ed., *Warren-Adams Letters: Being Chiefly a Correspondence among John Adams, Samuel Adams, and James Warren*, I ([Boston]), 1917, 184.

royal protection, and consequently discharged from our allegience."[26]
In his history written a few years after the Revolution, David Ramsay
marked the early months of 1776 as the time when the idea of Independence spread. The Prohibitory Act "proved that the colonists might
constitutionally declare themselves independent," and then "the hiring
of foreign troops to make war upon them, demonstrated the necessity
of their doing it immediately."[27]

On January 1, 1776, John Cleaveland, pastor in Ipswich writing as
"Johannes in Eremo," asked the Massachusetts public to attend to two
fundamental questions: "In what sense it must be taken, that the King
can do no wrong?" And the concomitant, "Whether, all things considered, it is not the indispensable duty of the *United Colonies* of *America*,
immediately, to form themselves into an independent Constitution, or
a Republick State?"[28] Two years earlier a radical voice in the *Boston
Gazette* had asked how a "prince, sworn to maintain the laws and constitution of his Empire, can connive at such villainy, without abolish-
ing his title to the crown."[29] But Cleaveland did more than snipe. He
dissected the logic of the established maxims. In defense of the king, he
pointed out, it has been said: "That the King does nothing, as King,
but by his Ministers, and, therefore, whatever wrong is done by the
Administration of the King, must be attributed to his Ministers, not to
him. But, according to this, what does the King do, as King? Why,
nothing, neither right nor wrong. And what is the King, but an absolute nothing?" Cleaveland dismissed this absurdity; obviously, some
acts were acts of the king, among them the royal charters which "contain the sacred compact between the King and them, by virtue of which
he is their King, and they his subjects; and, also, the King's oath to
protect them in the enjoyment of all the rights and privileges of *Englishmen*, and their oath of allegiance to obey him as King." If these are
acts of the king, why are not other acts his also? It is a commonplace
that "Kings do something, and what they do, they do by their Minis-

26. Charles Francis Adams, ed., *The Works of John Adams*, IV (Boston, 1851), 197.
27. David Ramsay, *The History of the American Revolution* (Trenton, N.J., 1811), I,
335–337. See also Frothingham, *Rise of the Republic*, 452–453, 497–498.
28. Force, ed., *American Archives*, 4th Ser., IV, 527. On the identity of Johannes in
Eremo, see Christopher M. Jedrey, *The World of John Cleaveland: Family and Community
in Eighteenth-Century New England* (New York, 1979), 131.
29. Oct. 18, 1773. Cf. Maier, *From Resistance to Revolution*, 208–209.

ters; then, it must follow that, whatever they do by their Ministers, is to be ascribed to them as their doing."[30]

In the light of that proposition, what had the king done? Was it not true that "whilst the *United Colonies* have been crying and praying to the King, as children to a father, for redress of grievances, asking only for children's bread, the stipulated rights and privileges of *Englishmen*, they have not had in return a stone, a serpent, and a scorpion—their petitions refused, themselves declared rebels—armed ships and troops sent to kill, destroy, lay waste, and spread desolation, by fire and sword, from one end of the Colonies to the other?" Did not his "cruel exertions" then "stab, to the very heart, the sacred compacts between the King and the Colonies, in which their allegiance to the King, and union to the empire are founded?"[31] The answer was obvious.

While radical opinion grew in strength with every dispatch from Great Britain, caution still marked official pronouncements from the Provincial Congress, reflecting the uncertainties of the populace as a whole. A proclamation of January 19, 1776, reviewing the province's course, thus far laid responsibility for the government's "barbarous extremities" at the feet of "the Administration of *Great Britain*," not the king.[32] On May 9, 1776, the House of Representatives resolved that at the upcoming election, town inhabitants were to instruct their new representatives on the question of independence. Worcester, Pittsfield, and a scattering of others came down firmly for independence; most were equivocal or silent.[33] Despite urgent appeals from Elbridge Gerry and John Adams in the Continental Congress, the Massachusetts legislature was unable to send instructions in favor of independence. The province paused at the final instant, reluctant still to cut the last fine thread binding them to their sovereign. It was not any affection for the king or trust in his goodness, but a reluctance to break free from the old foundation of government. Would government be legitimate without a king to complement the people? Not until July 3, 1776, did the House of Representatives feebly resolve that if the Congress "should think it proper to declare the colonies independent of the kingdom of Great Britain, this house will approve of the measure."[34] Massachusetts delegates were compelled to act on their own initiative.

30. Force, ed., *American Archives*, 4th Ser., IV, 527–529.
31. *Ibid.*
32. *Ibid.*, 268.
33. Patterson, *Political Parties*, 426–428.
34. Quoted in Jensen, *Founding of a Nation*, 677.

The concluding steps toward Independence were taken in Philadelphia, not Boston. Through 1775, delegates to the Continental Congress brought news of royal governments blinking out one by one up and down the seaboard. In November 1775 the Congress authorized South Carolina and New Hampshire to constitute governments simply to maintain order until the crisis passed. On May 10, 1776, the Congress passed a resolve with "remarkable unanimity" recommending the adoption of new governments wherever the old were ineffectual. Moderates supported the resolution in the belief that stable governments would not be affected. The leading moderate, John Dickinson, favored the measure unaware that John Adams and the radicals aimed particularly to undermine Pennsylvania's conservative government.[35]

Appointed to write a preamble for the resolve, John Adams took occasion to transform a resolve to stabilize government into a declaration of independence:

> Whereas, His Brittanic Majesty, in conjunction with the Lords and Commons of Great Britain, has, by a late Act of Parliament, excluded the inhabitants of these United Colonies from the protection of his Crown; and whereas, no answer whatever to the humble petitions of the colonies for redress of grievances and reconciliation with Great Britain has been or is likely to be given; but the whole force of that kingdom aided by foreign mercenaries, is to be exerted for the destruction of the good people of these colonies; and whereas, it appears absolutely irreconcileable to reason and good conscience for the people of these colonies now to take the oaths and affirmations necessary for the support of any government under the Crown of Great Britain, and it is necessary that every kind of authority under the said Crown should be totally suppressed, and all the powers of government exerted, under the authority of the people of these colonies, for the preservation of internal peace, virtue, and good order, as well as for the defence of their lives, liberties, and properties against the hostile invasions and cruel depredations of their enemies; therefore Resolved, That it be recommended to the respective Assemblies and Conventions of the United Colonies, where no government sufficient to the exigencies of their affairs have been hitherto established, to adopt such a government as shall, in the opinion of the representatives

35. Events are narrated *ibid.*, 682–685.

of the people, best conduce to the happiness and safety of their constituents in particular, and America in general.

The explosive power of the preamble lay in its evocation of the terms of the ancient covenant with the king. Monarchical authority arose from royal protection of the people. The preamble declared that the king of Great Britain had "excluded the inhabitants of these United Colonies from the protection of his Crown." He not only neglected their petitions, but exerted his whole force to destroy his colonial peoples. From being their protector, he had become their enemy. Conscience and reason forbade an oath of allegiance to such a monarch. Royal government was to be suppressed and a new government created. And this government was not to take the form of another covenant with another king. It was to be organized under "the authority of the people of these colonies." The people were to preserve internal peace and good order and to defend themselves against the depredations of their enemies. The people were to be their own protectors, and make a covenant of government with themselves.[36]

The preamble narrowly passed against the opposition of James Wilson of Pennsylvania and James Duane of New York. The Maryland delegation walked out. The close vote did not dampen John Adams's elation. "This day the Congress has passed the most important resolution that ever was taken in America."[37] He knew the significance of the words he had written. With the preamble, America had taken the last step toward complete separation from Britain, "a total absolute independence, not only of her Parliament, but of her Crown."[38]

The preamble passed on May 15, 1776. On June 7 Richard Henry Lee offered the Congress the resolution, "That these United Colonies are, and of right ought to be, free and independent States, that they are absolved from all allegiance to the British Crown, and that all political connection between them and the State of Great Britain is, and ought to be, totally dissolved."[39] After a flurry of exchanges between provincial congresses and their delegates, the Declaration of Independence was debated on July 1 and passed July 2. On July 4 the Congress ap-

36. Worthington Chauncey Ford *et al.*, eds., *Journals of the Continental Congress, 1774–1789* . . . (Washington, D.C., 1904–1937), IV, 352.
37. Adams to James Warren, in [Ford], ed., *Warren-Adams Letters*, I, 245.
38. Adams to Abigail Adams, May 17, 1776, in Butterfield *et al.*, eds., *Adams Family Correspondence*, I, 410.
39. Ford *et al.*, eds., *Journals of the Continental Congress*, V, 424–426.

proved Thomas Jefferson's draft. It indicted the king as enemy of his people with a lengthy list of his "injuries and usurpations." The failure of British government, Jefferson emphasized, lay not in royal incompetence or weakness, but in the king's will. "A long train of abuses" against his people evinced "a design to reduce them under absolute despotism." Events proved he purposely was destroying his people's rights. He was not their protector, but their enemy. They were by his acts "absolved from all allegiance to the British Crown."[40]

Ten days later the Declaration of Independence reached Worcester, always to the front in the Revolutionary movement. Isaiah Thomas, editor of the *Massachusetts Gazette and Spy*, read the Declaration from the porch of the Old South Meeting House, and Sunday after services, it was read again. The next day the townsmen assembled on the green near the Liberty Pole and heard the document read once more. Bells rang, drums were beaten, and people shouted their huzzahs. They fired muskets and cannons and lit bonfires. The crowd tore down the arms of George III from the courthouse and dumped them in the fire. Another company removed the sign of the King's Arms from a tavern with the innkeeper's cheerful approbation. Through the evening toasts were drunk to the United States of America, the president of the Congress, General Washington, officers of the army and navy, and patriots everywhere. Among the sentiments honored were "perpetual itching without the benefit of scratching, to the enemies of America." "The greatest decency and good order was observed, and at a suitable time each man returned to his respective home."[41]

The words of Johannes in Eremo written following the battles of Lexington and Concord now could serve as the province's final farewell to the king:

> King George the third adieu! no more shall we cry to you for protection! no more shall we bleed in defence of your person,—your breach of covenant! your violation of faith! your turning a deaf ear to our cries for justice, for covenanted protection and salvation

40. For congressional events of June 1776 through early July, see Jensen, *Founding of a Nation*, 687–701.

41. William Lincoln, *History of Worcester, Massachusetts, From Its Earliest Settlement to September, 1836* . . . (Worcester, Mass., 1862), 102–103. On the reception of the Declaration in the province, see John Henry Edmonds, "How Massachusetts Received the Declaration of Independence," American Antiquarian Society, *Proceedings*, XXXV (1925), 227–252.

from the oppressive, tyrannical and bloody measures of the British Parliament, and putting a sanction upon all their measures to enslave and butcher us, have DISSOLVED OUR ALLEGIANCE to your Crown and Government. your sword that ought *in justice to protect us*, is now drawn *with a witness* to destroy us!—O George see thou to thine own house.[42]

After much hesitation, Massachusetts with the other colonies at last acknowledged in July 1776 that royal protection had failed. The covenant was broken. Allegiance was at an end.

iii. Republican Government

There was never any doubt in Massachusetts or in the other colonies about the form of the new government. It was to be republican. John Adams assembled his thoughts on the proper form in January 1776, when the king's recent declarations made independence appear inevitable to many delegates to the Continental Congress. A reading of "Sidney, Harrington, Locke, Milton, Nedham, Neville, Burnet, and Hoadly," Adams observed, would "convince any candid mind, that there is no good government but what is republican."[43] That statement, taken by itself, makes it sound as if books persuaded Adams. But that was not true of the province as a whole, and probably not of Adams himself, although those authors doubtless confirmed his judgment. It was experience, not books, that made republican government seem inevitable in 1776, experience that went back nearly a century.

Massachusetts came to republicanism indirectly. Through its provincial period and up to the last minute of the Revolutionary crisis, the province did not oppose monarchy as a form of government. The affection for the king seems to have been genuine. As a person, he did not play enough of a role in colonial politics to make him a target in the years of revolutionary agitation. The problem that had disturbed Massachusetts for nearly a century was the presence of royal officials with interests opposed to the people's. Republican government came about as an attempt to solve that problem rather than to depose the

42. *Essex Gazette* (Salem), Apr. 18, 1775.
43. C. F. Adams, ed., *Works of John Adams*, IV, 194.

king. For more than a century Massachusetts had employed every device of law and politics to hold avaricious officials in check. Whether governors, customs officers, or surveyors of the woods, the royal appointees threatened to exploit the colony for personal gain. The problem lay less in the actual crimes of the officials than the fact that their interests ran contrary to the people's. The alien origin of many officials was troubling. Suffering in Massachusetts little affected family, friends, and property in England. Still more important was the source of the appointment. Governors received their office with its power, honors, and profits from the crown, not the people, and felt no compulsion to serve interests other than their own and their master's. The official's interests attached him to a separate order of persons—the order of rulers—rather than to the people. His hopes for security in office or for advancement depended on the superiors who appointed him, not on those whom he governed. His personal desires all moved a royal governor to oppress the people and to serve the ministry on whom he depended. The structure of monarchical government placed the interests of rulers and ruled in perpetual opposition. In time it became evident that to end this division, the source and foundation of the independent order of rulers—the crown—must itself be eliminated.

In the interim after the Provincial Congress took over in October 1774 and before Independence was declared in July 1776, the question of the best form of government inevitably came into public discussion. The moderate elements, still hoping against all odds for reconciliation with Britain, subscribed to the fictions supporting the Provincial Congress and the provisional government established in July 1775, fictions which left a place for the return of the king. More radical elements grew impatient with the delay. They wished to hurry toward Independence and a reform of government. It was obvious to them that royal government had to be abandoned. The radical leader Joseph Warren was disappointed with the Continental Congress's advice in June 1775 to govern the province under an adaptation of the 1691 charter because of the remnants of monarchism. The old charter, he said, "contains in it the seeds of despotism, and would, in a few years, bring us again into the same unhappy situation in which we now are." The charter still contained, like seeds of despotism, provisions for royal appointment of independent officials whose interests inevitably clashed with the people's. The only hope lay with a new government "so happily moulded, that the only road to promotion" was "through the affection of the people. This being the case, the interest of the governor and the governed will be the same; and we shall no longer be plagued by a group of unprincipled villains."[44] That was the key point: to bring the interest of rulers and ruled together. Noah Webster a little over a decade later summed up the grand lesson of the provincial period. A "*union of interests*," he wrote in the *American Magazine*, was not only "the *best*, but the *only* security" of the people's liberties. Rulers must have "an interest inseperable from that of the people."[45] The merit of republican government was that by giving to the people, rather than the king, the power of appointment, it blended the interests of rulers and people.

Boston radicals were not the only ones to think that a republican government was the best answer to villainy in office. In late 1775 the Reverend Thomas Allen in Pittsfield began to inveigh against the government formed in Massachusetts by instruction of the Continental Congress for the same reason that Joseph Warren objected to it, because it still had a monarchical element. He won enough support for the town to submit a petition in December 1775 favoring direct election of all officers. The petition identified precisely why Massachusetts had suffered under royal government through the provincial period. "The Nomination and appointment of our Governors by the King has been the Source of all the Evils and Calamities that have befallen this province and the united Colonies," the petition declared. Appointments descending from the king through the lesser offices sent a poison through the entire system. "At this Door all Manner of Disorders have been introduced into our Constitution till it has become an Engine of Oppression and deep Corruption and would finally, had it been continued, have brought upon us an eternal Destruction." The town had reviewed "our antient Mode of Government," the petition said, "with its dangerous Effects of nominating to office by those in power," and "must pronounce it the most defective discordant and ruinous System of Government of any that has come under our Observation."[46] The constitution was discordant because royal appointments set rulers

44. Warren to Samuel Adams, May 14, 1775, and to John Adams, June 21, 1775, in Frothingham, *Life and Times of Joseph Warren*, 483, 512.
45. *American Magazine*, I (1787–1788), 144, 142.
46. Petition of Pittsfield to the General Court, Dec. 26, 1776, in Robert J. Taylor, ed., *Massachusetts, Colony to Commonwealth: Documents on the Formation of Its Constitution, 1775–1780* (Chapel Hill, N.C., 1961), 18–19.

apart from the people, and ruinous because they were then free to exploit and oppress.

Although Pittsfield was critical of the General Court, that body would give the town no argument on the matter of general principle. The Court was as committed to popular control of officials as Berkshire County. In the Court's view, the monarchical element had been virtually eliminated under the provisional government set up in July 1775, although the form of the old charter was retained. To rally support, the Court issued a proclamation in January 1776 congratulating the people on the improvements in their government. The Continental Congress had instructed Massachusetts to call elections and convene an assembly, and the resulting government was of the people. "The present generation, therefore, may be congratulated on the Acquisition of a Form of Government more immediately, in all its Branches, under the Influence and controul of the People, and therefore more free and happy than was enjoyed by their Ancestors." The Council had "appointed Magistrates and Courts of Justice in every County, whose Happiness is so connected with that of the People, that it is difficult to suppose they can abuse the Trust."[47] Everyone agreed that government had to be under the control and influence of the people. Western farmers embraced republican principles along with Boston radicals. Even a conservative writing in May 1776 had to reassure his readers that he revered "a government in which regal power has no part."[48] Only by routing appointments as well as salaries through the people could the "discordant Constitution" be harmonized and the interests of people and rulers made one. Every person who argued for the election of officials, and their voices were heard everywhere in 1776 and 1777, made the end of monarchy and the establishment of republican government all the more inevitable.[49] When the time came after Independence to write a constitution for the state, it was a foregone conclusion that there would be no king, no independent fountain of power to appoint officials. There would be just one source of power, the people, and all of government would be dependent on them.

47. Proclamation of the General Court, Jan. 23, 1776, in Handlin and Handlin, *Popular Sources,* 67.
48. *Thomas's Massachusetts Spy Or, American Oracle of Liberty* (Worcester), May 18, 1776, in Taylor, ed., *Massachusetts, Colony to Commonwealth,* 30.
49. Elisha P. Douglass, *Rebels and Democrats: The Struggle for Equal Political Rights and Majority Rule during the American Revolution* (Chapel Hill, N.C., 1955), 171–172, 177.

Within the framework of republican government, however, there were innumerable possibilities for organizing authority differently. Pittsfield had raised one question in its 1775 petition. The town wanted more voice in the selection of officials than was permitted under the provisional government. Following the old charter, the Council still nominated county court officials, and the town wanted for itself "the previlege of electing our Civil and military officers." They wished to carry the republican impulse a step further toward democracy than the provincial government had. For "if the right of nominating to office is not invested in the people," the petitioners insisted, "we are indifferent who assumes it whether any particular persons on this or the other side of the [w]ater."[50] They wanted so much, they said, because the Council-appointed officers were back to their old tricks. They granted licenses, for example, and "divided the Money amongst themselves." Already they were showing "Independance of the People and Disposition triumphantly to ride over their heads and worse than renew all our former Oppresions."[51] In December 1775, to the dismay of conservative elements, a Berkshire County convention nominated county judges to submit to the Council for approval.[52] Pittsfield asked that "every Town may retain the Previlege of nominating their Justice of the peace and every County their Judges as well as the Soldiers of every Company of the Militia their officers."[53] As soon as the province found itself in "a state of nature," free to construct its own government, questions like these demanded answers.

Pittsfield's objection foreshadowed the disagreements about the nature of government that later expanded into extensive constitutional controversies as the state attempted to erect a republican government. As would be expected, most had to do with the melding of the people's and the ruler's interests, the issue that troubled the colonists throughout the provincial period and into the Revolution.[54] The question of two houses or one in the legislature, unicameralism or bicameralism, was actually a variant of that theme, the same issue as underlay popular election of officers. In both instances, the impulse was to bring the

---

50. Petition of Pittsfield, Dec. 26, 1776, in Taylor, ed., *Massachusetts, Colony to Commonwealth*, 19.
51. Petition of Pittsfield to the General Assembly, May 1776, in *ibid.*, 27.
52. Resolve of the Stockbridge Convention, Dec. 15, 1775, in *ibid.*, 16.
53. Petition of Pittsfield, Dec. 26, 1775, in *ibid.*, 19.
54. Wood, *Creation of the American Republic*, 55–59.

interest of rulers and people together to prevent an alien power in government from forming. Elections tied people and officials together, and thus the more officials that were elected, the better. By the same token, it seemed that the legislature should consist only of the popularly elected House of Representatives. Without a king as an independent force, there was presumably but one interest, the people's, to be represented. It followed naturally that the government should have only a single-house, or unicameral, legislature. That one body, representing the interests of the people, would have supreme authority. In *Common Sense*, Thomas Paine proposed as the natural form of government a unicameral legislature, chosen from the whole body of the people, having "the same concerns at stake which those have who appointed them and who will act in the same manner as the whole body would act were they present." By electing the delegates annually, "this frequent interchange will establish a common interest with every part of the community," and "they will mutually and naturally support each other."[55]

The appeal of a single-house legislature was all the greater for the momentary illusion that without rulers the people's interests were unitary. A writer in the *Pennsylvania Journal* in the spring of 1776 congratulated America for being the only country to frame a government, which "having no rank existing above that of freemen [it] has but one interest to consult."[56] The simple clarity of unicameralism won over Alexander Hamilton briefly in the spring of 1777 as the states were forming constitutions. Why should a democracy have a compound government, he asked, that is, one with an upper house and an executive representing different interests from those in the lower house? Instability in democracy, he speculated, "has proceeded from its being compounded with other principles and from its being made to operate in an improper channel. Compound governments, though they may be harmonious in the beginning, will introduce distinct interests; and these interests will clash, throw the state into convulsions and produce a change or dissolution."[57] Following the same logic, Benjamin Franklin zealously

55. Thomas Paine, *Common Sense: Addressed to the Inhabitants of America*, New Edition (Philadelphia, 1776), in Thomas Paine, *Common Sense and Other Political Writings*, ed. Nelson F. Adkins (Indianapolis, Ind., 1953), 6.

56. Mar. 13, 1776. See also *Massachusetts Spy Or, Thomas's Boston Journal* (Boston), Mar. 3, 1774.

57. Hamilton to Gouverneur Morris, May 19, 1777, in Harold C. Syrett and Jacob E. Cooke, eds., *The Papers of Alexander Hamilton*, I (New York, 1961), 254–256.

supported unicameralism for the Pennsylvania constitution. Looking back in his autobiography, John Adams said that, in November 1775, "every one of my friends, and all those who were the most zealous for assuming Government, had at that time no Idea of any other Government but a Contemptible Legislature in one assembly, with Committees for Executive Magistrates and Judges."[58] The number included Samuel Adams.

Voices were heard in Massachusetts in 1776 and 1777 favoring a single-house legislature and an executive with no veto. The radical democratic pamphlet, *The People the Best Governors, or, a Plan of Government founded on the Just Principle of Natural Freedom*, advocated unicameralism for the simple reason that the people "best know their wants and Necessities and therefore are best able to govern themselves."[59] The principle appealed to a newspaper essayist in 1777 because it made for an "easy, simple, and cheap" government.[60] The town of Ashfield wrote the House of Representatives on October 4, 1776, "that it [is] our opinan that the Asembelly of this Stat consist of one Colecttive body the members of which body shall Anually be Alected."[61] Enough towns favored unicameralism that the Council, which was threatened with elimination, opposed drafting a new constitution in 1777 for fear it would embody unicameralism. At least thirty town delegates, it was said, came to the assembly in May with instructions favoring a single-house legislature.[62]

Unicameralism lost ground, however, because it came into conflict with another element of republican political culture: mistrust of people in power. In the provincial period, the popular party believed that royal officials formed a separate interest in the government opposed to the people's. In the first days of Independence that suspicion came to envelop the new holders of power, the legislators. Even before Independence John Adams advocated two-house legislatures for new state con-

58. L. H. Butterfield *et al.*, eds., *Diary and Autobiography of John Adams* (Cambridge, Mass., 1961), IV, 358.

59. The pamphlet originally published in 1776 is reprinted as an appendix in Frederick Chase, *History of Dartmouth College and the Town of Hanover, New Hampshire* (Cambridge, Mass., 1891).

60. *Independent Chronicle. And the Universal Advertiser* (Boston), July 10, 1777.

61. Ashfield to the House of Representatives, Oct. 4, 1776, in Handlin and Handlin, *Popular Sources*, 112.

62. Patterson, *Political Parties*, 168. See also Douglass, *Rebels and Democrats*, 162, 167–169.

stitutions out of distrust of elected representatives. "A single assembly is liable to all the vices, follies, and frailties of an individual" and because it "is apt to be avaricious" when "possessed of all the powers of government, would make arbitrary laws for their own interest, execute all laws arbitrarily for their own interest, and adjudge all controversies in their own favor." Adams took this cautious position despite his insistence that the representative assembly "should be in miniature an exact portrait of the people at large." "Equal interests among the people should have equal interests in it."[63] A second house and an executive were necessary checks on the self-interest of the people's own elected representatives.

Others shared Adams's suspicions. In May 1776, while Massachusetts was still trying to rid itself of royal government, a newspaper correspondent complained that "the members of the Assembly have divided among themselves, and their particular friends, all the civil and military offices in the colony."[64] That charge, previously made against royal governors, was now directed at the House of Representatives. Similar complaints were voiced in the papers through the summer.[65] By the following spring suspicion of the legislature was crystallizing through the state. William Gordon, a friend of democracy and the Revolution, expressed his belief "that whenever the Supreme Legislature shall be vested in a single Assembly, ambitious men will have more than a little ground for building up their own particular greatness upon their country's ruin."[66] Provincial suspicions of power were so deeply ingrained that representatives of the people themselves were not exempt. Eventually a second house and an executive seemed to be a necessary restraint.[67]

63. C. F. Adams, ed., *Works of John Adams*, IV, 195–196.
64. *Thomas's Mass. Spy* (Worcester), May 18, 1776, in Taylor, ed., *Massachusetts, Colony to Commonwealth*, 32.
65. *New-England Chronicle* (Boston), June 20, July 11, Aug. 29, 1776.
66. Quoted in Douglass, *Rebels and Democrats*, 173.
67. Moderates joined in the suspicion of the legislature and used those doubts to advance the conservative idea of a two-house legislature. The Essex County response to the 1778 constitution, the Essex Result of April 29, 1778, declared: "The legislative power must not be trusted with one assembly. A single assembly is frequently influenced by the vices, follies, passions, and prejudices of an individual. It is liable to be avaricious, and to exempt itself from the burdens it lays upon it's constituents. It is subject to ambition, and after a series of years, will be prompted to vote itself perpetual." The Essex Result, 1778, in Handlin and Handlin, *Popular Sources*, 343.

In the convention that framed the constitution of 1780 and in the town ratification debates, politicians and freeholders pursued the tangled lines of republican logic. They did not succeed in unsnarling the knotted reasoning or in resolving the conflicts. John Adams admitted in 1787 in the *Defence of the Constitutions* that unicameralists persisted in Massachusetts to that very day.[68] Republicans could still argue that a single-house legislature was the natural form of government in a democracy. Others still believed the people, not the legislature or executive, should select civil and military officers. There were no clearcut solutions to the problems of a republican constitution, only judgments and decisions made on balance. By that time, the political impulses of the provincial period were intertwined with scores of new issues thrust on the state by Independence and war. Old problems took new forms and demanded new solutions.

But the provincial past was not forgotten. Concern for the corruptions of rulers, the lust for offices of honor and profit, and the dangers of slavery was ever present in popular thinking. Moreover, the issue underlying corruption, the regulation of the interests of rulers, received the closest attention. The most conservative opinion agreed on the necessity of representing all interests in government. The Essex County convention's response to the constitution of 1778 emphasized that "the rights of representation should be so equally and impartially distributed, that the representatives should have the same views, and interests with the people at large. They should think, feel, and act like them, and, in fine, should be an exact miniature of their constituents." In the same spirit, the Essex result advocated annual elections of the governor to prevent the abuse of his powers. Such an official could be trusted. "This Governor is not appointed by a King, or his ministry, nor does he receive instructions from a party of men, who are pursuing an interest diametrically opposite to the good of the state." "He knows he must soon return, and sink to a level with the rest of the community."[69]

Although Independence had entangled the people of Massachusetts in constitutional perplexities unforeseen when they declared for Independence, they did not lose sight entirely of what they fought for. In the debates of the late 1770s they still prized what they had first sought

68. C. F. Adams, ed., *Works of John Adams*, IV, 299–300.
69. The Essex Result, 1778, in Handlin and Handlin, *Popular Sources*, 341, 361.

in resorting to revolution, a "whole government of our choice, managed by persons whom we love, revere, and can confide in."[70] They were resolved to create a political system wherein the interests of rulers and people mingled and officials' private good gave them incentives to work for the good of all.

iv. Republican Society

After Independence, republican society received less attention than republican government. No town meeting was devoted to the implications of equality for society. Life went on without framing a constitution for a new social order. And yet the end of monarchy and its associated culture raised questions about society. Theoretically, in a republic each citizen was independent, free of the demeaning links that bound inferiors to superiors in traditional society. Under monarchy, the social hierarchy supported the political structure by making clients submissive to their patrons, just as the people as a whole were submissive to the king. Although radical Whigs in England criticized dependence, in actual fact the intimate, person-to-person connections of patron and client reinforced the overall dependence of the people on the protector. Government relied on these networks in virtually every aspect of the maintenance of order. Such dependencies were contradictory in a republic, where each voter was to speak his own mind in the selection of officials and no one was to have influence over another. Social relationships that were desirable under one form of government were reprehensible under the other.[71]

Americans soon came to understand that republican government had social implications. The introduction of the word "aristocracy" into common political use signified awareness of the need for a proper social order. While rarely heard before 1776, "aristocrat" came to be a frequent term of political opprobrium (along with "demagogue"). "Aristocracy" implied a small group exercising influence through the

70. Quoted in John Chester Miller, *Triumph of Freedom, 1775–1783* (Boston, 1948), 343.
71. English Whigs also honored the ideal of independence, but under circumstances that severely circumscribed its practical implications. J.G.A. Pocock, "The Classical Theory of Deference," *American Historical Review*, LXXXI (1976), 516–523.

patronage of property or office. By commanding his dependents, the aristocrat magnified his power and threatened to make government an instrument of his own will. Aristocracy led back directly to the evils of royal government, where a few officials used their authority for private gain. In making aristocracy a prime target for political attack, republicans signified their determination to end the dependencies that made some aristocrats and others their clients. The 1780 Massachusetts Declaration of Rights stated that " GOVERNMENT is instituted for the common good; for the protection, safety, prosperity and happiness of the people: and not for the profit, honor, or private interest of any one man, family, or class of men."[72]

The proper condition of republican society, and the opposite of aristocracy, was "equality." By "equality," the first generation of American republicans meant equality of dominion, that is, that no man had the right to rule or control another without his consent. The implications for government were clear, but so were they for society; every form of dependence had to be dissolved or overcome. Since men ruled others not only by virtue of political authority but also as patrons, patronage endangered the republic. Dependence on another for one's living was as surely a form of inequality as subjection to his rule and just as intolerable.[73]

Obviously the ideal of equality had the potential for drastically changing the countryside. Other than offices, the patronage of the landlord was the main source of dependence and thus of inequality in England.[74] Whig theorists recognized that the power of great landholders had to be dispersed in a republican society. In James Harrington's imaginary seventeenth-century commonwealth, Oceana, land was widely distributed on the principle, "If the whole people be landlords, or hold the lands so divided among them, that no one man, or number of men, within the compass of the few or aristocracy, overbalance them, the empire (without the interposition of force) is a commonwealth."[75]

---

72. In Handlin and Handlin, *Popular Sources*, 444. On the American desire for personal independence, see Richard L. Bushman, "This New Man: Dependence and Independence, 1776," in Richard L. Bushman *et al.*, eds., *Uprooted Americans: Essays to Honor Oscar Handlin* (Boston, 1979), 79–96.

73. On the rich meanings of the word "equality," see J. R. Pole, *The Pursuit of Equality in American History* (Berkeley, Calif., 1978).

74. Harold Perkin, *The Origins of Modern English Society, 1780–1880* (London, 1969), 42.

75. J.G.A. Pocock, ed., *The Political Works of James Harrington* (Cambridge, 1977), 164.

Distribution of property virtually made a commonwealth (or republic) without changes in the government. By the same token, no change in the government made a difference if land was concentrated in a few hands. Harrington proposed an agrarian law for England to prevent any person from holding land with annual rents exceeding two thousand pounds. His simple expedient was to divide estates equally among the heirs so long as any estate was larger than the prescribed amount. In the course of a few generations, all would be less.

In New England, where Harrington had influence among political writers, republican publicists similarly recognized the virtue of wide distribution of property. Noah Webster, the Connecticut educational theorist and political writer, though a Federalist, embraced Harrington's agrarian law. "An equality of property," Webster wrote, "with a necessity of alienation, constantly operating to destroy combinations of powerful families, is the very soul of a republic." Webster believed that liberty had advanced only as property was diffused.

> We observe that the power of the people has increased in exact proportion to their acquisitions of property. Wherever the right of primogeniture is established, property must accumulate and remain in families. Thus the landed property in England will never be sufficiently distributed, to give the powers of government wholly into the hands of the people. . . . Make laws, irrevocable laws in every state, destroying and barring entailments; leave real estates to revolve from hand to hand, as time and accident may direct; and no family influence can be acquired and established for a series of generations—no man can obtain dominion over a large territory—the laborious and saving, who are generally the best citizens, will possess each his share of property and power, and thus the balance of wealth and power will continue where it is, in the body of the people.

Other rights, such as trial by jury and liberty of the press, rested on this one fundamental principle. "Such rights are inseparably connected with the *power* and *dignity* of the people, which rest on their *property*."[76]

76. Noah Webster, *An Examination into the Leading Principles of the Federal Constitution* . . . (Philadelphia, 1787), in Paul Leicester Ford, ed., *Pamphlets on the Constitution of the United States* (Brooklyn, 1888), 58–60, 61n.
77. Ezra Stiles, *The United States elevated to Glory and Honor* . . . (New Haven, Conn., 1783), in John Wingate Thornton, ed., *The Pulpit of the American Revolution . . . ,* 2d ed. (Boston, 1876), 404.

Circumstances in Massachusetts enabled conservatives like Webster to contemplate Harrington's agrarian law without trepidation. Ezra Stiles, president of Yale College, in projecting the "Future Glory of the United States," laid down the familiar principle that "dominion is founded in property, and resides where that is, whether in the hands of the few or many." For that reason, "the feudal tenure of estate" is "not adapted to the circumstances of free citizens." The great lords exercised too much influence. "Large territorial property vested in individuals is pernicious to society." Independent freeholds were the correct social basis. Stiles thought, moreover, that a "free tenure of lands, an equable distribution of property, enters into the foundation of a happy state," for ownership made everyone desirous of defending property, liberty, and country. These radical principles did not trouble him in the least, because he believed New England already lived by them. His proof of their validity did not rest on an imaginary projection like Harrington's Oceana. He knew they worked because they had been "singularly verified in New England, where we have realized the capital ideas of Harrington's Oceana."[77] No reforms were necessary. New England was Oceana. In the convention that framed Massachusetts' 1780 constitution, someone proposed that the name of the state be changed to Oceana.[78]

Earlier, English observers had commented that Massachusetts had monarchical government but not a monarchical society, a disturbing contradiction for the friends of imperial government. It meant that the province lacked the networks of dependents required to make monarchical government work. Now that discrepancy was seen to have prepared the way for a revolution in government. For when monarchy was ended, Massachusetts society was republican and egalitarian with-

78. Oscar Handlin and Mary Flug Handlin, *Commonwealth: A Study of the Role of Government in the American Economy: Massachusetts, 1774–1861*, rev. ed. (Cambridge, Mass., 1969), 30. See also Wood, *Creation of the American Republic*, 99. Abigail Adams worried about Virginia society: "Are not the Gentery Lords and the common people vassals, are they not like the uncivilized Natives Brittain represents us to be?" she asked John. He admitted that "this Inequality of Property, gives an Aristocratical Turn to all their Proceedings. . . . But the Spirit of these Barons, is coming down, and it must submit." Abigail Adams to John Adams, Mar. 31, 1776; John Adams to Abigail Adams, Apr. 14, 1776, in Butterfield *et al.*, eds., *Adams Family Correspondence*, I, 369, 381. Jeremy Belknap thought that none of the states had realized the equal distribution of property required in a republic. Gerald Stourzh, *Alexander Hamilton and the Idea of Republican Government* (Stanford, Calif., 1970), 230.

out the necessity for further change. Government and society were already basically in harmony.

The effortless acceptance of such radical ideas did not, however, add to their strength. The prevalence of independent freeholders actually weakened efforts for further reforms, even where needed. The state did go so far toward an agrarian law as to regulate the inheritances of people who died without making a will. A 1784 law provided that the heirs of a man who died intestate should receive equal shares, except the first son, who received a double portion. In 1789, the legislature went still further and provided that all the children were to take equally. But no regulations were imposed on those who made wills.[79] Harringtonian sentiments likewise had an effect, at least temporarily, on the sales of state lands in Maine and elsewhere. The state was cautious at first about granting large tracts. A newspaper article in 1779 offering a new constitution proposed a clause restricting the amount of land held by individuals, lest they "denominate their landed estates, manners or lordships, as has been practised in other parts of the world."[80] Until 1790 Massachusetts land offices sold the land in small quantities, hoping to help small farmers get a start while contributing to state revenues. But sales were so poor that financial exigency forced the state in 1791 to make large grants to speculators to raise badly needed funds. There were complaints of impending feudalism and warnings about the "safety and future prosperity" of the republic, but the tracts were sold.[81]

The fate of Massachusetts land sales and the limited reform of inheritance laws typified the effect of republican principles on society. Belief in the benefits of property ownership to prevent dependence constrained rather than directed policy. When ideal and reality confronted one another, economic need or vested interests usually thwarted reform impulses. A freehold for every citizen was more an aspiration than a practical goal. Rather than becoming an imperative for legislation, the aversion to aristocracy and dependence served as a source of

79. James Sullivan, *The History of Land Titles in Massachusetts* (New York, 1972 [orig. publ. Boston, 1801]), 147.
80. *Boston Gazette, and the Country Journal*, July 19, 1779.
81. Quoted in Robert E. Moody, "Samuel Ely: Forerunner of Shays," *New England Quarterly*, V (1932), 127. See also statement of Holland Land Company representative in Walter Hill Crockett, *Vermont: The Green Mountain State* (New York, 1921), II, 507–508.

rhetoric for denouncing political enemies or unpopular measures. A preacher in 1795 noted the "clamours daily made" that the government was "too aristocratic in its form and oppressive in its operation,"[82] and yet no constitutional revisions followed. John Adams in the late 1780s worried about the creation of an aristocracy on the frontier as land speculators accumulated large blocks, but did nothing to change policy.[83] The western paper money men in the same decade thought the monopolizers of money would "swallow up all us little folks, like the great leviathan," recreating a feudal order, but lost to hard money men.[84] And so on through succeeding decades, whenever it was thought that the accumulation of wealth in a few hands threatened to make great lords of some and pliant dependents of others, antimonarchical language was heard. Even an opponent of rapid western land sales in 1833 claimed that speculators would turn ordinary farmers into "large masses of laboring tenants . . . the menials of some wealthy landlord, who fattens on the spoils of the industry and hard earnings of this valuable class of our citizens."[85] But republican principles were preeminent in the realm of words, not in the making of policy. In direct confrontations with powerful interests, independence and equality yielded.

Still, the pliability of republican ideals in the practical world should not be mistaken for feebleness. Those ideals were indelibly engraved in thought and belief. America was defined as not monarchical, not aristocratic, and not feudal, and its citizens as independent, not servile or submissive. In his 1794 poem "Greenfield Hill," Timothy Dwight said of New England freeholders:

> A prince, a king, each independent swain;
> No servile thought, no vile submission, known;
> No rent to lords, nor homage to a throne.[86]

Antimonarchical values and language infused political discourse and social criticism for more than a century after the Revolution, giving to

82. Henry Ware, *The Continuance of Peace and increasing Prosperity A Source of Consolation and just Cause of Gratitude to the Inhabitants of the United States* . . . (Boston, 1795), 26.
83. C. F. Adams, ed., *Works of John Adams*, IV, 359.
84. Quoted in Taylor, *Western Massachusetts in the Revolution*, 173.
85. Quoted in Rowland Berthoff, "Independence and Attachment, Virtue and Interest: From Republican Citizen to Free Enterpriser, 1787–1837," in Bushman *et al.*, eds., *Uprooted Americans*, 111.
86. Timothy Dwight, *Greenfield Hill: A Poem in Seven Parts* (Hartford, Conn., 1794), 155.

republican ideology the strength as well as the weakness of a cultural force.[87]

From the start, expressive works attempted to capture and propagate the meaning of republican society and government in a self-conscious effort to create a republican culture. New York crowds knew the statue of George III in Bowling Green must be toppled, and Boston had to change the name of Orange Street (after King William's House of Orange) to Washington. More complex efforts involved the organization of republican civic pageantry.[88] The elaborate celebrations for the first republican president, for example, reflected as precisely the ideals governing American republican culture as coronation processions expressed the principles of monarchy.

To greet President Washington on his tour of the states in the fall of 1789, Boston constructed an arch and a colonnade, wrote an ode, and designed a procession to escort and follow him from his entrance into the city to the center of the town.[89] Washington arrived at the Vassal house in Cambridge at 10:00 A.M. on Saturday, October 24. In the house that served as his headquarters when he took command of the Continental army in 1775, he changed into army uniform. Although he toured in a carriage with six servants and two secretaries, Washington entered Boston on horseback. He knew enough to shed the trappings of his office, anything that hinted of elegance or grandeur, and to present himself as a simple soldier.

The intended impact of his demeanor was preserved later in the most famous American portrait of the age, Gilbert Stuart's head of

---

87. Eric Foner, *Free Soil, Free Labor, Free Men: The Ideology of the Republican Party before the Civil War* (New York, 1970).

88. Frothingham, *Rise of the Republic*, 549–550; Neil Harris, *The Artist in American Society: The Formative Years, 1790–1860* (New York, 1966); Kenneth Silverman, *A Cultural History of the American Revolution: Painting, Music, Literature, and the Theatre in the Colonies and the United States from the Treaty of Paris to the Inauguration of George Washington, 1763–1789* (New York, 1976); Robert Middlekauff, "The Ritualization of the American Revolution," in Stanley Coben and Lorman Ratner, eds., *The Development of an American Culture* (Englewood Cliffs, N.J., 1970), 31–43. For retention of older forms, see Louise Burnham Dunbar, *A Study of "Monarchical" Tendencies in the United States from 1776 to 1801*, University of Illinois Studies in the Social Sciences, X,' No. 1 (Urbana, Ill., 1922).

89. Descriptions of the events can be found in "Historic Processions in Boston from 1689–1824," the Bostonian Society, *Publications*, V (Boston, 1908), 74–81; Mary Caroline Crawford, *Old Boston Days and Ways . . .* (Boston, 1909), 277–281. The broadside with instructions for participants is in James H. Stark, *Antique Views of the Town of Boston* (Boston, 1901), 282–284.

Washington. It contrasts strongly with official court portraits of royalty, such as Alan Ramsay's portrait of George III. George III is magnificent in his intricate attire, colorful, sparkling, rich. George Washington's clothes are simple, plain, and almost dull. In one, the emphasis is on the setting; in the other, on the person. George III is amiable, stately, and strong despite his somewhat babyish round face; but his head is lost amidst the ermine robes, the gold brocade fabric, the jeweled necklace, the draperies, the column, and the rug. The setting overwhelms the king's private person. In George Washington's portrait, we see nothing but face. Particularly are we aware of the jaw, the firm line of the lips, and the serene eyes. All the stories of a mouthful of ill-fitting dentures cannot remove the effect of oaklike integrity and will. Such was the impact intended for the school children who stood before the balcony at the statehouse to view the president.[90]

The order of Washington's procession contrasted as sharply to the coronation procession of George III as the countenances of president and king in the two portraits. Twenty-eight years earlier, in newspaper accounts of the coronation, Bostonians read of the processional stair ascending from clerks in Chancery, chaplains, sheriffs and aldermen, through barons and baronesses, bishops, viscounts, earls, and dukes, to the queen and king, both canopied, and in robes, surrounded by and bearing the royal regalia. Interspersed among the ranks were trumpeters, kettle drums, and liveries of crimson velvet.[91] It was such a procession that caused tears of joy to swim in the eyes of Thomas Prince and transported the multitudes who lined the streets of Westminster in 1714.

Bostonians, not to be outdone completely, attempted a degree of splendor to honor Washington, including an eighteen-foot triumphal arch across Washington Street designed by Charles Bulfinch, supporting a canopy twenty feet high, topped by an American eagle. The colonnade built out from the statehouse and supporting the balcony measured forty-four feet, the better to "exhibit in a strong light, 'The Man of the People.'"[92] The gallery to which he descended was furnished with armchairs sitting on rich carpets.

90. Richard L. Bushman, "Freedom and Prosperity in the American Revolution," in Larry R. Gerlach et al., eds., *Legacies of the American Revolution* ([Logan, Utah], 1978), 61–83.
91. *Bost. Gaz.*, Nov. 16, 1761.
92. *Massachusetts Magazine, or, Monthly Museum of Knowledge and Rational Entertainment* (Boston), X (Oct. 1789), 633–634. Note pagination errors for Oct. and Nov. issues.

But the procession itself was of a simpler nature. At the head were a military troop, town and county officials, Council and lieutenant governor, consuls of France and Holland, and then clergy, lawyers, physicians, merchants, traders, and masters of vessels, in places of eminence. But no trumpet fanfares, scarlet liveries, or flower girls accompanied the notables. Moreover, they did not predominate. Following patterns familiar from processions celebrating the ratification of the federal constitution, tradesmen composed the bulk of the procession. There were forty-six entries, ranged in alphabetical order from bakers to wheelwrights, each bearing a yard-square white silk flag on a seven-foot staff, marked with an appropriate device. The artisans were asked to "display such insignia of their craft, as they can conveniently carry in their hands."[93] The procession formed on the mall and marched out to greet Washington as he entered the city. They opened ranks as he approached, and he passed between them into the town. Officials and artisans followed, with "the Scholars of the several Schools in town, with quills in their hands," bringing up the rear.[94]

From the vantage point of the cordwainers and ropemakers in Washington's procession, society looked much different than it did to the anonymous London workers observing the coronation procession. Society and government did not tower above the citizens of Boston to such stupefying heights. Not only were the heights reduced, but the lower orders were raised. They were given a position, a name, and an identity in the procession of state. The presence of citizens in the procession instead of on the sidelines in an undifferentiated mass signified their active role in the republic. Under monarchy there were height, magnificence, and exclusiveness; republican society was level, simple, and inclusive.[95]

The 1789 procession in Boston did not foretell the way society was to develop in Massachusetts or anywhere in the United States in the succeeding years. Contrary to the expression of republican ideals in

93. "Procession" instructions in Stark, *Antique Views*, 284. On the ratification processions, see Whitfield J. Bell, Jr., "The Federal Processions of 1788," *New-York Historical Society Quarterly*, XLVI (1962), 5–39.
94. *Mass. Mag.*, X (Oct., 1789), 633.
95. For an analysis of the origins and meaning of the federal processions, see Alfred F. Young, "English Plebeian Culture and Eighteenth-Century American Radicalism," in Margaret Jacob and James Jacob, eds., *The Origins of Anglo-American Radicalism* (Hemel Hempstead, England, 1984). Alfred Young generously permitted me to see his essay in proof.

pageants, works of art, and poetry, society became less egalitarian in the early nineteenth century. Increasing prosperity separated the richest citizens from the poorest, and more and more workers lost their independent status to become employees and tenants.[96] But these tendencies did not signify the death of the republican spirit or its irrelevance to American life. In the triumph of republican government over monarchy in 1776, the basic values of the American nation were forged, and though often thwarted or denied, those values exerted unrelenting pressure on the remnants of the old order carried over from our beginnings under a king. Republican culture has always been a resource, often the only resource, of the powerless and oppressed. In time, republican principles wrought great changes in the lives of women, slaves, and the poor. To this day, symbols in political discourse are turned into forces in political action, giving us cause to believe that the last outcome of America's passage to a republic is yet unknown.

96. On the evolution of the ideal of independence, see Berthoff, "Independence and Attachment," in Bushman *et al.*, eds., *Uprooted Americans*, 97–124.

AFTERWORD

The foregoing account departs from political history as it is often written these days in emphasizing political ideas, values, and attitudes more than social and economic conditions. The coming of the Revolution is seen, as is common, as a reaction to imperial reforms, beginning with the Sugar Act of 1764 and going through the Massachusetts Government Act of 1774.[1] But rather than refer to social conflicts to understand the colonists' response, the book attempts to explain what parliamentary taxation, a colonial civil list, and the reorganization of Massachusetts government meant in terms of political culture.

Society and the economy have not been neglected as a matter of principle. It is simply that in my opinion there is insufficient evidence of a crisis in colonial society. There were, to be sure, social strains in the decade before the Revolution: less land in settled areas, more poor and unemployed in the cities, merchant complaints about bad markets, large debts to British creditors, religious dissent, and recalcitrant children.[2] But these did not add up to more stress than was experienced in many decades before or after the Revolution. Moreover, the revolutionaries themselves did not blame the government for their various

1. For an account emphasizing the impact of British policies, see David Ammerman, *In the Common Cause: American Response to the Coercive Acts of 1774* (Charlottesville, Va., 1974), esp. 145–146.
2. For discussions of social forces in the Revolution: James A. Henretta, "Economic Development and Social Structure in Colonial Boston," *William and Mary Quarterly*, 3d Ser., XXII (1965), 75–92; Kenneth A. Lockridge, "Social Change and the Meaning of the American Revolution," *Journal of Social History*, VI (1973), 403–439; Bruce G. Merritt, "Loyalism and Social Conflict in Revolutionary Deerfield, Massachusetts," *Journal of American History*, LVII (1970–1971), 277–289; Robert A. Gross, *The Minutemen and Their World* (New York, 1976); Stephen E. Patterson, *Political Parties in Revolutionary Massachusetts* (Madison, Wis., 1973); Gary B. Nash, *Urban Crucible: Social Change, Political Consciousness, and the Origins of the American Revolution* (Cambridge, Mass., 1979).

social problems. We are the ones to hypothesize cause and effect. The participants gave other explanations of why they revolted, and it is their reactions to imperial policies which I have tried to understand and describe.[3]

Attributing so much to political culture does not drop society and the economy out of the picture altogether. Taking the words of politicians seriously, and not as a flimsy cover thrown over the real forces in political life, leads, rather, to a perception of social forces as the participants understood them. And they were intensely aware of the social relationships governing action. Above all, they were conscious of how interest bound people into networks of patrons and clients, the one dependent on the other for office, land, or favor, and how dependence compelled inferiors to yield to commands from above.

From an eighteenth-century perspective, the most notable fact about provincial Massachusetts society was the weakness of the dependency networks in the lower reaches. The governor was the dependent of the ministry, and the thin upper layer of royal appointees in the colonies was in turn dependent on him. But below that the ties of superior to inferior were frail and thin. Too large a proportion of Massachusetts families owned land and too few held offices or received substantial favors from their social superiors for unpopular measures coming from the top to be respected at the bottom of society. As innumerable observers noted, the heavy superstructure of royal government lacked an adequate social base.

That lack proved to be important in the Revolution. When events broke patriots and loyalists apart, the county elites whom the governor had made into colonels of the militia and judges of the courts of common pleas were the only ones on whom he could rely. There were others who tagged along, but the county elites (along with a few eminent professionals and merchants trading to England) were the only well-defined groups with strong sympathies for the crown.[4] Massachu-

3. For the potential pitfalls in this empathetic approach, see Robert Eccleshall, *Order and Reason in Politics: Theories of Absolute and Limited Monarchy in Early Modern England* (Oxford, 1978), 10–11. Mary Fulbrook summarizes the critique of the social interpretation of the English Revolution and argues for holding on to a modified class analysis nevertheless in "The English Revolution and the Revisionist Revolt," *Social History*, VII (1982), 249–264.

4. Merritt, "Loyalism and Social Conflict," *WMQ*, 3d Ser., LXVII (1970), 285–289; Wallace B. Brown, *The King's Friends: The Composition and Motives of the American Loyalist Claimants* (Providence, R.I., 1965), 22–25.

setts tore along the line dividing the small group of dependents on royal patronage from the mass of those who were independent and thus available for recruitment into the Revolutionary cause.

Beyond the question of the tories, the colonists conceived of the entire Revolutionary movement as a struggle over dependence. Judging from what was written, the people of Massachusetts as a whole before Independence did not regret the lack of dependencies and yearn to be more like traditional societies. Quite to the contrary, what troubled the colonists most before 1776 was the fear that independence was being eroded. The payment of salaries from crown revenues and royal appointment of sheriffs, justices, and juries spread what Pittsfield called the poison of corruption through society. More and more officials were falling under the influence of the ministry, extending the patronage networks into every little village. At the same time, taxes threatened to create lordships in America, bringing to life social and economic dependence to match the political dependence growing out of patronage.

Lordships were the evil opposite to the independent freeholds which most Americans enjoyed, and fear of them was the ultimate social reason for the opposition to parliamentary taxation. Excessive taxes, it was thought, led to impoverishment, foreclosure, and finally a few great lords and the rest tenants and laborers. The colonists did not say explicitly that taxes, like debt, would bring their lands to the auction block, but the dangers of foreclosure were well known. The currency advocates of earlier decades and Shays's rebels in the 1780s understood exactly how farmers lost their land and great owners gained it when debts could not be paid. Assuming that everyone understood the reality of the threat, Revolutionary whigs warned of impending lordships as a direct consequence of unchecked taxation. The actual prevalence of rural indebtedness gave substance to the fear that excessive taxes would in time jeopardize independent freeholds and reduce small farmers to tenantry. Like the disconsolate land bank men in 1741 and currency-poor farmers in 1786, farmers in 1775 were willing to take up arms to stop the course of oppression.

In whig thinking, lordships and patronage were thematically related. Both were forms of dependence, and both were the consequence of parliamentary taxation. The sequence from taxes to lordships, it was believed, would create in America the very dependencies at the foundation of society from which America had always been free, just as royal salaries and appointments made more and more government officials dependent on the ministry. American farmers would become tenants and laborers as their political leaders were becoming placemen and lackeys. Parliamentary taxes would simultaneously form a social and a political system made up of servile dependents bound by interest to their superiors.

In the largest sense, the Revolution was fought not only to achieve independence from Great Britain but also to preserve independence in America. For a century and a half, the colonies embodied the contradiction of a monarchical government lacking a monarchical society, that is, rulers appointed by the crown governing people whose shops and farms made them independent of all superiors. In the Revolutionary crisis, that contradiction demanded resolution. The aim of the revolutionaries came to be the formation of a government consistent with their society, a government in which rulers were dependent on the people rather than the reverse. The alternative, as it seemed to them, was the formation of a society consistent with monarchical government, a society in which a subordinate people composed of laborers, tenants, and placemen were entirely dependent on their rulers and superiors.

Viewed from an eighteenth-century perspective, then, society and the economy are seen to have played an important part in the coming of the American Revolution, but still it cannot be said that ours was a social revolution. The large majority of Massachusetts farmers were independent freeholders before the Revolution, and they remained so afterward. Where tenantry was more prevalent, as in Maryland, the Revolution had little effect on changing conditions. The debt that worried farmers before the Revolution continued to worry them long after. Troubling social conditions in Massachusetts did not change after 1776.

We must look elsewhere for significant change. The American Revolution can be considered a true revolution, but in another sense. It did not overthrow a ruling class, but it did overthrow the class of rulers. Under monarchy, rulers were a class apart. Their appointments by the king, the fountain of power, separated and elevated them. In the Revolution, the moral foundation of the rulers' separate status was destroyed. When the two centers of moral authority, king and people, became one, the people were the only fountain of power. In a republic, popular appointment made rulers morally and politically dependent on the people, tied closely by common interests to the populace they governed. Government was of the people.

That was more of a change than we might think, looking back. Our own preconceptions lead us to conceive of economic power as more ominous and more fundamental than government. But in the eighteenth century, political power was thought to be the greater of the two. The authority of the state to tax, to dispose of offices and salaries, and to enlist labor far exceeded the capacities of the greatest merchants and landowners. In eighteenth-century thinking, threats to the prosperity and peace of farmers and artisans came less from commercial magnates and landlords than from those individuals, whether rich or poor, who controlled the powers of government. That is why officials more than merchants were the object of provincial jealousy and fear. In attacking government, the revolutionaries engaged the most ominous and powerful force in their world.[5]

At the same time, these very rulers were benefactors, the protectors of the people against foreign invasions and domestic disorder. In their weakness and insufficiency, ordinary people were helpless against the malignant forces at large in the world. The monarch commanded the loyalties of the populace because he promised to protect them. That was the very basis of the state. To cast off their protectors because they seemed to endanger more than defend was an act of great courage. It helped, of course, that the colonists for a century had largely managed their own affairs and had long practice with self-government. Still, in provincial political culture, a class of rulers had always borne the responsibility for protection and governance, and for the people to take the responsibility of ruling and protecting on themselves was truly a revolutionary act.

What drove them to it, as I have argued at length, was the belief that interest, the force that ultimately governed all men, led colonial officials to plunder rather than to protect the people. The Declaration of Independence did not end this worry. The regulation of interest continued to preoccupy the nation after 1776 and, indeed, remained as the

---

5. In some respects the American Revolution was reminiscent of the French peasant uprisings of an earlier era described by Emmanuel Le Roy Ladurie. Peasant uprisings, he says "were opposed to change and in particular to that unpardonable 'novelty'—the proliferation of royal offices and the rise of a coterie of wealthy tax farmers surrounding the still revered figure of the sovereign. Basically, the peasant revolt of the classic age, as painted in contrasting colors by Porchenev and Mousnier, constitutes a rejection of the bourgeois state, the military-financial complex and rising taxes." "Motionless History," *Social Science History*, I (1977), 133.

central problem of politics for at least a decade. Once rid of royal officials, people worried about other combinations forming to pursue their interests at the public expense. With suspicions heightened by the preceding agitation, Massachusetts towns came to doubt the honesty of their own representatives and took precautions to prevent them from combining against the public. Even though elected, the representatives, it was feared, would form a separate interest of their own. A second house of the legislature to check the first was one result of these doubts; a separate convention to frame the state constitution was another. People wished to prevent the legislature, the people's representatives, from organizing government for their own benefit. It seemed safer to assign constitution-making to a temporary convention that would disappear as a body once the framing was complete and thus have nothing to gain from conniving.[6] From these apprehensions came the idea of Massachusetts' constitutional convention. These same doubts carried over to the Federal Convention, where the delegates from the small states feared the large states would combine to favor their own interests. It mattered little that no conceivable economic or religious similarities united the large states. It was believed that any collection of persons, no matter how unlikely, given access to power, would devise ways to use it for their own benefit.

The framers learned many lessons about self-interest in the 1780s. Above all, they realized as never before that the people as a whole had diverse and conflicting interests. The Revolutionary agitation had focused attention almost solely on the alien interests of rulers. The people had been treated as unitary, threatened not by each other, but by government. The people were one interest; rulers were another. Popular interests, of course, were not one, and the colonists had ample reason to know that before Independence. But the conflicts of the 1780s drove the point home once again, with the rancorous debates over paper money, distribution of taxes, and the disposal of western lands.[7]

6. On the way these issues worked themselves out in the state constitutional conventions, see Gordon S. Wood, *The Creation of the American Republic, 1776–1787* (Chapel Hill, N.C., 1969), chaps. 5–9; Willi Paul Adams, *The First American Constitutions: Republican Ideology and the Making of the State Constitutions in the Revolutionary Era*, trans. Rita Kimber and Robert Kimber (Chapel Hill, N.C., 1980).

7. Lester H. Cohen, "Explaining the Revolution: Ideology and Ethics in Mercy Otis Warren's Historical Theory," *WMQ*, 3d Ser., XXXVII (1980), 200–218.

In their despair over the ensuing confusion, the would-be Federalist elements saw no alternative but to reconstruct a partially independent class of rulers, in contradiction to the basic impulse of the Revolution. The conservatives understood the risks they took in separating rulers from the people; the dangers of oppression would reemerge. But somehow a balance had to be struck and an authority formed capable of mediating among the interests. Madison stated the dilemma with perfect clarity in his "Vices of the Political System":

> The great desideratum in Government is such a modification of the sovereignty as will render it sufficiently neutral between the different interests and factions, to controul one part of the society from invading the rights of another, and at the same time sufficiently controuled itself, from setting up an interest adverse to that of the whole Society.[8]

He did not want a return to monarchy, where the sovereign sacrificed the people's happiness "to his ambition or avarice." Nor did he favor the pure democracy of a small republic in which government could never be sufficiently neutral to serve as arbiter of conflicting interests. The large republic was his answer, and in the Constitutional Convention it became the American answer.

In the midst of formulating constitutional measures for dealing with the problem of interests, Americans began to reflect on the meaning of their independence. They had not set out to overthrow the king or to set up a republic. Up until the end, Massachusetts would have accepted a return to their first charter, giving them larger powers of government while still upholding allegiance to the monarch.[9] They repudiated the king only when there was no other way to control appointed officials. Only gradually did it dawn that in dissolving their ties to the monarch, the American colonies had rid themselves of a weight that had bowed mankind for centuries. Throwing off monarchy and aristocracy would

8. James Madison, "Vices of the Political System of the United States: April 1787," in Marvin Meyers, ed., *The Mind of the Founder: Sources of the Political Thought of James Madison* (Indianapolis, Ind., 1973), 91.

9. Lord Mansfield summarized accurately the American position when he said they "would allow the king of Great Britain a nominal sovereignty over them, but nothing else. They would throw off the dependency on the crown of Great Britain, but not on the person of the king, whom they would render a cypher." Quoted in Robert W. Tucker and David C. Hendrickson, *The Fall of the First British Empire: Origins of the War of American Independence* (Baltimore, Md., 1982), 410.

let the human spirit take flight. Republican government opened possibilities for unprecedented growth in the arts, in learning, and in commercial enterprise. Optimism flushed the speeches of those who saw the age-old shackles falling away. "Possessed of absolute freedom and Independency," George Washington observed at the end of the war, the Americans were "peculiarly designated by Providence for the display of human greatness and felicity."[10]

At other times, the sobering realization that the people might be incapable of ruling themselves tempered the enthusiasm. Without a monarch to head the state, the nation would descend into bitter chaos, ending at last in a tyranny worse than the first. In the same message where he spoke of America's hopeful prospect, Washington warned the states that they must soon decide whether "they will be respectable and prosperous, or contemptable and miserable as a nation."[11]

In the despairing moments, politicians comforted themselves with the thought that the attempt was worth making. To release the human spirit from its traditional bondage warranted taking risks. In the midst of capricious legislation and social turmoil, conservatives reminded each other that the American republic was launched on a grand experiment. Must popular government necessarily perish in time, the victim of its own weakness, or could it survive and flourish in freedom? America was a test to see whether a self-governing people, liberated from the oppression of monarchy and aristocracy, could stand among the nations of the earth, free of both the shield and the burden of a king.

10. John C. Fitzpatrick, ed., *The Writings of George Washington from the Original Manuscript Sources, 1745–1799,* XXVI (Washington, D.C., 1938), 484–485.
11. *Ibid.,* 486.

APPENDIX

Country Party Rhetoric in Massachusetts

The imposition of royal government on Massachusetts in the late seventeenth century coincided with the emergence in England of that group of country party political polemicists variously termed Old Whigs, Real Whigs, or Commonwealthmen who ultimately exercised great influence on American political thought. This loosely connected group of publicists, scholars, and active politicians was not notable for its political ideas taken one by one, most of which were conventional and familiar by 1679 when the Exclusion Crisis first crystallized their principles. Separation of powers, rotation in office, a wider franchise, annual parliaments, and an end to undue ministerial influence in the legislature, all Old Whig reforms, had been advocated in the parliamentary party well before 1679. What distinguished the Real Whigs was the connection of political reforms with criticism of bureaucratic and financial forces coming into being in Restoration and Augustan England, and a masterful employment of the press to dramatize and propagate their views.[1]

The hallmark of Real Whig writing was a passionate hatred of corruption in all of its forms: the selling of political places for votes in Parliament, the betrayal of English rights for private gain, the excessive influence of stock-jobbers and financiers in politics, the pandering of courtiers for office, the repulsive servility of all who yielded to the influence of money or favor, and the impending tyranny and slavery that hovered over all, as corruption sapped the strength of English society. The Real Whig imperative was to warn the nation

---

1. For an introduction to the large literature on country party ideology, see Caroline Robbins, *The Eighteenth-Century Commonwealthman: Studies in the Transmission, Development and Circumstance of English Liberal Thought from the Restoration of Charles II until the War with the Thirteen Colonies* (Cambridge, Mass., 1959); J.G.A. Pocock, "Machiavelli, Harrington, and English Political Ideologies in the Eighteenth Century," *William and Mary Quarterly*, 3d Ser., XXII (1965), 549–583; and *The Machiavellian Moment: Florentine Political Thought and the Atlantic Republican Tradition* (Princeton, N.J., 1975). For further bibliography, see Robert E. Shalhope, "Toward a Republican Synthesis: The Emergence of an Understanding of Republicanism in American Historiography," *WMQ*, 3d Ser., XXIX (1972), 49–80; and "Republicanism and Early American Historiography," *WMQ*, XXXIX (1982), 334–356.

of these dangers. The movement expanded rapidly after Parliament's failure to renew the Licensing Act in 1695 removed restrictions on the press. London and provincial newspapers multiplied, and a flood of political pamphlets poured from the presses. Appreciating the opportunity, Real Whig polemicists used poetry, drama, history, sermons, and essays as well as newspapers to express their distress. Beginning in 1726, the Tory opposition to Robert Walpole, which had by this time ironically adopted Old Whig attitudes in many respects, sponsored a weekly, the *Craftsman*, to keep up the assault, and Walpole in self-defense engaged the *London Journal* to return the fire.[2]

Real Whig rhetoric, moving out from London along the avenues of cultural dispersion, ultimately reached the American provinces. Radical modes of speech were all the more accessible to the colonies because in Whig eyes America was a case in point. The crown's attack on the Massachusetts charter and the suspension of colonial liberties under Governor Andros, for example, provided English Whigs with an ideal subject. *The Humble Address of the Publicans*, published in London in 1691, exemplified both Real Whig modes of social analysis and their extravagant language as applied to the colonies. The source of New England's miseries under Andros, the anonymous author argued, was "Persons brought up and educated in all manner of Debauchery and Depravation: a sort of People who may of right, and will stile themselves Gentlemen: *for they cannot work, and will not beg*, and therefore are fain to turn Sharpers, and practise little Tricks and Inventions for Bread." "These Cormorants are insatiable, so that a few *Publicans* are capable to ruine a great People," although they never grow, because "the holes of their Bags are commonly wider than their mouths."[3] *The Humble Address* gave a foretaste of how Real Whig writers for the next eighty years would deal with the colonies, seeing them as another field for corrupt officials and sharpers to exercise their craft at the expense of the public.

Charles Davenant, the friend of Shaftesbury and contemporary of the Real Whig publicist John Trenchard, was another who warned of "hungry courtiers at home" who schemed to become one of those "governors sent from hence, whose most common aim is to grow rich by fleecing the inhabitants." In 1698 Davenant was worrying just as much about "effeminacy, pride, ambition and luxuries of all kind" corrupting the colonial peoples and making it

---

2. Isaac Kramnick, *Bolingbroke and His Circle: The Politics of Nostalgia in the Age of Walpole* (Cambridge, Mass., 1968).

3. *The Humble Address of the Publicans of New-England, to which King you please; with some Remarks Upon it*, in William H. Whitmore, ed., *Andros Tracts: Being a Collection of Pamphlets and Official Papers Issued during the Period between the Overthrow of the Andros Government and the Establishment of the Second Charter of Massachusetts . . .* (The Prince Society, *Publications*, V–VII [New York, 1868–1874]), II, 241.

easy for avaricious officials to form a party.[4] Trenchard himself argued that the only way to keep the colonies attached to the mother country was to use them well. British policy should aim at binding the colonies through mutual commercial interests. Colonies held by force would soon separate or produce no profit. "Any Body of Troops considerable enough to awe them, and keep them in Subjection, under the Direction too of a needy Governor, often sent thither to make his Fortune, and at such a Distance from any Application for Redress, will soon put an End to all Planting, and leave the Country to the Soldiers alone; and if it did not, would eat up all the Profit of the Colony."[5]

The Real Whig interest in the colonies, however, did not evoke an immediate response in New England. For fifty years after the issuance of the second charter, Massachusetts Bay politicians kept the English radicals at a distance. Edward Randolph and Edward Cranfield reported that English Whigs were in touch with the popular party in Massachusetts in the 1680s, as well they might have been, but the models for Thomas Danforth and the two Elisha Cookes were the parliamentary politicians of an earlier generation, not the febrile radicals of the Exclusion Crisis.[6] Massachusetts popular leaders focused on charter and British constitutional principles in their published writings and in the debates in the lower house, so far as they are recorded. Attacks on corruption were carefully restrained. In public, popular politicians were almost exclusively preoccupied with technical constitutional issues: the right to elect a speaker, adjourn the House, audit accounts, or frame money bills.[7] The popular party's agreement with the Real Whigs' forthright charges of corruption surfaced only at certain moments—after the downfall of Andros, or in 1708 when Dudley appeared to be implicated in illicit trade, or in 1729 when Burnet demanded a permanent salary. Otherwise the American leaders carefully maintained the appearance of respect and restricted themselves to the language of right.

The outspoken agent of Massachusetts and Connecticut, Sir Henry Ashurst, who was associated with the Real Whigs until his death in 1711, futilely attempted to educate the colony in the radical language of the Commonwealthmen. He repeatedly admonished his New England correspondents to speak out against the vices of their governor. Ashurst told Increase Mather

4. Charles Davenant, *The Political and Commercial Works* . . . , ed. Sir Charles Whitworth (London, 1771), II, 55; see also 32–35, 56.
5. John Trenchard and William Gordon, *Cato's Letters: or, Essays on Liberty, Civil and Religious, and Other Important Subjects*, 3d ed. (New York, 1969 [orig. publ. London, 1724]), IV, 7–8.
6. David S. Lovejoy, *The Glorious Revolution in America* (New York, 1972), 149, 152–153.
7. Country Whigs under Anne were similarly restrained in the House of Commons. Dennis Rubini, *Court and Country, 1688–1702* (London, 1967), 24.

that Massachusetts under Dudley was in danger of a slavery worse than the Turks'. The Council vote to clear Dudley of bribery charges in 1708 infuriated Ashurst. "Is there no courage left?" he asked Wait Winthrop.[8] He feared self-serving persons would persuade New England to yield to the pressures and "have you give up your liberties, and be slaves to some oppressing governors to flay you at their pleasure." Ever impatient, Ashurst threatened to stop defending them unless he saw "a better spirit among you."[9]

Ashurst showed the way for New England in his 1708 tract, *The Deplorable State of New England By Reason of a Covetous and Treacherous Governor, and Pusillanimous Counsellors.* Although published anonymously by "A.H.," there is strong internal and external evidence that the tract was Ashurst's attempt to discredit Dudley and at the same time to reprove the Council for backing down on its charges against the governor.[10] References in the *Deplorable State* to "an Hungry Governour, who has been willing to Enrich himself and his Family on the Ruines of his country," could have been written by Cotton Mather or Elisha Cooke. But in the Real Whig manner, Ashurst carried the analysis further in accusing Dudley of multiplying offices and distributing them to councillors and assemblymen to win their votes. The people could not gain redress for their wrongs, he said, because "the Governour may have so Modell'd the *General Assembly*, that they shall pass wretched *Votes* to his Advantage." Ashurst explained the province's timidity as a result of Dudley's

8. Henry Ashurst to Wait Winthrop, Aug. 24, 1708, Massachusetts Historical Society, *Collections*, 6th Ser., V (Boston, 1892), 174.

9. Henry Ashurst to Gurdon Saltonstall, June 27, 1709, *ibid.*, 196. See also Ashurst to Increase Mather, May 10, 1710, *ibid.*, 210, and 109–110, 131–132, 138, 151. On Ashurst, see Philip Arthur Muth, "The Ashursts: Friends of New England," (Ph.D. diss., Boston University, 1967).

10. For evidence of the Ashurst attribution, see Richard L. Bushman, "Corruption and Power in Provincial America," in *The Development of a Revolutionary Mentality*, Library of Congress Symposia on the American Revolution (Washington, D.C., 1972), 86n; and John Gorham Palfrey, *History of New England* (Boston, 1858–1890), III, 527. Richard R. Johnson attributes *The Deplorable State* to Cotton Mather, as others have done, and cites a letter of Mather's in 1707 that Johnson believes closely parallels the tract. *Adjustment to Empire: The New England Colonies in the Era of the Glorious Revolution, 1675–1715* (New Brunswick, N.J., 1981), 344n. The letter does indict Dudley for bribery, but says nothing of winning votes in the assembly through the distribution of offices. Mather also sent Sewall "an account of one small article that occurred" in the recent ferment over Dudley's illicit French trade. This "small article" cannot be the sweeping, general analysis of *The Deplorable State*. Mather to Stephen Sewall, Dec. 13, 1707, in Kenneth Silverman, comp., *Selected Letters of Cotton Mather* (Baton Rouge, La., 1971), 74–76. Johnson also discovered a statement of Ashurst's that the "booke is just as it came over from New England," which is consistent with the persona adopted in the tract, but not proof that he did not write it.

influence, but he also admonished Massachusetts to drop its apparent diffidence and speak out. "Why will the *Massachusetts* Counsellors permit themselves to be made the Tools of their Governour's particular designs?" he wanted to know. Councillors should be "Thorns in the Sides of Evil Governours." "Where is your Courage?" Abandon the "Obsequious Strain," and "say before the Governour's Face, what you Talk so freely behind his back." [11]

The retention of Ashurst as agent over many years indicated approval of his animus against the governors. Ashurst shipped Cotton Mather two hundred copies of *The Deplorable State* for distribution in New England. The tract made enough of an impression that it was reprinted in Boston in 1720, and the House referred to it in 1721 when Governor Shute objected to the way it talked back to him. Deprived of its right to defend popular privileges, the House said, Massachusetts "might in a short process of time be brought into miserable streights and difficulties, and every one among us furnished with subject matter to write the deplorable State of *New-England.*" [12] The comment implied both a feared deterioration of colonial rights were the House to let down its guard and a threat to speak more bluntly if privileges were lost. Neither the 1721 House nor any politicians of that decade carried out the threat. The delegates suspected every official of self-aggrandizement, but restricted themselves in public discourse almost entirely to constitutional issues. They spoke with force, but with unvarying restraint.

James Franklin came back from his English apprenticeship in 1717 determined to provide Massachusetts with the most candid forms of whiggish political comment. His *New-England Courant* from 1721 to 1723 attacked the clerical power in Massachusetts with as much gusto as John Trenchard and Thomas Gordon's *Independent Whig* of 1720 and 1721 criticized the intolerance of High Churchmen in the English establishment. Franklin reprinted essays from *Cato's Letters*, also written by Trenchard and Gordon, but for the *London Journal* in late 1720. Not content with the *Courant* alone, Franklin published tracts like *English Advice to the Freeholders etc., of the Province of the Massachusetts-Bay*. The pamphlet warned against the election of "Sheriffs, Military Officers," and other placemen likely to "become Wax to receive every Impression the Enemies of our Constitution shall think fit to make on them." One *Courant* essay told the story of Major Ball-Face, a tool of the governor, intimidating James Trueman to gain a vote for the Ball-Face candidate in a town election. [13] All this was ripe country party rhetoric.

Franklin's experiment with London journalism, however, was short-lived.

11. Mass. Hist. Soc., *Colls.*, 5th Ser., VI (Boston, 1879), 103, 113–114; see also 115–116, 118, 119.
12. *Journals of the House of Representatives of Massachusetts* (Boston, 1919–), III, 98.
13. *English Advice to the Freeholders etc., of the Province of the Massachusetts-Bay* (Boston, 1722), 2; *New-England Courant* (Boston), May 7–14, 1722.

Many of his charges were unbelievable. The democratically organized congregational churches did not make a credible enemy of liberty. By the same token, frequent elections and a broad franchise in Massachusetts towns prevented the exercise of influence in town elections even where the Major Ball-Faces wanted control. The Franklin tract, *English Advice to the Freeholders,* was not suited to the provinces. Moreover, the radical journalist and popular party leaders never joined forces in Massachusetts as they did in England. The *New-England Courant* gave scant attention in its pages to the issues that concerned the House of Representatives: the governor's salary, selection of a speaker, and audit of accounts. And on his side, Elisha Cooke saw no reason to complain of undue influence in a House that consistently backed him by large majorities. Massachusetts observed the *Courant* with wonder and increasing annoyance until Franklin so offended his potential supporters that in 1723 the House closed the paper down. Franklin pulled back and gave up trying to sell fashionable London journalism in Boston. After 1723 the *Courant* and his subsequent publishing venture, the *Rhode Island Gazette,* were as dully circumspect as the rest of the New England press.[14]

The blowup over the salary and the audit of accounts under Burnet and Belcher had no more effect in turning Cooke and the House to the political style of English radicals. In 1733 Lewis Morris and his party in New York briefly sponsored John Peter Zenger's *New-York Weekly Journal* to carry on a war against Governor William Cosby, exactly as Pulteney and the opposition Tories used the *Craftsman* against Walpole.[15] The language, the tone, the method were the same. Cooke and his associates by contrast saw no need to mobilize an opposition press or resort to the ferocious language of Walpole's critics. Without political and financial support from popular party leaders, printers prudently avoided the inflammatory writings of political radicals, which were sure to alienate the sources of government printing business.[16] When the anonymous "Americanus" published a tract in 1739 with "some Helps from *Cato's Letters,*" warning against patronage in the legislature, no one in Boston dared to print it. Americanus had to send to Rhode Island to

14. Stephen Botein, "'Meer Mechanics' and an Open Press: The Business and Political Strategies of Colonial American Printers," *Perspectives in American History,* IX (1975), 198, 207–209; Bushman, "Corruption and Power," in *Development of a Revolutionary Mentality,* 68–73; Elizabeth Christine Cook, *Literary Influences in Colonial Newspapers, 1704–1750* (New York, 1912).

15. James Alexander, *A Brief Narrative of the Case and Trial of John Peter Zenger, Printer of The New York Weekly Journal,* ed., Stanley Nider Katz (Cambridge, Mass., 1963), 1–34. Morris and his friends soon abandoned the journal, and radical rhetoric faded from New York for more than a decade. Zenger's later newspapers sank into conventionality, as had Franklin's. Botein, "'Meer Mechanics' and an Open Press," *Perspectives in American History,* IX (1975), 207.

16. *Boston News-Letter,* Mar. 7, 1723.

have his work published.[17] The popular party's dominance in the House and subsequent control of the printed journals satisfied the party's need to reach the public, and the necessity of its leaders to meet the governor face to face in the course of everyday political business moderated their tone of voice. The very strength of the opposition party prevented English radical rhetoric from getting a purchase in Massachusetts in the first half of the eighteenth century.[18]

The province's orientation toward English political writing perceptibly changed after 1745. A growing number of Massachusetts politicians and publicists broke through the reserve of their predecessors and adopted radical political language as their own. The probable cause was the shift away from the classic constitutional controversies with the governor, over which the two Cookes had so confidently presided until 1736, toward internecine domestic conflicts on the one hand and uneven contests with vast imperial forces on the other. The Cookes had easily held their own against the governor and managed all the propaganda devices of the House—petitions, addresses, journals—to the advantage of the popular cause. In the domestic controversies of the 1750s, the minority party lost control of the House media and knew the anguish of powerlessness. So did the provincials who ran up against unmanageable imperial forces during and after the French wars. The extravagant charges of the radical rhetoric, with its apocalyptic sense of doom, seemed to suit circumstances at mid-century better than it had the times of the two Cookes.

Daniel Fowle's *Independent Advertiser*, which ran its life from January 1748 to December 1749, was, like James Franklin's *New-England Courant*, the work of a printer-editor with one eye on London fashions and another on the Boston market. Fowle reprinted *Cato's Letters* nearly as liberally as had Franklin. But

17. *A Letter to the Freeholders and other Inhabitants of the Massachusetts-Bay, relating to their Approaching Election of Representatives* (Newport, R.I., 1739), advertisement.
18. Orthodox Calvinist politicians such as Cooke may have sensed the incompatibility of radical rhetorical styles with the outlook of New England Puritans. As a critic of the *Craftsman* charged in 1729, "The business of your Paper hath been to prove the World *mad*; that is, according to the Principles of *Stoicism*, governed by a strange Medley of Ambition, Ignorance, Luxury and Corruption." Quoted in Herbert M. Atherton, *Political Prints in the Age of Hogarth: A Study of the Ideographic Representation of Politics* (New York, 1974), 107. Puritans could not wholeheartedly embrace such a despairing view of the world. Richard L. Bushman, "Caricature and Satire in Old and New England before the American Revolution," Mass. Hist. Soc., *Proceedings*, LXXXVIII (1976), 19–34. For the view that libertarian thought was heavily represented in American newspapers before 1740, see Gary Huxford, "The English Libertarian Tradition in the Colonial Newspaper," *Journalism Quarterly*, XLV (1968), 677–686. Botein concludes that Huxford's evidence does not warrant his conclusions. "'Meer Mechanics' and an Open Press," *Perspectives in American History*, IX (1979), 197.

the *Advertiser* differed from the *Courant* in speaking to issues that troubled Massachusetts: impressment, the return of Louisburg to France after the Treaty of Aix-la-Chappelle, and the exchange of Massachusetts' inflated paper for silver. Moreover, local politicians such as the young Samuel Adams and William Douglass wrote for the *Advertiser*. The *Advertiser* expressed the mood of provincials frustrated by the implacable British war machine and by the growing divisions in their own society, not only the opportunism of a flashy young journalist trying to attract subscribers.

The *Independent Advertiser* having prepared the way, other journalists soon followed. For the previous thirty years, currency regulation had engendered an extensive and impassioned literature, but nothing as outraged as the pamphlets published against the redemption of Massachusetts paper currency in 1750. In January 1749, the House approved the exchange of the £183,649 sterling received for the province's part in the Louisburg expedition for £2,000,000 of paper money. The inflationist elements, which had previously prevailed in the assembly, foresaw a sharp curtailment of the money supply and sudden profits to the merchants who had acquired large quantities of paper. For extravagance of language, the tracts which the opposition produced to vent their anger went beyond anything ever before seen in Massachusetts. The title of one, *Massachusetts in Agony*, epitomized the despairing tone and the rage at oppressive merchants who were believed to be carrying the province to ruin. The merchants "*forced*" inflation upon the colony "by Cunning, and by Power, through Lust of Power, Lust of Fame, Lust of Money; through Envy, Pride, Covetousness, and *violent* Ambition. The Bite of a mad Dog is not more dangerous or incurable, than Ambition."[19]

Less than three years later, Boston publicists turned again to English political models when the House in 1754 passed an excise tax on domestic distillers and liquor merchants. Opposition politicians thought at once of Pulteney's campaign against Walpole's 1733 excise proposal. In August 1754 the *Boston Evening-Post* reprinted an essay from the December 1733 issue of the *London Magazine*. The eleven antiexcise pamphlets which appeared between June 1754 and May 1755 borrowed imagery and arguments and occasionally made explicit references to the 1733 precedent. In the course of the controversy, Daniel Fowle attacked the House of Representatives so viciously that it or-

---

19. *Massachusetts in Agony: or, Important Hints To the Inhabitants of the Province . . .* (Boston, 1750), in Andrew McFarland Davis, ed., *Colonial Currency Reprints, 1682–1751* (New York, 1964 [orig. publ. Boston, 1910–1911]), IV, 438. The pamphlet exemplified the sentimentalist tendency noted by Kenneth Silverman to overload political language with emotion. *A Cultural History of the American Revolution: Painting, Music, Literature, and the Theatre in the Colonies and the United States from the Treaty of Paris to the Inauguration of George Washington, 1763–1789* (New York, 1976), 82–88.

dered the public hangman to burn Fowle's tract and jailed him for five days.[20]

Though Fowle left the province for New Hampshire, his departure did not end radical journalism in the 1750s as James Franklin's withdrawal had deflated radical rhetoric in the 1720s. In 1755 Benjamin Edes and John Gill purchased the *Boston Gazette* from Samuel Kneeland. The new owners foreshadowed their journalistic tastes when the *Gazette* masthead juxtaposed a cut from Kneeland's *Gazette* with one from the *Independent Advertiser*.[21] On May 12, the *Gazette* printed an essay warning of governors who were "jaylors and Sponges" of their people, "who chain them and squeeze them, and yet take it very ill if they do but murmur." "What a melancholy Reflection is this, that the most terrible and mischievous Foes to a Nation should be its own Magistrates! And yet in every enslaved Country, which is almost every Country, this is their woful Case."[22] In 1756 the governor objected to the licentiousness of the press, and even the Boston selectmen complained that the *Gazette* printed essays injurious to religion. Edes and Gill, however, were not to be silenced. They had a market for their paper, and they assiduously wrote for that market from the moment they purchased their press until the *Gazette* finally closed its doors in Boston on the eve of the Revolution and moved to Watertown.[23]

Spiritually joining forces with these political publicists, a few members of the Boston clergy in the 1750s also took up with English radicals. Samuel Cooper of the Brattle Street Church was one of two identifiable authors of the antiexcise pamphlets, and a parishioner, John Lovell, the distinguished Boston schoolmaster, was another.[24] The most strident voice was Jonathan Mayhew's, pastor of the West Church, with its congregation of newly rich merchants. Mayhew had broken with Boston's Calvinist orthodoxy in 1749 in a series of seven sermons whose broad Arminian principles reflected his reading in English latitudinarian theology.[25] His politics were equally radical.

20. Paul S. Boyer, "Borrowed Rhetoric: The Massachusetts Excise Controversy of 1754," *WMQ*, 3d Ser., XXI (1964), 328–351.

21. Botein, "'Meer Mechanics' and an Open Press," *Perspectives in American History*, IX (1975), 201–202.

22. *Boston Gazette, or Country Journal*, May 12, 1755.

23. Clyde Augustus Duniway, *The Development of Freedom of the Press in Massachusetts* (Cambridge, Mass., 1906), 121; Rollo G. Silver, "Benjamin Edes, Trumpeter of Sedition," Bibliographical Society of America, *Papers*, XLVII (1953), 250–251; Botein, "'Meer Mechanics' and an Open Press," *Perspectives in American History*, IX (1975), 216, 220–225.

24. Boyer, "Borrowed Rhetoric," *WMQ*, 3d Ser., XXI (1964), 338; Charles W. Akers, *The Divine Politician: Samuel Cooper and the American Revolution in Boston* (Boston, 1982).

25. Republished in England, the seven sermons brought Mayhew a congratulatory note from Dr. Benjamin Avery, chairman of the nonconformist lobby in the House of

In January 1750 Mayhew delivered a sermon on Rom. 13:1–8 that borrowed heavily from English sources. For centuries the biblical text had afforded religious support for government. In New England the clergy frequently referred to the passage in the annual election sermons delivered on the day when the lower house of the assembly chose the upper house. Through the eighteenth century, the ministry emphasized the mutual obligation of rulers and people. Every soul was to "be subject unto the higher powers" on the one hand, while on the other rulers were to be "the minister of God to thee for good." Mayhew signaled his intention to throw over the traditional balance when he selected January 30 as the occasion for his *Discourse concerning Unlimited Submission and Non-Resistance to the Higher Powers*, the anniversary of the execution of Charles I in 1649.[26] In England the church marked the day with a fast and a prayer book service, while English ultra-Whigs turned the observation upside down and dined off calves' heads to show their approval of Charles's decapitation. Mayhew's sentiments all lay with the enemies of the king and the opponents of nonresistance. Rather than balancing the obligations of rulers and people, Mayhew bowed briefly to the people's duty to obey good rulers and expounded instead on the moral responsibility to overthrow tyrants. When rulers "rob and ruin the public instead of being guardians of its peace and welfare, they immediately cease to be the *ordinance* and *ministers of God* and no more deserve that glorious character than common *pirates* and *highwaymen*." From the biblical obligation to submit to a good king, it followed that "when he turns tyrant and makes his subjects his prey to devour and to destroy instead of his charge to defend and cherish, we are bound to throw off our allegiance to him and to resist." As for Charles I, "during a reign, or rather a tyranny, of many years, he governed in a perfectly wild and arbitrary manner." "It was the oppression and violence of his reign that brought him to his untimely and violent end at last."[27]

Mayhew sent a copy of the sermon to Benjamin Hoadly, the great dissenting bishop from whom Mayhew had borrowed ideas and language, and in 1752 Richard Baron, editor and propagator of Commonwealth writings, printed the *Discourse* in a collection entitled *The Pillars of Priestcraft and Orthodoxy Shaken*.[28] Through Baron, Mayhew came under the tutelage of Thomas

Commons, and in 1750 an honorary degree from Aberdeen University. Bernard Bailyn, ed., *Pamphlets of the American Revolution, 1750–1776* (Cambridge, Mass., 1965), I, 205. On Mayhew, Charles W. Akers, *Called unto Liberty: A Life of Jonathan Mayhew, 1720–1766* (Cambridge, Mass., 1964); and Alden Bradford, *Memoir of the Life and Writings of Rev. Jonathan Mayhew, D.D. . . .* (Boston, 1838).

26. Mayhew delivered the sermon in early Feb., but Jan. 30 was noted as the occasion.

27. Jonathan Mayhew, *A Discourse concerning Unlimited Submission and NonResistance to the Higher Powers . . .* (Boston, 1750), in Bailyn, ed., *Pamphlets of the American Revolution*, I, 228, 232, 239, 244.

28. Bailyn, ed., *Pamphlets of the American Revolution*, I, 210.

Hollis, the retiring but energetic advocate of radical Whig principles who thereafter used Mayhew as a contact point for disseminating libertarian principles in New England. Mayhew proved worthy of the trust. Prompted by Hollis, Mayhew in the 1760s took a leading part in the campaign against the appointment of an Episcopal bishop and in mobilizing resistance to the Stamp Act.[29] In Mayhew and Samuel Cooper, English radical Whiggery received the support of two well-placed, articulate, and persistent spokesmen who argued libertarian causes not as an incidental, but as a central theme of their lives.

The fact that radical Whig language sounded most loudly in Boston is partly to be associated with the city's growing isolation in the colony after 1740. As the popular party consensus broke down after the conclusion of the last major constitutional controversy in 1736, Boston found itself ever more frequently in the minority in crucial assembly votes. The old consensus held through the fight with Belcher over currency contraction and the land bank. Then underlying conflicts over the distribution of taxes among the towns came to the surface. The excise tax on liquor was only the most notorious of a series of debates over Boston's fair share. Numerically at a hopeless disadvantage in the assembly, Boston was at the mercy of the country representatives.[30]

Just as city politicians adopted the language of radical Whiggery, so Boston raised up political leaders as excessive and intense in their actions as was the diction of radical rhetoric. As early as the 1740s, this new type of politician foreshadowed a style of leadership which was to carry the province into revolution. The first of the new breed was James Allen, merchant, town meeting moderator, tax collector, and Boston's representative to the General Court. Nothing in his background foreshadowed his turn toward radical politics. By birth James Allen could claim political power in Boston as rightfully as Thomas Hutchinson. The grandson of the Reverend James Allen and the son of a merchant who served as colony treasurer for twenty-two years, Allen ranked fifth socially in his Harvard class. His marriage in 1725 to the daughter of Colonel Thomas Fitch was a social event attended by members of the provincial council.[31]

After an appropriate interlude as a merchant and supporter of the Congregationalist West Church in Boston, Allen aspired to replace his father,

29. Bernhard Knollenberg, ed., "Thomas Hollis and Jonathan Mayhew: Their Correspondence, 1759–1766," Mass. Hist. Soc., *Proc.*, LXXI (Boston, 1947–1950), 102–193; Bernard Bailyn, "Religion and Revolution: Three Biographical Studies," *Perspectives in American History*, IV (1970), 83–169.

30. Robert Zemsky, *Merchants, Farmers, and River Gods: An Essay on Eighteenth-Century American Politics* (Boston, 1971), 263–264; G. B. Warden, *Boston, 1689–1776* (Boston, 1970), 127–148.

31. For biographical information on Allen, see Clifford K. Shipton, *Sibley's Harvard Graduates: Biographical Sketches of Those Who Attended Harvard College*, VI (Boston, 1942), 159–164.

Jeremiah Allen, in the treasurer's office. Governor Belcher vetoed the assembly's nomination of Jeremiah in 1736 ostensibly on account of ill health. The son won election in the House as the replacement, but to the chagrin of both Allens, Belcher refused concurrence. That rebuff turned Allen to the opposition, just as Lewis Morris turned against Governor Cosby in New York in 1733 when removed from the chief justiceship. For a year the Allens refused to turn over the treasury or to surrender marred currency for burning, on the grounds that the province owed Jeremiah Allen seven thousand pounds. In 1739 Boston elected Allen to the House, where he firmly opposed Belcher's effort to contract the currency. Belcher complained that the Allens were making "attempts against the Government" out of "inveterate" and "rancorous malice."[32]

Allen's eccentricities and excesses at first prevented him from getting more than a tenuous hold on his Boston constituents and on his associates in the assembly. He won his first election to the Council in 1743. By the end of the decade, however, as inflation, war, and suffering in Boston reduced the city to desperation, Allen's talents seemed better suited to the town's needs. Boston elected him to the House again in 1747 and for every year thereafter until his death in 1755. In the assembly, Allen took his place among the leading men on the committees, but his style was too excessive to win much support. In opposing Thomas Hutchinson's proposal to replace the province's paper currency with sterling, Allen's tongue got him in trouble. In December 1748, he declared on the floor that "Former Houses (I do not mean this House, Mr. Speaker) have passed many villainous resolves, which the Governor unluckily gave his fiat to."[33] When Allen refused to apologize, the House expelled him.

Allen immediately took his case to the public in a *Letter to the Freeholders and Qualified Voters*. Elisha Cooke had defended himself publicly in 1720 when Governor Shute vetoed his nomination as speaker and impugned his loyalty to the crown. Cooke's *Just and Seasonable Vindication* was a cautious, legalistic brief for himself and the right of the House to elect its speaker. Allen's *Letter* of 1749 was an inflammatory diatribe in the mode of Thomas Gordon, whose dedication to the translation of Tacitus was quoted on the title page. Besides defending himself, Allen enlarged the controversy and pointed to deeper and

32. Quoted in *ibid.*, 161. On Belcher's rejection of Allen, see *Journals of the House*, XIV, 51, 70, 88, 121–122. The governor also negatived Thomas Cushing, Jr., the House's third nominee for treasurer. *Ibid.*, 90–92. On Allen's 1740 controversy with Roland Cotton, representative from Woburn, see [James Allen], *A Letter to a Friend in the Country* . . . (Boston, 1740), 4; and for Cotton's objections, *Journals of the House*, XVIII, 7–8. See also Zemsky, *Merchants, Farmers, and River Gods*, 247–248.

33. Quoted in George R. Minot, *Continuation of the History of the Province of Massachusetts Bay From the Year 1748*, I (Boston, 1798), 104. See also *Journals of the House*, XXV, 119, 137, 148, 150–151, 158; Zemsky, *Merchants, Farmers, and River Gods*, 167–168.

more ominous forces. "The present Circumstances of the Province are so very distressing and dark, as that to look critically into them, would have a Tendency to drive us into Despair." Is it not true, he asked, "whether the Interest and Power of Prerogative has not been inconceivably increased since the Success at Louisburg? Whether the Friends of Power have not thereby acquired a leading and *Influence* over the Hearts and Minds of the People dangerous to Liberty, and alluring to Ambition . . . Has not the Syren Voice of Flattery become almost universal, delusively enchanting the People to forge their own Chains . . . ?" The moral of it all was not to elect "those who have been backed by Bills of Ech——ge and com——s——ns which by their Actions they seem to value more than their necessary Food."[34]

Boston endorsed Allen by immediately reelecting him to the House by a vote of 346 to 127; when the House refused him a seat, the town elected him to the next House, which did seat him. From 1749 until the day in 1755 when he was stricken with apoplexy just after delivering a speech in the assembly, Allen served as Boston's representative. The writer of the eulogy in the *Boston Evening-Post* expressed the town's ambivalence. His sharp tongue and fierce candor troubled people, even though he struck at deserving targets. "He had a natural Flow of Satire, which tho' from its too frequent Use, might be sometimes disadvantageous to himself and to his Cause, was yet never employ'd to insult the innocent, and overwhelm the unfortunate." And yet Allen's abrasive language did not sound like the vent of personal disappointment or the fantasies of an overheated mind. He spoke the truth for Boston. His excesses were taken as a sign of purity. "His Heart was inaccessible to Corruption, his Ear impenetrable by Flattery; neither the Whispers nor the Clamours of the Great could shake or soften his Independency." As the *Evening-Post* said, "With these Qualities he could not be belov'd by the Hypocrite, the mean Dependent, the Tool of Party, and the Friend and Patron of Arbitrary Power."[35]

James Allen had little immediate impact on Massachusetts politics. Although he took a large share of everyday committee assignments in the House as Cooke had done, Allen spoke for Boston, not for a provincial popular party. The measures he opposed most vehemently, the redemption of paper currency and the excise on liquor, passed in the House. In 1747, when he was expelled, the House refused to reinstate him until after the next election. Allen's main achievement was to introduce into the legislature radical

34. James Allen, *Letter to the Freeholders and Qualified Voters, Relating to the Ensuing Election* (Boston, 1749), 3, 5, 12.

35. Quoted in Shipton, *Sibley's Harvard Graduates*, VI, 162, 163. Boston regularly elected Allen as tax collector, a post reserved for town favorites. Warden, *Boston*, 130; John A. Schutz, *William Shirley: King's Governor of Massachusetts* (Chapel Hill, N.C., 1961), 142.

Whig ideology from the streets of Boston and to forge in his own person a model of the radical politician for successors to follow. What had been written anonymously in pamphlets, in the *Independent Advertiser*, and in the *Gazette*, Allen said in his own name, and probably on the floor of the House. He brought together Elisha Cooke's leadership of the opposition with the radical language and confrontive style which Sir Henry Ashurst had advocated fifty years earlier. In his bellicosity, passion, and ideology, Allen was a precedent for James Otis, Jr., Samuel Adams, and the cadre of Revolutionary radicals.

James Otis, Jr., particularly resembled Allen. Both were from established, wealthy families. James Otis, Sr., was a merchant, Barnstable County magnate, a member of the Governor's Council, and at one time a candidate for the office of chief justice. Both Otis Junior and Allen turned against the governor when he denied office to family members. Both had temperaments well suited to the emotional extravagances of radical Whig rhetoric. After he went into opposition in 1760, Otis had only slightly more success than Allen in rallying majorities in the House. He set John Adams's heart aflame with a defense of merchants' rights in the writs of assistance case, but he often could not get the votes in the House.[36] Upon his first election to the House from Boston in 1761, Otis was admonished to constrain the impassioned speeches that had won him fame in the courtroom. "You have great abilities," a member of the delegation warned, "but you are too warm, too impetuous, your opponents though they cannot meet you in argument, will get the advantage of you by interrupting you, and putting you in a passion." True to the prediction, Timothy Ruggles and John Choate, old hands in assembly politics, goaded Otis into a fury by interrupting his speech and releasing the uncontrolled sarcasm they knew would discredit him. The House expelled a fellow Bostonian, John Tyng, for rude language.[37] Otis's feisty but prudent father spoke for many when he observed that "sometimes the Whiggs a Little overdo as to the Strick Truth of things." His brother called Otis Junior "Esq. Bluster."[38] The new language bewildered some House members. One colleague wrote his son that Otis's attack on the governor in 1762 was all out of proportion to the offense. Otis's analysis of political dynamics seemed fantastic, and his reflections on

36. In 1762 after some initial successes, Otis lost on the selection of a candidate for Massachusetts' agent in England, and again on the passage of a place bill. John J. Waters, Jr., *The Otis Family in Provincial and Revolutionary Massachusetts* (Chapel Hill, N.C., 1968), 140, 146, 149. For a description of Otis's "reckless vitality," see Page Smith, *John Adams* (Garden City, N.Y., 1962), I, 40.

37. The Otis episode is told in William Tudor, *The Life of James Otis* . . . (Boston, 1823), 92–94; and Tyng's expulsion can be followed in *Journals of the House*, XXXIII, 127–128.

38. Both quoted in Waters, *The Otis Family*, 130, 163.

the motives of rulers at best impolitic. In 1763 Otis's party lost badly at the polls. Influential as Otis was at times, his hour had not yet come.[39]

The mood of the House and the countryside swiftly changed after 1763. The parliamentary taxation bills placed all of Massachusetts in the powerless position Boston had occupied in the debates over taxes in the 1740s and 1750s. The older prudence became obsolete in the assembly and in the province. James Otis, Jr., and Samuel Adams took command of a House majority of a size unknown since the days of Elisha Cooke. Their language rang true to a growing number of representatives. They invariably controlled the House on imperial issues, and conservatives with the temerity to oppose popular causes risked losing their seats. Governors Bernard and Hutchinson faced a popular party as large and implacable as the bloc that backed Cooke against Shute. This time, however, to Cooke's tradition of constitutionalism, the new leaders added the ideas, the manner, and the tactics of England's radical Whigs.

39. *Ibid.*, 147. An essayist in the *Boston Evening-Post*, Feb. 14, 1763, noted that pious countrymen who came to the city found that with Otis and Samuel Adams, "downright scurrility and gross impudence, was really the most exalted Patriotism, the most perfectly refined, disinterested Amor Patriae." Lawrence Henry Gipson recognized a similar disparity in Virginia in 1760, dividing "young, hotheaded" burgesses from "cool, old Members." *The Coming of the Revolution, 1763–1775* (New York, 1965), 141. In the address to king, Lords, and Commons of 1764, George Wythe wrote with so much freedom, Jefferson reported, that "his colleagues of the Committee shrunk from it as wearing the aspect of treason, and smoothed its features to it's present form." Quoted in J. A. Leo Lemay, "John Mercer and the Stamp Act in Virginia, 1764–1765," *Virginia Magazine of History and Biography* XCI (1983), 9.

INDEX